Cornerstone
Phila

DATE DUE

This item is Due on
or before Date shown.
3200100086832

1225 –

SAINT THOMAS AQUINAS

SUMMA CONTRA GENTILES

BOOK TWO: CREATION

University
of
Notre Dame Press
Notre Dame
London

Translated,
with an Introduction
and Notes,
by
JAMES F. ANDERSON

University of Notre Dame Press edition 1975

Copyright © 1956 by Doubleday & Company, Inc.

First published in 1956 by Hanover House as

On the Truth of the Catholic Faith

First paperback edition 1956 by Image Books

Published by arrangement with Doubleday & Company, Inc.

Printed in the United States of America

Library of Congress Cataloging in Publication Data

Thomas Aquinas, Saint, 1225?-1274.
  Summa contra gentiles.

  Reprint of the ed. published by Hanover House,
Garden City, N.Y., under title: On the truth of
the Catholic faith.
  Includes bibliographies.
  CONTENTS: book 1. God, translated, with an
introd. and notes, by A. C. Pegis. —book 2. Crea-
tion, translated, with an introd. and notes, by
J. F. Anderson. [etc.]
  1. Apologetics—Middle Ages, 600-1500. I. Ti-
tle.
[BX1749.T4 1975]   239   75-19883
ISBN 0-268-01675-5
ISBN 0-268-01676-3 pbk.

Contents

5

Introduction

While St. Thomas, on the whole problem of the creation of the world, owes much to his predecessors, he differs from them all. In a sense the Thomistic position lies mid-way between that of the Averroists and that of the Augustinians. The former maintained the eternal existence of the world as a matter of rational demonstration, while the latter held that a beginning of the world in time was not only a matter of revelation but of rational demonstration as well. St. Thomas Aquinas, however, maintains the possibility of a beginning of the world in time, along with the possibility of its eternity, denying that either possibility can be shown by reason to be the fact.

Indeed, in developing his solution of the problem of creation, St. Thomas owes much to his mediaeval forerunners, above all, no doubt, to his master, St. Albert the Great, and to Maimonides. Nevertheless, St. Thomas' teaching departs from theirs significantly. Thus, Maimonides would admit creation as a matter of revelation only, whereas St. Thomas holds that it can be demonstrated rationally. And yet both thinkers agree that it is impossible to demonstrate the beginning of the world in time, and that it is always possible to deny the eternal existence of the world. Again, St. Albert admits, with Maimonides, that the creation of the world ex nihilo cannot be known except by faith, while St. Thomas (closer in this respect to the Augustinian tradition than his master, St. Albert) considers this demonstration possible. On the other hand, the creation of the universe in time is indemonstrable according to St. Thomas but demonstrable according to St. Albert, who, in this respect, joins the Augustinian tradition. Now, against both these thinkers St. Thomas maintains the possibility of demonstrating the creation of the world ex nihilo; and here we see him in opposition likewise to Averroes and his school. Moreover, while conceding, with Maimonides, the possibility of a universe created from all eternity, St. Thomas refuses steadfastly to confuse the truths of faith with things that can be demonstrated.

The central insight, which St. Thomas makes unmistakably clear, is that creation is essentially a matter of dependence in being—total and absolute—, and that if one adds the idea of the world's newness, it is only to refer to a fact (acknowledged by Christians on grounds of revelation alone), not to anything pertaining to the essence of creation in itself. It is on this point that the entire Judaeo-Christian tradition parts company with Greek and pagan thought, for which there never was any question of a creation *ex nihilo*—no problem of seeking the cause of being in the complete universality of its meaning, namely, of being taken precisely as such. For all being was thought to constitute an eternal, necessary, underived totality. The action of the divine causality within this whole, then, presupposed something as necessary and, so to speak, as aboriginal as itself, whether one call this a kind of primordial chaos, with the Platonists, or matter, with the Aristotelians.

Having in Book I of the *Summa Contra Gentiles*[1] treated of God in Himself, St. Thomas now considers the procession of creatures from God, namely, creation. Book I was basically concerned with two problems: the existence of God; and His perfections, or attributes, as they are more commonly called. The latter problem, in turn, was itself divided into two problems: the perfections or attributes pertaining to God's being; and those pertaining to His action or operation.

There are, however, two types of action or operation: one which remains in the agent and which does not pass into an external effect; and another which issues in an effect outside the agent. The former type of action or operation is called "immanent," and thus belongs to the consideration of God in Himself; while the latter is called "transient," and therefore pertains to the problem of creation, that is to say, the study of God, not in Himself but in His works.

[1] See A. C. Pegis, General Introduction to *St. Thomas Aquinas, On The Truth of the Catholic Faith, Summa Contra Gentiles, Book One: God*, Hanover House, Garden City, New York, 1955, pp. 15 ff.

That Book II is not simply philosophical (any more than the other three) is clear at the outset. St. Thomas is expressly concerned with showing the relevance—indeed, the necessity —of the study of creatures for the instruction of faith in God (ch. 2), as well as for refuting errors against the true knowledge of God (ch. 3). Moreover, the whole treatment of creation in Book II complies with what St. Thomas understands to be the requirements of "the teaching of the faith"—doctrina fidei (ch. 4), and it is "the truth of faith"—veritas fidei (ch. 5) which for St. Thomas determines the things to be treated and the order of their treatment. Assuredly, there is a metaphysics— a straight philosophy—of creation contained in Book II of the Summa Contra Gentiles, but this Book is not merely a metaphysics of creation. For while St. Thomas uses arguments purely natural in character, as well as arguments appealing to the revealed word of God, the purpose of the entire argumentative structure is to convince his audience (consisting chiefly, in St. Thomas' mind, of the Moslem theologians and apologists) of the truth of the Catholic faith. In short, the general procedure is theological, inasmuch as it concerns an exposition and a defense of doctrine pertaining to God and man's relation to God.

The treatise on creation deals with three main problems: the act of bringing things into being; the distinction of things from one another; the nature of those things which were brought into being and made distinct from one another, in so far as this consideration is relevant to the truth of the faith— quantum ad fidei pertinet veritatem (ch. 5).

As to the first problem, having shown that it befits God to be the very source or cause of the being of other things, St. Thomas proves that God is in fact that cause (ch. 15), and he proceeds to explain the mode of operation of the divine causality, turning next to consider the question of the nature and especially the duration of the effects of that causality (chs. 16–39).

Now, since God is pure Being, containing in Himself the total perfection of being, it is His proper function to give being—dare esse. But being is absolutely prior to any perfection or determination thereof. And this is tantamount to saying that God gives being, or creates, "from nothing," that is, from no pre-existing being whatever; since, prior to being, nothing whatever is.

This action, called "creation," is absolutely *sui generis*; all other productions are effected by means of some kind of change or movement, that is to say, by somehow transforming something already existing. It follows that God alone is able to create, properly speaking, and that no creature can share in this act even instrumentally, since (to cite but one consideration) creation of its very nature requires an *infinite* power; it demands omnipotence because the ontological gap between non-being and being is infinite, and only an almighty Agent can close it. The further inference may be drawn that the divine creative causality is free, and hence intellectual and voluntary in character; that it is therefore false to say that things depend on God's simple will without any reason; for a free, a voluntary agent is an intellectual agent, and an intellectual agent is one that produces its effects and orders them in accordance with its knowledge and wisdom. Nor does the fact that God has created things voluntarily, and not necessarily, stand in the way of His having willed certain things to exist which are incorruptible, things whose substantial being is necessary (namely, all immaterial things and those whose matter is not subject to contrary forms or determinations), as well as others whose substantial being is inherently contingent, and which, therefore, are by nature corruptible. Neither are we to suppose that creatures must have always existed, although it is impossible for human reason to demonstrate either that creatures always existed or that they did not always exist. Revelation alone is decisive in informing us that the latter is true.

The question of the so-called eternity of the world occupies an important place in Book II because mediaeval Moslem theology was largely based on the doctrine of the newness of the world, whence one argued to God's existence; while in the camp of Moslem philosophy, which, at least in the High Middle Ages, was predominantly an Averroistic brand of Aristotelianism, the theory of the eternity of the world was deemed centrally significant. And St. Thomas addresses himself here especially to the Moslems—philosophers as well as theologians—who for the most part advocated theories which excluded man from any real relationship to God by placing man's ultimate end in a union with a separate intellect which is not God, God being conceived as an utterly transcendent entity that must ever remain in its ineffable unity inaccessible to the human spirit.

The second general problem dealt with in this Book is that of the distinction of things—their multiplication and diversification. This problem follows logically from the first one, for, having considered those matters which concern the bringing of things into being, the whole question of their distinction from one another arises at once. Why are there things at all? Obviously, that is the first question. Why are these things many and distinct? This, no less clearly, is the second question. And it is certainly an important question because of its bearing upon "the true knowledge of God"; for, as St. Thomas had already remarked (ch. 3), "errors about creatures sometimes lead one astray from the truth of faith," and this occurs "in so far as they disagree with true knowledge of God."

For one to ascribe the distinction of things to the wrong cause would be a radical error concerning creatures. Therefore, St. Thomas is at pains to show: that the multiplicity and variety of things in the created universe did not, as the ancient Greek cosmologists supposed, result from chance movements or convergences of material principles; that, on the contrary, matters were created diverse and mutually distinct *in order that* they might be suitable recipients for various forms; that the diversity and distinction of things cannot have resulted from any pair of contrary agents or active principles, the one good, the other evil by nature, as some of the ancient philosophers and even some heretics in Christian times had taught; that, in fact, the primary cause of the distinction of things cannot be found at all in the order of secondary (even angelic) agents, as Avicenna and certain early heretics averred; that it cannot be attributed to a diversity of merits on the part of rational creatures, as Origen maintained; but that there is distinction—multiplicity and variety and diversity—among created things primarily for this reason, that they may more adequately represent the perfection of God. As St. Thomas points out (ch. 45): "The highest degree of perfection should not be lacking in a work made by the supremely good workman. But the good of order among diverse things is better than any of the members of an order, taken by itself . . . It was not fitting, therefore, that God's work should lack the good of order. And yet, without the diversity and inequality of created things, this good could not exist." In short, "the diversity and inequality in created things are not the result of chance, nor of a diversity of matter, nor of the intervention of certain causes or merits, but of the intention of God Himself, who wills to give the creature such perfection as it is possible for it to have."

Having at some length dealt with the question of the cause of the distinction or diversity among things, St. Thomas addresses himself to the third, and last, problem which he had proposed (in ch. 5) to investigate, namely, the *nature of the distinct and diversified creatures, as far as this concerns the truth of faith.* Quantitatively, the treatment of this problem occupies by far the largest part of the Book, and it consists of one long treatise on the intellectual substance.

The connection of this part with the preceding is clear. We have seen that, according to St. Thomas, the perfection (or completeness) of the universe required diversity among things. Now he proceeds to show, in this third part (beginning with ch. 46), that the perfection of the universe required the existence of some intellectual creatures, "in order that creatures might perfectly [that is, in a generally complete manner] represent the divine goodness" (ch. 46).

The Angelic Doctor then goes on (chs. 47–55) to consider the nature of such creatures, showing that they are possessed of will and of free will; that they are incorporeal and immaterial; that there is in them, as in all creatures, a composition of essence and being, of potency and act (though, of course, not of matter and form); and that they are therefore by nature incorruptible. Then (chs. 56–90) the problem of the union of an intellectual substance to a body is considered; for, as Thomas says, "having shown that an intellectual substance is neither a body, nor a power dependent upon a body, it remains for us to inquire whether an intellectual substance can be united to the [human] body" (ch. 56). After proving that such a union could not be by way of a mixture, or of corporeal or quantitative contact, he argues that the intellect is the very form and act of the body, on the grounds that only this position can account for the fact that man *is* a substantial unity of soul and body, and not, as the Platonists, for example, would have it, *a soul using a body.*

After showing (ch. 58) that the nutritive, sensitive, and intellective powers in man are not three souls, but that all the soul's operations proceed from one soul, St. Thomas successively tackles: the doctrine of Averroes, that the possible intellect whereby the soul understands is a separate substance existing apart from the body and is not the form of the body; the doctrine of Alexander of Aphrodisias, according to whom the possible intellect is not rooted in an intellectual substance, but is consequent on the mixture of the elements in the human body; the doctrine of Galen, that the soul is a temperament; the doctrine that the soul is a harmony (not of sound but of contraries); that the soul is a body. He then proceeds to show how the intellect, or the intellective soul, is distinguished from the sense power, as well as the imagination, explaining at length (against all major objections known to him) how an intellectual substance, such as the human soul, can be and is the very form of the human body, being united to it immediately and present in its totality in the whole body and in each part thereof.

Still another formidable adversary remains to be dealt with —the Arabian philosopher, Avicenna, with his doctrine of the separate agent intellect. St. Thomas confronts this doctrine with the simple principle that a power must exist in that of which it is a power, declaring that "if the possible intellect [which is in potentiality to all intelligible objects] is a part of the soul and not a separate substance, as we have shown, then the agent intellect, by whose action the intelligible species result therein, [also] will not be a separate substance, but an active power of the soul" (ch. 76)—as, indeed, Aristotle, correctly interpreted, likewise maintained, according to St. Thomas (ch. 78)—together with the doctrine that the intellect, or the intellective part of the soul, is independent of the body, and therefore does not (unlike the souls of brute animals) perish with the body, but, on the contrary, is by nature incorruptible or immortal.

St. Thomas then goes on to treat the problem of the origination of the human soul, arguing that it begins to exist with the body and had no prior existence; that it is not made of the very substance or nature of God, although the human soul is made in the image of God; that it is not transmitted or generated or formed through any physical or biological causality; that, on the contrary, it is brought into being by the creative act of God alone, for, being immaterial, it cannot be made from anything, and hence is made from nothing; that is to say, it is created. Yet, no intellectual substance (and such is the soul) can be united to any other body than the human, although there are, St. Thomas maintains (ch. 91), some intellectual substances which are not united to bodies at all. In fact, Chapters 91–101 constitute a treatise on separate intellectual substances.

A number of arguments are advanced in order to show that such substances do, in fact, exist. For example, it is pointed out that to exist in separation from bodies does not belong to human souls essentially, but accidentally, since such souls are by their very nature forms of bodies. Yet, as Aristotle observes, the essential must be prior to the accidental; so that there are some intellectual substances, naturally prior to souls, to which extra-corporeal existence belongs essentially. Moreover, there is the consideration that, although it pertains to the nature of some intellectual substance, namely, the soul, to be united to something else, this does not pertain to the nature of the intellectual substance, as such; for, enjoying an operation by virtue of its own nature, such a substance is by nature a self-subsistent reality; whence it is inferred that there are some intellectual substances which are not united to bodies. Then, too, we find, with Aristotle, that above the imperfect in any genus there is the perfect in that genus; wherefore, above forms that exist in matter and thus are imperfectly actual, there are some forms which are, as forms, complete acts, subsisting in themselves, namely, separate intellectual substances. The perfect way of understanding, furthermore, consists in the knowledge of things that are intelligible of themselves, whereas to grasp things which are not intelligible in themselves but are made intelligible by the (agent) intellect is an imperfect way of understanding. Therefore, if prior to every imperfect thing there must be something perfect in the same genus, then there are, above human souls (which understand by receiving intelligible forms from phantasms), some intellectual substances which understand things that are intelligible in themselves, without receiving knowledge from sensible things—substances which, therefore, are by their nature completely separate from bodies.

Although some considerations like these may seem, from a "rationalistic" point of view, to argue the fittingness, rather than the fact, of the existence of separate substances, St. Thomas, as we shall see, does not limit himself to the so-called purely rational order. He proceeds to argue, on Scriptural as well as rational grounds, that such substances are exceedingly numerous, being far greater in number, for instance, than the movers of the spheres or the heavenly bodies or the heavenly movements, more numerous, indeed, than the whole multitude of material things. Scripture itself bears witness not only to the existence but to the very great number of separate substances: "Thousands of thousands ministered to Him, and ten thousand times a hundred thousand stood before Him" (Dan. 7:10). Certainly, there are rational and natural considerations. (Thus, the lower are for the sake of the higher, which exist for their own sake, and should therefore be as numerous as possible; and so it is that the elemental bodies are found to be inconsiderable in number as compared with the heavenly bodies.) But it is the Word of God which is fully conclusive in this matter.

St. Thomas goes on to argue that the separate substance is not multiplied in the one species, as is man, for instance, because (to give but one fundamental reason) the separate substance is altogether devoid of matter; nor, then, are the separate substance and the human soul of the same specific nature; nor do the concepts of genus and species apply to the separate substance in the way in which they apply to other created substances; neither is the separate substance's knowledge derived from sensible things, as man's knowledge is; nor are separate substances, as we, sometimes understanding and sometimes not understanding; rather, understanding, which is their proper operation, is continuous and perpetual in them.

The Angelic Doctor completes his treatise on separate substances by dealing with the mode, and the objects, of the knowledge proper to them. This short treatise is a fitting conclusion to the long treatise on creation (which Book II is), because it is in the being of separate substances that the perfection of created reality primarily consists.

It is a pleasure to thank Dmitri Gloss, of South Bend, Indiana, as well as Robert Perusse and Robert Haertle of Marquette University, for their generous assistance.

Marquette University   JAMES F. ANDERSON
Milwaukee, Wisconsin

Bibliography

The following list falls into two main groups: primary sources used in the preparation and annotation of this translation of *Summa Contra Gentiles*, Book II, and some modern studies relevant to matters treated therein.

I. SOURCES

1. Alexander of Aphrodisias
De intellectu et intellecto, in G. Théry, *Alexandre d'Aphrodise* (*Autour du décret de 1210*, II), *Bibliothèque Thomiste*, vol. 7, Kain, Le Saulchoir, 1926, pp. 74–82.

2. Aristotle
Aristotelis Opera, 2 vols. Berlin Academy Edition based on I. Bekker, Berlin, G. Reimer, 1831.
The Works of Aristotle, English translation, edited by W. D. Ross, 11 vols., Oxford, Clarendon Press, 1928–1931.

3. Averroes
Averrois Cordubensis Commentarium Magnum in Aristotelis de Anima Libros, edited by F. Stuart Crawford, Cambridge, Mass., The Mediaeval Academy of America, 1953.

4. Avicenna
Avicennae perhypatetici philosophi ac medicorum facile primi opera in luce redacta, Venetiis, 1508.

5. *Liber de Causis*, edited by R. Steele, in *Opera hactenus inedita Rogeri Baconi*, fasc. 12, Oxford, Clarendon Press, 1935.

6. Moses Maimonides
The Guide for the Perplexed, translated from the original Arabic text by M. Friedländer, 2nd edition, London, G. Routledge, 1936.

7. Plato

Platonis Opera, 5 vols. in 6, edited by J. Burnet, Oxford, Clarendon Press, 1905–1913.

The Dialogues of Plato, 5 vols., translated by B. Jowett, Oxford, Clarendon Press, 1871.

The Dialogues of Plato, 2 vols., translated by B. Jowett, with an introduction by R. Demos, New York, Random House, 1937.

8. Porphyry

Isagoge, IV, 1 (edited by A. Busse, Berlin, 1887), in *Commentaria in Aristotelem graeca*, 23 vols., Berlin Academy Edition, Berlin, G. Reimer, 1882–1909.

Isagoge, translated into Latin by Boethius, J. P. Migne, *Patrologia Latina*, vol. 64, coll. 77–158.

9. St. Albert the Great

B. *Alberti Magni Commentarii in II Sententiarum*, dist. 1, art. 8 (in *Opera Omnia*, vol. 27, edited by A. Borgnet, Paris, Vivès, 1890–1899).

B. *Alberti Magni Summa Theologiae*, II, tract. 1, Quaest. 3, memb. 2 (in *op. cit.*, vol. 32).

10. St. Thomas Aquinas

S. *Thomae Aquinatis Doctoris Angelici Opera Omnia, iussu impensaque Leonis XIII P. M. edita*, 16 vols., Ex Romae Typographia Polyglotta, 1882–1948.

S. *Thomae Aquinatis Scriptum Super Sententiis*, 4 vols. (incomplete), edited by P. Mandonnet (vols. 1–2) and M. F. Moos (vols. 3–4), Paris, P. Lethielleux, 1929–1947.

S. *Thomae de Aquino Doctoris Angelici Summa Contra Gentiles*, Romae, Apud Sedem Commissionis Leoninae, 1934.

St. *Thomae Aquinatis Opuscula Omnia*, 5 vols., edited by P. Mandonnet, Paris, Lethielleux, 1927.

St. *Thomae Aquinatis Quaestiones Disputatae et Quaestiones duodecim Quodlibetales*, 5 vols., 7th edition, Rome, Marietti, 1942.

Basic Writings of Saint Thomas Aquinas, 2 vols., edited and annotated, with an Introduction, by Anton C. Pegis, New York, Random House, 1945.

11. Latin writers (St. Augustine, St. Hilary, St. Gregory the

Great, Boethius, Gennadius) are quoted from J. P. Migne, *Patrologia Latina*, 221 vols., Paris, 1844–1864 (with later printings).

12. St. John Damascene, St. Gregory of Nyssa, St. Basil the Great, the Pseudo-Dionysius, Nemesius, and Origen are quoted from J. P. Migne, *Patrologia Graeca*, 162 vols., Paris, 1857–1866 (with later printings).

Abbreviations used in the footnotes:
PL: *Patrologia Latina*
PG: *Patrologia Graeca*
SCG: *Summa Contra Gentiles*

II. STUDIES

1. The creation and distinction of things

Anderson, James F., *The Cause of Being*, St. Louis, Herder, 1952.

Chevalier, Jacques, *La notion du nécessaire chez Aristote et ses prédecesseurs*, Paris, Alcan, 1915.

Donnelly, P. T., "St. Thomas and the Ultimate Purpose of Creation", *Theological Studies*, 2 (1941), 53–83.

Durantil, J., "La notion de la création dans Saint Thomas", *Annales de philosophie chrétienne*, 14 (1912).

Forest, A., *La structure métaphysique du concert selon S. Thomas d'Aquin*, Paris, Vrin, 1931, pp. 46–71.

Garrigou-Lagrange, R., O. P., *The Trinity and God the Creator*, translated from the French by Frederic C. Eckhoff, St. Louis, Herder, 1952, ch. 18–27.

Geiger, L.-B, O. P., *La participation dans la philosophie de s. Thomas*, Paris, Vrin, 1942, ch. 14.

Gilson, Etienne, *Being and Some Philosophers*, Toronto, Pontifical Institute of Mediaeval Studies, 1949, ch. 3–4.

————, *The Spirit of Mediaeval Philosophy*, translated from the French by A. H. C. Downes, New York, Scribners, 1940, ch. 5.

————, *La philosophie au moyen âge*, 2nd edition, Paris, Payot, 1944, part 11, ch. 2.

Joyce, G. H., S. J., *Principles of Natural Theology*, London, Longmans, 1924, part 3, ch. 14.

Maritain, Jacques, *Approaches to God*, translated from the French by P. O'Reilly, New York, Harper, 1954.

Mascall, E. L., *He Who Is*, London, Longmans, 1948, ch. 8.

Meyer, H., *The Philosophy of St. Thomas Aquinas*, translated from the German by Frederic C. Eckhoff, St. Louis, Herder, 1944, ch. 12–14.

Pegis, A. C., *St. Thomas and the Greeks*, Milwaukee, Marquette University Press, 1937.

———, "The Dilemma of Being and Unity", in *Essays in Thomism* (Symposium edited by R. Brennan), New York, Sheed and Ward, 1942.

Penido, M. T.-L., *Le rôle de l'analogie en théologie dogmatique*, Paris, Vrin, 1931, part 2, ch. 2.

Rickaby, J., S. J., *Studies in God and His Creatures*, London, Longmans, 1924, ch. 4.

Sertillanges, A. D., O. P., *Foundations of Thomistic Philosophy*, translated from the French by Godfrey Anstruther, O. P., London, Sands, 1931, ch. 4.

———, *L'idée de création et ses retentissements en philosophie*, Paris, Aubier, 1945.

———, "La création", Revue Thomiste, 11 (1928), 97–115.

———, "La notion de création", Revue Thomiste, 13 (1930), pp. 48–57.

Smith, Gerard, S. J., *Natural Theology*, New York, Macmillan, 1951, ch. 15.

———, "Avicenna and the Possibles", *New Scholasticism*, 17 (1943), pp. 340–357.

2. The nature of created things, with special reference to man and the angels

Brennan, R. E., O. P., *Thomistic Psychology*, New York, Macmillan, 1941, ch. 1–3, 7, 11–12.

Collins, James, *The Thomistic Philosophy of the Angels*, Washington, The Catholic University of America Press, 1947.

Del Prado, N.. *De Veritate Fundamentali Philosophiae Christianae*, Fribourg (Switzerland), 1911, Book 3, ch. 4; Book 4, ch. 2.

Eslick, E. J., "The Thomistic Doctrine of the Unity of Creation", *New Scholasticism*, 13 (1939), pp. 49–70.

Gilson, Etienne, *The Spirit of Mediaeval Philosophy*, translated from the French by A. H. C. Downes, New York, Scribners, 1940, ch. 9–10.

——, *Le Thomisme*, 5th edition, in series, *Études de philosophie médiévale*, I, Paris, Vrin, 1945, Part 2, ch. 1–4.

——, *History of Christian Philosophy in the Middle Ages*, New York, Random House, 1955, part 3, ch. 1; part 8, ch. 1 and 3.

Grabmann, M., O. P., *Thomas Aquinas*, translated from the German by Virgil Michel, New York, Longmans, 1928, ch. 9.

Harmon, F. L., *Principles of Psychology*, Milwaukee, Bruce, 1938, ch. 22.

Klubertanz, G. P., S. J., *The Philosophy of Human Nature*, New York, Appleton-Century-Crofts, 1953, ch. 2–4, 8, 13–14.

Maher, M., S. J., *Psychology*, 9th edition, New York, Longmans, 1933, ch. 12–14, 21–26.

Pegis, A. C., *St. Thomas and the Problem of the Soul in the Thirteenth Century*, Toronto, Institute of Mediaeval Studies, 1934.

Riedl, J. O., "The Nature of the Angels", in *Essays in Thomism*, (Symposium edited by R. Brennan), New York, Sheed and Ward, 1942.

Sertillanges, A. D., O. P., *Foundations of Thomistic Philosophy*, translated from the French by Godfrey Anstruther, O. P., London, Sands, 1931, ch. 7.

Wild, John, *Introduction to Realistic Philosophy*, New York, Harper, 1948, pp. 304–402.

Saint Thomas Aquinas

ON THE TRUTH OF THE CATHOLIC FAITH

BOOK TWO: CREATION

Chapter 1.

THE CONNECTION BETWEEN THE FOLLOWING
CONSIDERATIONS AND THE PRECEDING ONES

"I meditated upon all Thy works: I medi-
tated upon the works of Thy hands"
(Ps. 142.5).

[1] Of no thing whatever can a perfect knowledge be obtained unless its operation is known, because the measure and quality of a thing's power is judged from the manner and type of its operation, and its power, in turn, manifests its nature; for a thing's natural aptitude for operation follows upon its actual possession of a certain kind of nature.

[2] There are, however, two sorts of operation, as Aristotle teaches in *Metaphysics* IX[1]: one that remains in the agent and is a perfection of it, as the act of sensing, understanding, and willing; another that passes over into an external thing, and is a perfection of the thing made as a result of that operation, the acts of heating, cutting and building, for example.

[3] Now, both kinds of operation belong to God: the former, in that He understands, wills, rejoices, and loves; the latter, in that He brings things into being, preserves them, and governs them. But, since the former operation is a perfection of the operator, the latter a perfection of the thing made, and since the agent is naturally prior to the thing made and is the cause of it, it follows that the first of these types of operation is the ground of the second, and naturally precedes it, as a cause precedes its effect. Clear evidence of this fact, indeed, is found in human affairs; for in the thought and will of the craftsman lie the principle and plan of the work of building.

[4] Therefore, as a simple perfection of the operator, the first type of operation claims for itself the name of *operation*, or, again, of *action*; the second, as being a perfection of the

1. Aristotle, *Metaphysics*, IX, 8 (1050a 25).

thing made, is called *making* so that the things which a craftsman produces by action of this kind are said to be his *handiwork*.

[5]   Of the first type of operation in God we have already
spoken in the preceding Book of this work, where we treated
of the divine knowledge and will.[2] Hence, for a complete
study of the divine truth, the second operation, whereby
things are made and governed by God, remains to be dealt
with.

[6]   In fact, this order we can gather from the words quoted
above. For the Psalmist first speaks of meditation upon the
first type of operation, when he says: "I have meditated on all
Thy operations"; thus, *operation* is here referred to the divine
act of understanding and will. Then he refers to meditation on
God's works: "and I meditated on the works of Thy hands";
so that by "the works of Thy hands" we understand heaven
and earth, and all that is brought into being by God, as the
handiwork produced by a craftsman.

Chapter 2.

THAT THE CONSIDERATION OF CREATURES IS
USEFUL FOR INSTRUCTION OF FAITH

[1]   This sort of meditation on the divine works is indeed
necessary for instruction of faith in God.

[2]   First, because meditation on His works enables us in
some measure to admire and reflect upon His wisdom. For
things made by art are representative of the art itself, being
made in likeness to the art. Now, God brought things into
being by His wisdom; wherefore the Psalm (103:24) declares:
"Thou hast made all things in wisdom." Hence, from reflection upon God's works we are able to infer His wisdom, since,
by a certain communication of His likeness, it is spread abroad
in the things He has made. For it is written: "He poured her

2. SCG, I, ch. 44–102.

out," namely, wisdom, "upon all His works" (Eccli. 1:10). Therefore, the Psalmist, after saying: "Thy knowledge is become wonderful to me: it is high, and I cannot reach it," and after referring to the aid of the divine illumination, when he says: "Night shall be my light," etc., confesses that he was aided in knowing the divine wisdom by reflection upon God's works, saying: "Wonderful are Thy works, and my soul knoweth right well" (Ps. 138:6, 11, 14).

[3] Secondly, this consideration [of God's works] leads to admiration of God's sublime power, and consequently inspires in men's hearts reverence for God. For the power of the worker is necessarily understood to transcend the things made. And so it is said: "If they," namely, the philosophers, "admired their power and effects," namely of the heavens, stars, and elements of the world, "let them understand that He that made them is mightier than they" (Wisd. 13:4). Also it is written: "The invisible things of God are clearly seen, being understood by the things that are made: His eternal power also and divinity" (Rom. 1:20). Now, the fear and reverence of God result from this admiration. Hence, it is said: "Great is Thy name in might. Who shall not fear Thee, O King of Nations?" (Jer. 10:6–7).

[4] Thirdly, this consideration incites the souls of men to the love of God's goodness. For whatever goodness and perfection is distributed to the various creatures, in partial or particular measure, is united together in Him universally, as in the source of all goodness, as we proved in Book I.[1] If, therefore, the goodness, beauty, and delightfulness of creatures are so alluring to the minds of men, the fountainhead of God's own goodness, compared with the rivulets of goodness found in creatures, will draw the enkindled minds of men wholly to Itself. Hence it is said in the Psalm (91:5): "Thou hast given me, O Lord, a delight in Thy doings, and in the works of Thy hands I shall rejoice." And elsewhere it is written concerning the children of men: "They shall be inebriated with the plenty of Thy house," that is, of all creatures, "and Thou shalt make them drink of the torrent of Thy pleasure: for with Thee is the fountain of life" (Ps. 35:9–10). And, against

1. SCG, I, ch. 28 and 40.

certain men, it is said: "By these good things that are seen," namely, creatures, which are good by a kind of participation, "they could not understand Him that is" (Wis. 13:1), namely, truly good; indeed, is goodness itself, as was shown in Book I.[2]

[5]   Fourthly, this consideration endows men with a certain likeness to God's perfection. For it was shown in Book I that, by knowing Himself, God beholds all other things in Himself.[3] Since, then, the Christian faith teaches man principally about God, and makes him know creatures by the light of divine revelation, there arises in man a certain likeness of God's wisdom. So it is said: "But we all beholding the glory of the Lord with open face, are transformed into the same image" (II Cor. 3:18).

[6]   It is therefore evident that the consideration of creatures has its part to play in building the Christian faith. And for this reason it is said: "I will remember the works of the Lord, and I will declare the things I have seen: by the words of the Lord are His works" (Ecclus. 42:15).

Chapter 3.

THAT KNOWLEDGE OF THE NATURE OF CREATURES SERVES TO DESTROY ERRORS CONCERNING GOD

[1]   The consideration of creatures is further necessary, not only for the building up of truth, but also for the destruction of errors. For errors about creatures sometimes lead one astray from the truth of faith, so far as the errors are inconsistent with true knowledge of God. Now, this happens in many ways.

[2]   First, because through ignorance of the nature of creatures men are sometimes so far perverted as to set up as the first cause and as God that which can only receive its being from something else; for they think that nothing exists beyond

2. *SCG*, 1, ch. 38.   3. *SCG*, I, ch. 49–55.

the realm of visible creatures. Such were those who identified God with this, that, and the other kind of body; and of these it is said: "Who have imagined either the fire, or the wind, or the swift air, or the circle of the stars, or the great water, or the sun and moon to be the gods" (Wis. 13:2).

[3] Secondly, because they attribute to certain creatures that which belongs only to God. This also results from error concerning creatures. For what is incompatible with a thing's nature is not ascribed to it except through ignorance of its nature—as if man were said to have three feet. Now, what belongs solely to God is incompatible with the nature of a created thing, just as that which is exclusively man's is incompatible with another thing's nature. Thus, it is from ignorance of the creature's nature that the aforesaid error arises. And against this error it is said: "They gave the incommunicable name to stones and wood" (Wis. 14:21). Into this error fell those who attribute the creation of things, or knowledge of the future, or the working of miracles to causes other than God.

[4] Thirdly, because through ignorance of the creature's nature something is subtracted from God's power in its working upon creatures. This is evidenced in the case of those who set up two principles of reality; in those who assert that things proceed from God, not by the divine will, but by natural necessity; and again, in those who withdraw either all or some things from the divine providence, or who deny that it can work outside the ordinary course of things. For all these notions are derogatory to God's power. Against such persons it is said: "Who looked upon the Almighty as if He could do nothing" (Job 22:17), and: "Thou showest Thy power, when men will not believe Thee to be absolute in power" (Wis. 12:17).

[5] Fourthly, through ignorance of the nature of things, and, consequently, of his own place in the order of the universe, this rational creature, man, who by faith is led to God as his last end, believes that he is subject to other creatures to which he is in fact superior. Such is evidently the case with those who subject human wills to the stars, and against these it is

said: "Be not afraid of the signs of heaven, which the heathens fear" (Jer. 10:2); and this is likewise true of those who think that angels are the creators of souls, that human souls are mortal, and, generally, of persons who hold any similar views derogatory to the dignity of man.

[6]   It is, therefore, evident that the opinion is false of those who asserted that it made no difference to the truth of the faith what anyone holds about creatures, so long as one thinks rightly about God, as Augustine tells us in his book *On the Origin of the Soul*.[1] For error concerning creatures, by subjecting them to causes other than God, spills over into false opinion about God, and takes men's minds away from Him, to whom faith seeks to lead them.

[7]   For this reason Scripture threatens punishment to those who err about creatures, as to unbelievers, in the words of the Psalm (27:5): "Because they have not understood the works of the Lord and the operations of His hands, Thou shalt destroy them, and shalt not build them up"; and: "These things they thought and were deceived," and further on: "They esteemed not the honor of holy souls" (Wis. 2:21–22).

Chapter 4.

THAT THE PHILOSOPHER AND THE THEOLOGIAN CONSIDER CREATURES IN DIFFERENT WAYS

[1]   Now, from what has been said it is evident that the teaching of the Christian faith deals with creatures so far as they reflect a certain likeness of God, and so far as error concerning them leads to error about God. And so they are viewed in a different light by that doctrine and by human philosophy. For human philosophy considers them as they are, so that the different parts of philosophy are found to correspond to the different genera of things. The Christian faith, however, does

1. St. Augustine, *De anima et ejus origine*, IV, 4, (PL, 44, col. 527).

not consider them as such; thus, it regards fire not as fire, but as representing the sublimity of God, and as being directed to Him in any way at all. For as it is said: "Full of the glory of the Lord is His work. Hath not the Lord made the saints to declare all His wonderful works?" (Ecclus. 42:16–17).

[2] For this reason, also, the philosopher and the believer consider different matters about creatures. The philosopher considers such things as belong to them by nature—the upward tendency of fire, for example; the believer, only such things as belong to them according as they are related to God—the fact, for instance, that they are created by God, are subject to Him, and so on.

[3] Hence, imperfection is not to be imputed to the teaching of the faith if it omits many properties of things, such as the figure of the heaven and the quality of its motion. For neither does the natural philosopher consider the same characters of a line as the geometrician, but only those that accrue to it as terminus of a natural body.

[4] But any things concerning creatures that are considered in common by the philosopher and the believer are conveyed through different principles in each case. For the philosopher takes his argument from the proper causes of things; the believer, from the first cause—for such reasons as that a thing has been handed down in this manner by God, or that this conduces to God's glory, or that God's power is infinite. Hence, also, [the doctrine of the faith] ought to be called the highest wisdom, since it treats of the highest cause; as we read in Deuteronomy (4:6): "For this is your wisdom and understanding in the sight of nations." And, therefore, human philosophy serves her as the first wisdom. Accordingly, divine wisdom sometimes argues from principles of human philosophy. For among philosophers, too, the first philosophy utilizes the teachings of all the sciences in order to realize its objectives.

[5] Hence again, the two kinds of teaching do not follow the same order. For in the teaching of philosophy, which considers creatures in themselves and leads us from them to the knowledge of God, the first consideration is about crea-

tures; the last, of God. But in the teaching of faith, which considers creatures only in their relation to God, the consideration of God comes first, that of creatures afterwards. And thus the doctrine of faith is more perfect, as being more like the knowledge possessed by God, who, in knowing Himself, immediately knows other things.

[6]   And so, following this order, after what has been said in Book I about God in Himself, it remains for us to treat of the things which derive from Him.

Chapter 5.

ORDER OF PROCEDURE

[1]   We shall treat of these matters in the following order: first, the bringing forth of things into being;[1] second, their distinction;[2] third, the nature of these same things, brought forth and distinct from one another, so far as it is relevant to the truth of the faith.[3]

Chapter 6.

THAT IT IS PROPER TO GOD TO BE THE SOURCE OF THE BEING OF OTHER THINGS

[1]   Presupposing the things already demonstrated in Book I, let us now show that it belongs to God to be the principle and cause of being to other things.

[2]   For in Book I of this work it was shown, by means of Aristotle's demonstration, that there is a first efficient cause, which we call God.[1] But an efficient cause brings its effects into being. Therefore, God is the cause of being to other things.

1. See below, ch. 6.
2. See below, ch. 39.
3. See below, ch. 46.
1. SCG, I, ch. 13.

[3] Also, it was shown in Book I, by the argument of the same author, that there is a first immovable mover, which we call God.[2] But the first mover in any order of movements is the cause of all the movements in that order. Since, then, many things are brought into existence by the movements of the heaven, and since God has been shown to be the first mover in the order of those movements, it follows necessarily that God is the cause of being to many things.

[4] Furthermore, that which belongs to a thing through itself must be in it universally; as for man to be rational and fire to tend upwards. But to enact an actuality is, through itself, proper to a being in act; for every agent acts according as it is in act. Therefore, every being in act is by its nature apt to enact something existing in act. But God is a being in act, as was shown in Book I.[3] Therefore, it is proper to Him to enact some being in act, to which He is the cause of being.

[5] It is, moreover, a sign of perfection in things of the lower order of reality that they are able to produce their like, as Aristotle points out in his *Meteorology*.[4] But, as was shown in Book I, God is supremely perfect.[5] Therefore, it belongs to Him to produce something actual, like Himself, so as to be the cause of its existence.

[6] Then, too, it was shown in Book I that God wills to communicate His being to other things by way of likeness.[6] But it belongs to the will's perfection to be the principle of action and of movement, as is said in *De anima* III.[7] Therefore, since God's will is perfect, He does not lack the power of communicating His being to a thing by way of likeness. And thus He will be the cause of its being.

[7] Moreover, the more perfect is the principle of a thing's action, to so many more and more remote things can it extend its action: thus, fire, if weak, heats only things nearby; if

2. *Ibid.*
3. SCG, I, ch. 16.
4. Aristotle, *Meteorology*, IV, 3 (380a 15).
5. SCG, I, ch. 28.
6. SCG, I, ch. 75.
7. Aristotle, *De anima*, III, 10 (433a 22).

strong, it heats even distant things. But pure act, which God is, is more perfect than act mingled with potentiality, as it is in us. But act is the principle of action. Since, then, by the act which is in us we can proceed not only to actions abiding in us, such as understanding and willing, but also to actions which terminate in things outside of us, and through which certain things are made by us, much more can God, because He is in act, not only understand and will, but also produce an effect. And thus He can be the cause of being to other things.

[8] Hence, it is said: "Who doth great things and unsearchable things without number" (Job 5:9).

Chapter 7.

THAT ACTIVE POWER EXISTS IN GOD

[1] Now, from this it is clear that God is powerful, and that active power is fittingly attributed to Him.

[2] For active power is the principle of acting upon another, as such. But it is proper to God to be the source of being to other things. Therefore, it pertains to Him to be powerful.

[3] Again, just as passive potency follows upon being in potency, so active potency follows upon being in act; for a thing acts in consequence of its being in act, and undergoes action because it is in potency. But it is proper to God to be in act. Therefore, active power belongs to Him.

[4] The divine perfection, furthermore, includes in itself the perfections of all things, as was shown in Book I.[1] But active power belongs to the perfection of a thing; for the more perfect any thing is, so much the greater is its power found to be. Therefore, active power cannot be wanting in God.

[5] Moreover, whatever acts has the power to act, since that which has not the power to act cannot possibly act; and what

1. SCG, I, ch. 28.

cannot possibly act is necessarily non-active. But God is an acting and a moving being, as was shown in Book I.[2] Therefore, He has the power to act; and active, but not passive, potency is properly ascribed to Him.

[6] Thus it is said in the Psalm (88:9): "Thou art mighty, O Lord," and elsewhere: "Thy power and Thy justice, O God, even to the highest great things Thou hast done." (Ps. 70: 18–19).

Chapter 8.

THAT GOD'S POWER IS HIS SUBSTANCE

[1] Now, from this the further conclusion can be drawn that God's power is His very substance.

[2] For active power belongs to a thing according as it is in act. But God is act itself, not a being whose actuality is due to an act that is other than itself; for in God there is no potentiality, as was shown in Book I of this work.[1] Therefore, God is His own power.

[3] Again, we argue from the fact that whatever is powerful and is not its own power is powerful by participation of another's power. But nothing can be said of God participatively, since He is His very own being, as was shown in Book I.[2] Therefore, He is His own power.

[4] Then, too, active power pertains to a thing's perfection, as we have just seen.[3] But every perfection of God is contained in His very being, as was shown in Book I.[4] Therefore, God's power is not other than His very being, as we likewise proved in Book I.[5] Therefore, He is His own power.

2. *SCG*, I, ch. 13.
1. *SCG*, I, ch. 16.
2. *SCG*, I, ch. 22.
3. See above, ch. 7.
4. *SCG*, I, ch. 28.
5. *SCG*, I, ch. 22.

[5]   Again, in things whose powers are not their substance, the powers themselves are accidents. Hence, natural power is placed in the second species of *quality*.[6] But in God there can be no accident, as was shown in Book I.[7] Therefore, God is His power.

[6]   Moreover, everything which is through another is reduced to that which is through itself, as to that which is first. But other agents are reduced to God as first agent. Therefore, God is agent through His very self. But that which acts through itself acts through its essence, and that by which a thing acts is its active power. Therefore, God's very essence is His active power.

Chapter 9.

THAT GOD'S POWER IS HIS ACTION

[1]   From this it can be shown that God's power is not other than His action.

[2]   For things identical with one and the same thing are identical with one another. But God's power is His substance, as was just proved. And His action is His substance, as was shown in Book I[1] with regard to His intellectual operation; for the same argument applies to His other operations. Therefore, in God power is not distinct from action.

[3]   The action of a thing, moreover, is a complement of its power; for action is compared to power as second act to first. But God's power is not completed by another than Himself, since it is His very essence. Therefore, in God power and action are not distinct.

[4]   Then, too, just as active power is something acting, so is its essence something being. But, as we have seen, God's power is His essence. Therefore, His action is His being. But His being is His substance.[2] Therefore, God's action is His substance; and thus the same conclusion follows as before.

6. Cf. Aristotle, *Categories*, VI, 7.   7. *SCG*, I, ch. 23.
1. *SCG*, I, ch. 45, ¶6.   2. Cf. *SCG*, I, ch. 22.

[5] Furthermore, an action that is not the substance of the agent is in the agent as an accident in its subject; and that is why *action* is reckoned as one of the nine categories of accident.[3] But nothing can exist in God in the manner of an accident.[4] Therefore, God's action is not other than His substance and His power.

Chapter 10.

HOW POWER IS ATTRIBUTED TO GOD

[1] But, since nothing is its own principle, and God's action is not other than His power, it is clear from the foregoing that power is attributed to God, not as principle of action, but as principle of the thing made. And since power implies relation to something else as having the character of a principle (for active power is the principle of acting on something else, as Aristotle says in *Metaphysics* v[1]), it is evident that power is in truth attributed to God in relation to things made, not in relation to action, except according to our way of understanding, namely, so far as our intellect considers both God's power and His action through diverse conceptions. Hence, if certain actions are proper to God which do not pass into something made but remain in Him, power is not attributed to Him in their regard, except according to our manner of understanding, and not according to reality. Such actions are understanding and willing. Properly speaking, therefore, God's power does not regard such actions, but only effects. Consequently, intellect and will are in God, not as powers, but only as actions.

[2] From the foregoing it is clear, also, that the multifarious actions attributed to God, as understanding, willing, producing things, and the like are not diverse realities, since each of these actions in God is His very being, which is one and the same. Indeed, from what has been shown in Book I,[2] it can

3. Cf. Aristotle, *Categories*, IV (2a 3).
4. *SCG*, I, ch. 23.
1. Aristotle, *Metaphysics*, V, 12 (1019a 18).
2. *SCG*, I, ch. 31 and 35.

be clearly seen how a thing may be signified in many ways without prejudice to the truth of its oneness in reality.

Chapter 11.

THAT SOMETHING IS SAID OF GOD IN
RELATION TO CREATURES

[1]   Now, since power is proper to God in relation to His effects, and since power, as was said,[1] has the character of a principle, and since *principle* expresses relationship to that which proceeds from it, it is evident that something can be said of God relatively, with regard to His effects.

[2]   It is, moreover, inconceivable that one thing be said in relation to another unless, conversely, the latter be said in relation to it. But other things are spoken of in relation to God; for instance, as regards their being, which they possess from God, they are dependent upon Him, as has been shown.[2] Conversely, therefore, God may be spoken of in relation to creatures.

[3]   Further. Likeness is a certain kind of relation. But God, even as other agents, produces something like to Himself.[3] Therefore, something is said of Him relatively.

[4]   Then, too, knowledge is spoken of in relation to the thing known. But God possesses knowledge not only of Himself, but also of other things. Therefore, something is said of God in relation to other things.

[5]   Again. Mover is spoken of in relation to thing moved, and agent in relation to thing done. But, as was shown,[4] God is an agent and an unmoved mover. Therefore relations are predicated of Him.

[6]   And again. *First* implies a relation, and so does *highest*.

1. See above, ch. 10, ¶1.   2. See above, ch. 6.
3. *SCG*, I, ch. 29, ¶2.   4. *SCG*, I, ch. 13, ¶3–29.

But it was shown in Book I that God is the first being and the highest good.[5]

[7] It is, therefore, evident that many things are said of God relatively.

Chapter 12.

THAT RELATIONS PREDICATED OF GOD IN REFERENCE TO CREATURES DO NOT REALLY EXIST IN HIM

[1] Now, these relations which refer to God's effects cannot possibly exist in Him really.

[2] For they cannot exist in Him as accidents in a subject, since there is no accident in Him, as was shown in Book I.[1] Neither can they be God's very substance, because, as Aristotle says in the *Categories*,[2] relative terms are those "which in their very being refer somehow to something else"; so that God's substance would then have to be referred to something else. But that which is essentially referred to another depends upon it in a certain way, since it can neither be nor be understood without it. Hence, it would follow that God's substance would depend on something else extrinsic to it, so that He would not be, of Himself, the necessary being, as He was shown to be in Book I.[3] Therefore, such relations do not really exist in God.

[3] It was shown in Book I, moreover, that God is the first measure of all things.[4] Hence, He stands in relation to other beings as the knowable to our knowledge, which is measured by the knowable; for "opinion or speech is true or false according as a thing is or is not," as Aristotle says in the *Categories*.[5] But, although a thing is said to be knowable in relation to knowledge, the relation is not really in the knowable,

5. *SCG*, I, ch. 13 and 41.
1. *SCG*, I, ch. 23.
2. Aristotle, *Categories*, VII (6a 36).
3. *SCG*, I, ch. 13, ¶35.　　4. *Ibid*.
5. Aristotle, *Categories*, V (4b 9).

but only in the knowledge. Thus, as Aristotle observes in *Metaphysics* v, the knowable is so called relatively, "not because it is itself related, but because something else is related to it."[6] Therefore the relations in question have no real being in God.

[4]   A further point. The aforesaid relations are predicated of God with respect not only to those things that are in act, but to those also that are in potency; for He both has knowledge of them and in relation to them is called the first being and the supreme good. But there are no real relations of that which is actual to that which is not actual, but potential; otherwise, it would follow that there are actually an infinity of relations in the same subject, since potentially infinite numbers are greater than the number two, which is prior to them all. God, however, is not referred to actual things otherwise than to potential things, for He is not changed as the result of producing certain things. Therefore, He is not referred to other things by a relation really existing in Him.

[5]   Furthermore, we observe that whatever receives something anew must be changed, either essentially or accidentally. Now, certain relations are predicated of God anew; for example, that He is Lord or Governor of this thing which begins to exist anew. Hence, if a relation were predicated of God as really existing in Him, it would follow that something accrues to God anew, and thus that He is changed either essentially or accidentally; the contrary of this having been proved in Book I.[7]

Chapters 13 and 14.

HOW THE AFORESAID RELATIONS ARE
PREDICATED OF GOD

[1]   It cannot be said, however, that these relations exist as realities outside God.

6. Aristotle, *Metaphysics*, IV, 15 (1021a 30).
7. *SCG*, I, ch. 13, ¶3–29.

[2]   For, if they did, we should have to consider yet other relations of God to those that are realities, seeing that God is the first of beings and highest of goods. And if these also are realities, we shall be compelled to find third relations; and so on endlessly. The relations by which God is referred to other things, therefore, are not realities existing outside Him.

[3]   Moreover, there are two ways in which a thing is predicated denominatively: first, from something external to it; as from place a person is said to be *somewhere*; from time, *somewhen*; second, from something present in it; as *white* from *whiteness*. Yet in no case is a thing denominated from a relation as existing outside it, but only as inhering in it. For example: a man is not denominated *father* except from the fatherhood which is in him. Therefore, the relations by which God is referred to creatures cannot possibly be realities outside Him.

[4]   Having proved that these relations have no real existence in God, and yet are predicated of Him, it follows that they are attributed to Him solely in accordance with our manner of understanding, from the fact that other things are referred to Him. For in understanding one thing to be referred to another, our intellect simultaneously grasps the relation of the latter to it, although sometimes that thing is not really related.

[5]   And so it is evident, also, that such relations are not said of God in the same way as other things predicated of Him. For all other things, such as wisdom and will, express His essence; the aforesaid relations by no means do so really, but only as regards our way of understanding. Nevertheless, our understanding is not fallacious. For, from the very fact that our intellect understands that the relations of the divine effects are terminated in God Himself, it predicates certain things of Him relatively; so also do we understand and express the knowable relatively, from the fact that knowledge is referred to it.

[6]   [Chapter 14]   From these considerations it is clear, also, that it is not prejudicial to God's simplicity if many relations are predicated of Him, although they do not signify His es-

sence; because those relations are consequent upon our way of understanding. For nothing prevents our intellect from understanding many things, and being referred in many ways to that which is in itself simple, so as to consider that simple reality under a manifold relationship. And the more simple a thing, the greater is its power, and of so many more things is it the principle, so that it is understood as related in so many more ways. Thus, a point is the principle of more things than a line is, and a line than a surface. Therefore, the very fact that many things are predicated of God in a relative manner bears witness to His supreme simplicity.

Chapter 15.

THAT GOD IS TO ALL THINGS THE CAUSE
OF BEING

[1]   Now, because it has been proved[1] that God is the source of being to some things, it must be demonstrated further that everything besides God derives its being from Him.

[2]   For whatever does not belong to a thing as such appertains to it through some cause, as *white* to man; that which has no cause is primary and immediate, so that it must needs be through itself and as such. But no single entity can as such belong to two things and to both of them; for what is said of a thing as such is limited to that very thing; the possession of three angles equal to two right angles is proper to the triangle exclusively. So, if something belongs to two things, it will not belong to both as such. Therefore, no single thing can possibly be predicated of two things so as to be said of neither of them by reason of a cause. On the contrary, either the one must be the cause of the other—as fire is the cause of heat in a mixed body, and yet each is called *hot*—or some third thing must be the cause of both, as fire is the cause of two candles giving light. But being is predicated of everything that is. Hence, there cannot possibly be two things neither of which

1. See above, ch. 6.

has a cause of its being, but either both of them must exist through a cause, or the one must be the cause of the other's being. Everything which is in any way at all must then derive its being from that whose being has no cause. But we have already shown[2] that God is this being whose existence has no cause. Everything which is in any mode whatever, therefore, is from Him. Now, to say that *being* is not a univocal predicate argues nothing against this conclusion. For *being* is not predicated of beings equivocally, but analogically, and thus a reduction to one must be made.

[3] Furthermore, whatever a thing possesses by its own nature, and not from some other cause, cannot be diminished and deficient in it. For, if something essential be subtracted from or added to a nature, another nature will at once arise, as in the case of numbers, where the addition or the subtraction of the unit changes the species of the number. If, however, the nature or quiddity of a thing remains integral, and yet something in it is found to be diminished, it is at once clear that this diminution does not derive simply from that nature, but from something else, by whose removal the nature is diminished. Therefore, whatever belongs to one thing less than to others belongs to it not by virtue of its own nature alone, but through some other cause. Thus, that thing of which a genus is chiefly predicated will be the cause of everything in that genus. So we see that what is most hot is the cause of heat in all hot things; and what is most light, the cause of all illuminated things. But as we proved in Book I, God is being in the highest mode.[3] Therefore, He is the cause of all things of which *being* is predicated.

[4] Then, too, the order of causes necessarily corresponds to the order of effects, since effects are commensurate with their causes. Hence, just as effects are referred to their appropriate causes, so that which is common in such effects must be reduced to a common cause. Thus, transcending the particular causes of the generation of this or that thing is the universal cause of generation—the sun; and above the particular governors of the kingdom, as, indeed, of each city in it, stands

2. *SCG*, I, ch. 13, ¶34.
3. *SCG*, I, ch. 13, ¶35.

the king, the universal cause of government in his whole realm. Now, being is common to everything that is. Above all causes, then, there must be a cause whose proper action is to give being. But we have already shown in Book I that God is the first cause.[4] Everything that is must, therefore, be from God.

[5] Moreover, the cause of everything said to be such and such by way of participation is that which is said to be so by virtue of its essence. Thus, fire is the cause of all hot things as such. But God is *being* by His own essence, because He is the very act of being. Every other being, however, is a being by participation. For that being which is its own act of being can be one only, as was shown in Book I.[5] God, therefore, is the cause of being to all other things.

[6] Again, everything that can be and not-be has a cause; for considered in itself it is indifferent to either, so that something else must exist which determines it to one. Since, then, it is impossible to go on to infinity, there must exist a necessary being which is the cause of all things that can be and not-be. Now, there is a certain kind of necessary being whose necessity is caused. But in this order of things, also, progression to infinity is impossible; so that we must conclude to the existence of something which is of itself necessary being. There can be but one such being, as we proved in Book I.[6] And this being is God. Everything other than God, therefore, must be referred to Him as the cause of its being.

[7] Moreover, as we proved above,[7] God is the maker of things inasmuch as He is in act. But by virtue of His actuality and perfection God embraces all the perfections of things, as was shown in Book I;[8] and thus He is virtually all things. He is, therefore, the maker of all things. But this would not be the case if something besides God were capable of being otherwise than from Him; for nothing is of such a

4. *SCG*, I, ch. 13, ¶34.
5. *SCG*, I, ch. 42, ¶17.
6. *SCG*, I, ch. 42, ¶8.
7. See above, ch. 7, ¶3.
8. *SCG*, I, ch. 28, ¶7, 8.

nature as to be from another and not from another, since if a thing is of a nature not to be from another, then it is through itself a necessary being, and thus can never be from another. Therefore, nothing can be except from God.

[8]   A final argument. Imperfect things originate from perfect things, as seed from the animal. But God is the most perfect being and the highest good, as was shown in Book I.[9] Therefore, He is the cause of the being of all things, and this is especially so in view of the truth already demonstrated[10] that such a cause cannot but be one.

[9]   Now, this truth is confirmed by divine authority; for it is said in the Psalm (145:6): "Who made heaven and earth, the sea, and all the things that are in them"; and: "All things were made by Him, and without Him was made nothing" (John 1:3); and: "Of Him, and by Him, and in Him are all things: to Him be glory for ever" (Rom. 11:36).

[10]   The error of the natural philosophers of old, who asserted that certain bodies exist without a cause, is by this truth abolished, as well as the error of those who say that God is not the cause of the substance of the heaven, but only of its motion.

Chapter 16.

THAT GOD BROUGHT THINGS INTO BEING
FROM NOTHING

[1]   Now, what has been said makes it clear that God brought things into being from no pre-existing subject, as from a matter.

[2]   For, if a thing is an effect produced by God, either something exists before it, or not. If not, our assertion stands, namely, that God produces some effect from nothing pre-existing. If something exists before it, however, we must either

9. *SCG*, I, ch. 28 and 41.
10. *SCG*, I, ch. 42.

go on to infinity, which is impossible in natural causes, as Aristotle proves in *Metaphysics* II,[1] or we must arrive at a first being which presupposes no other. And this being can be none other than God Himself. For we proved in Book I that God is not the matter of any thing;[2] nor, as we have shown,[3] can there be anything other than God which is not made to be by Him. It therefore follows that in the production of His effects God requires no antecedent matter to work from.

[3] Every matter, furthermore, is limited to some particular species by the form with which it is endowed. Consequently, it is the business of an agent limited to some determinate species to produce its effect from pre-existing matter by bestowing a form upon it in any manner whatsoever. But an agent of this kind is a particular agent; for causes are proportionate to their effects. So, an agent that necessarily requires pre-existent matter from which to produce its effect is a particular agent. Now, it is as the universal cause of being that God is an agent, as we proved in the preceding chapter. Therefore, in His action He has no need of any pre-existing matter.

[4] Again. The more universal an effect is, the higher its proper cause; for the higher the cause, to so many more things does its power extend. But *to be* is more universal than *to be moved*, since, as the philosophers also teach, there are some beings—stones and the like—which are immobile. So, above the kind of cause which acts only by moving and changing there must exist that cause which is the first principle of being, and this, as we have proved in the same place, is God. Thus, God does not act only by moving and changing. On the other hand, every agent which cannot bring things into being except from pre-existing matter, acts only by moving and changing; for to make something out of matter is the result of some kind of motion or change. Therefore, to bring things into being without pre-existing matter is not impossible. Hence, God brings things into being without pre-existing matter.

1. Aristotle, *Metaphysics*, Ia, 2 (994a 2).
2. SCG, I, ch. 17.
3. See above, ch. 15.

[5] Moreover, to act only by motion and change is incompatible with the universal cause of being; for, by motion and change a being is not made from absolute non-being, but this being from this non-being. Yet, as was shown, God is the universal principle of being. Therefore, to act only by motion or by change is contrary to His nature. Neither, then, is it proper to Him to need pre-existing matter in order to make something.

[6] An additional argument. Every agent produces something in some way like itself. But every agent acts according as it is in act. Therefore, to produce an effect by somehow causing a form to inhere in a matter will be the proper function of an agent actualized by a form inherent in it, and not by its whole substance. Hence, in *Metaphysics* VII Aristotle proves that material things, which possess forms in matter, are generated by material agents having forms in matter, not by forms existing through themselves.[4] But God is a being in act, not through anything inherent in Him, but through His whole substance, as was proved above.[5] Therefore, the proper mode of His action is to produce the whole subsisting thing, and not merely an inhering entity, namely, a form in a matter. Now, every agent which does not require matter for its action acts in this way. In His action, consequently, God requires no pre-existing matter.

[7] Then, too, matter stands in relation to an agent as the recipient of the action proceeding from that agent. For that same act which belongs to the agent as proceeding therefrom belongs to the patient as residing therein. Therefore, matter is required by an agent in order that it may receive the action of the agent. For the agent's action, received in the patient, is an actuality of the patient's, and a form, or some inception of a form, in it. But God acts by no action which must be received in a patient, for His action is His substance, as was proved above.[6] Therefore, He requires no pre-existing matter in order to produce an effect.

[8] Again. Every agent whose action necessitates the prior

4. Aristotle, *Metaphysics*, VII, 8 (1033b 10).
5. SCG, I, ch. 22 and 23.   6. See above, ch. 8 and 9.

existence of matter possesses a matter proportioned to its action, so that whatever lies within the agent's power exists in its entirety in the potentiality of the matter; otherwise, the agent could not actualize all that lies within its active power, and hence, as regards the things it could not actualize, it would possess that power in vain. But matter stands in no such relation to God. For in matter there does not exist potentiality to any particular quantity, as Aristotle points out in *Physics* III;[7] whereas God's power is absolutely infinite, as we proved in Book I of this work.[8] No pre-existing matter, therefore, is required by God as necessary ground for His action.

[9]   Diverse things, furthermore, have diverse matters; for the matter of spiritual things is not the same as that of corporeal things, nor is the matter of the heavenly bodies the same as that of corruptible bodies. This, indeed, is clear from the fact that receptivity, which is the property of matter, is not of the same nature in these things. For receptivity in spiritual things is intelligible in character; thus, the intellect receives the species of intelligible things, though not according to their material being; while the heavenly bodies acquire new positions, but no new existences, as the lower bodies do. Hence, there is no one matter which is in potentiality to universal being. But God is universally productive of the total being of things.[9] There is, then, no matter corresponding, in proportionate fashion, to Him. Hence, He stands in no need of matter.

[10]   Moreover, wherever in the universe we find some mutual proportion and order among things, one of those things must derive its being from another, or both from some one thing. For an order must be founded in one term by it corresponding to another; otherwise, order or proportion would be the result of chance, which cannot be allowed in the first principles of things, since it would then follow with even greater force that all else are fortuitous. So, if a matter commensurate with God's action exists, it follows either that the one is derived from the other, or both from a third thing. But, since God is the first being and the first cause, He cannot

7. Aristotle, *Physics*, III, 6 (206b 15).
8. SCG, I, ch. 43.
9. See above, ch. 15.

be the effect of matter, nor can He derive His being from any third cause. It remains, therefore, that, if any matter proportioned to God's action exists, then He Himself is the cause of it.

[11] The first existent, furthermore, is necessarily the cause of the things that exist; for, if they were not caused, then they would not be set in order from that first being, as we have just shown. Now, the order that obtains between act and potentiality is this: although in one and the same thing which is sometimes in potentiality and sometimes in act, the potentiality is prior in time to the act, which however is prior in nature to the potentiality, nevertheless, absolutely speaking, act is necessarily prior to potentiality. This is evident from the fact that a potentiality is not actualized except by a being actually existing. But matter is only potentially existent. Therefore, God who is pure act, must be absolutely prior to matter, and consequently the cause of it. Matter, then, is not necessarily presupposed for His action.

[12] Also, prime matter in some way is, for it is potentially a being. But God is the cause of everything that is, as was shown above.[10] Hence, God is the cause of prime matter—in respect to which nothing pre-exists. The divine action, therefore, requires no pre-existing nature.

[13] Holy Scripture confirms this truth, saying: "In the beginning God created heaven and earth" (Gen. 1:1). For to create means nothing else than to bring something into being without any pre-existing matter.

[14] This truth refutes the error of the ancient philosophers who asserted that matter has no cause whatsoever, for they perceived that in the actions of particular agents there is always an antecedent subject underlying the action; and from this observation they assumed the opinion common to all, that from nothing, comes nothing. Now, indeed, this is true of particular agents. But the ancient philosophers had not yet attained to the knowledge of the universal agent which is productive of the total being, and for His action necessarily presupposes nothing whatever.

10. *Ibid.*

Chapter 17.

THAT CREATION IS NEITHER MOTION NOR CHANGE

[1]   In the light of what has been proved, it is evident that God's action, which is without pre-existing matter and is called *creation*, is neither a motion nor a change, properly speaking.

[2]   For all motion or change is the "act of that which exists potentially, as such."[1] But in the action which is creation, nothing potential pre-exists to receive the action, as we have just shown.[2] Therefore, creation is not a motion or a change.

[3]   Moreover, the extremes of a motion or change are included in the same order, either because they fall under one genus, as contraries—for example, in the motion of growth or alteration and of carrying a thing from one place to another—or because they share in one potentiality of matter, as do privation and form in generation and corruption. But neither of these alternatives can be attributed to creation; for in this action no potentiality is present, nor does there exist anything of the same genus as this action and which is presupposed for it, as we have proved. In creation, therefore, neither motion nor change exists.

[4]   Again, in every change or motion there must be something existing in one way now and in a different way before, for the very word *change* shows this.[3] But, where the whole substance of a thing is brought into being, there can be no same thing existing in different ways, because such a thing would not itself be produced, but would be presupposed to the production. Hence, creation is not a change.

[5]   Furthermore, motion or change must precede that which

1. Cf. Aristotle, *Physics*, III, 6 (201a 10).
2. See above, ch. 16.
3. Cf. Aristotle, *Physics*, V, 1 (225a 1).

results therefrom; for in the being of the made lies the beginning of rest and the term of motion. Every change, then, must be a motion or a terminus of motion, which is successive. And for this reason, what is being made is not; because so long as the motion endures, something is coming to be, and is not; whereas in the very terminal point of motion, wherein rest begins, a thing no longer is coming to be; it is. In creation, however, this is impossible. For, if creation preceded its product, as do motion or change, then some subject would have to be prior to it; and this is contrary to the nature of creation. Creation, therefore, is neither a motion nor a change.

Chapter 18.

HOW OBJECTIONS AGAINST CREATION ARE SOLVED

[1] Now, what has been said makes apparent the fruitless effort of those who impugn creation by arguments derived from the nature of motion or change—the contention, for example, that creation, like other motions or changes, must take place in a subject, or that in creation non-being must be transmuted into being, just as fire is changed into air.

[2] For creation is not a change, but the very dependency of the created act of being upon the principle from which it is produced. And thus, creation is a kind of relation; so that nothing prevents its being in the creature as its subject.

[3] Nevertheless, creation appears to be a kind of change from the point of view of our way of understanding only, namely, in that our intellect grasps one and the same thing as not existing before and as existing afterwards.

[4] But, clearly, if creation is some sort of relation, then it is a certain reality; and neither is it uncreated nor is it created by another relation. For, since a created effect depends really upon its creator, a relation of real dependency, such as this, must itself be something real. But everything real is brought

into being by God; it therefore owes its being to God. It is not, however, created by a creation other than that whereby this first creature itself is said to be created. For just as accidents and forms do not exist by themselves, so neither are they created by themselves; creation is the production of a being.[a] Rather, just as accidents and forms exist in another, so are they created when other things are created. Moreover, a relation is not referred through another relation, for in that case we would fall into an infinite regress; but it is referential of itself, because it is a relation by essence. Hence, there is no need for another creation by which creation itself is created, and so on to infinity.

Chapter 19.

THAT IN CREATION NO SUCCESSION EXISTS

[1]   From the foregoing it is also clear that all creation is successionless.

[2]   For succession characterizes motion. But creation is not a motion, nor the term of a motion, as a change is; hence, there is no succession in it.

[3]   In every successive motion, furthermore, there exists some mean between the extremes of the motion; for a mean is that which a continuously moved thing attains first before reaching the terminal point. But between being and non-being, which are as it were the extremes of creation, no mean can possibly exist. Therefore, in creation there is no succession.

[4]   Again, in every making involving succession, a thing is in process of becoming prior to its actual production, as is shown in *Physics* VI.[1] But this cannot occur in creation. For the becoming which would precede the creature's actual production would require a subject. The latter could not be the creature itself, of whose creation we are speaking, since, before being made, the creature is not. Nor would that subject lie in the maker, because to be moved is an act not of the

a. Cf. St. Thomas Aquinas, *Summa Theologiae*, I–II, 110, 2, ad 3.
1. Aristotle, *Physics*, VI, 6 (237b 10).

mover, but of the thing moved. It therefore remains that some pre-existing matter of the thing produced would be the subject of the process of becoming. This is contrary to the idea of creation. It is therefore impossible that creation should involve succession.

[5] And again. Every successive making must take place in time; since before and after in motion are numbered by time.[2] But time, motion, and the thing that is in motion are all simultaneously divided.[3] This, indeed, is manifestly so in local motion; for, if the motion is regular, half the motion will occupy half the time. Now, the division in forms corresponding to the division of time is in terms of intensification and diminution; thus, if a thing is heated to a certain degree in so much time, it is heated to a less degree in less time. Hence, there can be succession in motion, or in any making, so far as that which is affected by motion is divisible, either in point of quantity, as in local motion and in growth, or as regards intensity and remission, as in alteration. The latter[4], however, takes place in two ways: *in one way*, because the form, which is the term of the motion, is divisible with respect to intensity and remission, as is evidently the case when a thing is in process of motion toward whiteness; *in another way*, because a division of this kind occurs in dispositions to such a form; thus, the process whereby the form of fire comes to exist is successive on account of preceding alteration in the dispositions towards the form. But the very substantial being of the creature is not divisible in this way; for "substance is not susceptible of degrees."[5] Nor do any dispositions precede creation, since there is here no pre-existing matter, and disposition is on the side of matter. It follows that in creation no succession is possible.

[6] Successiveness in the making of things, moreover, derives from a defect of the matter, which is not suitably disposed from the beginning for the reception of the form; so that, when the matter is already perfectly disposed for the form, it

---

2. Aristotle, *Physics*, IV, 11 (219b 1).
3. Cf. Aristotle, *Physics*, VI, 4 (235a 15).
4. Divisibility of motion according to intensity and remission.
5. Cf. Aristotle, *Categories*, V (3b 33).

receives it immediately. For instance, because a transparent body is always in a state of complete readiness to receive light, it is illuminated at once by the presence of a luminous object; nor is there here any antecedent motion on the part of the illuminable thing, but only the illuminating agent's local motion by which it becomes present. But nothing having the character of matter is prerequisite to creation; nor for the accomplishment of His action does God as agent lack anything which might accrue to Him afterwards through movement, because He is immobile, as we proved in Book I of this work.[6] It therefore remains that creation is instantaneous. Thus, a thing simultaneously is being created and is created, even as a thing at the same moment is being illuminated and is illuminated.

[7]   And so it is that holy Scripture proclaims the creation of things to have been effected in an indivisible instant; for it is written: "In the beginning God created heaven and earth" (Gen. 1:1). And Basil explains that this beginning is "the beginning of time";[7] and is necessarily indivisible, as Aristotle proves in *Physics* vi.[8]

Chapter 20.

THAT NO BODY IS CAPABLE OF CREATIVE ACTION

[1]   The preceding considerations make it perfectly clear that no body can produce anything by creation.

[2]   A body acts only if it is moved, for the agent acting and the patient being acted upon, or the maker making and the thing being made, must exist together, simultaneously. Now, "those things are simultaneously existent which are in the same place," as is pointed out in *Physics* v,[1] and it is only by motion

6. *SCG*, I, ch. 13.
7. St. Basil the Great, *Homilia I in Hexaemeron*, V (PG, 29, col. 14).
8. Aristotle, *Physics*, VI, 3 (233b 33).
1. Aristotle, *Physics*, V, 3 (226b 22).

that a body acquires a place. But no body is moved except in time. Therefore, whatever is made by the action of a body comes to be successively. Yet, as we have just shown,[2] creation is successionless. Therefore, nothing can be produced creatively by any bodily thing whatsoever.

[3] Again. Every agent that acts so far as it is moved, necessarily moves that upon which it acts; the thing made and the thing acted upon are determined by the disposition of the maker and agent, for every agent produces its like. So, if an agent, while varying in disposition, acts in that it is changed by movement, a succession of new dispositions must also arise in the patient and in the thing made; and this cannot take place without motion. But, as was shown, a body does not move unless it is moved. Therefore, nothing is made by the action of a body except through the motion or change of the thing made. It was, however, shown above[3] that creation is neither a change nor a motion. It remains that no body can cause anything by creating it.

[4] Moreover, since agent and effect must be similar to each other, a thing that does not act by its total substance cannot produce the total substance of its effect. Thus, Aristotle proves, conversely,[4] that an immaterial form, which acts by its whole self, cannot be the proximate cause of a process of generation whereby the form alone is actualized. But no body acts by its total substance, although the whole substance acts. For, since every agent acts through the form by which it is in act, only that thing whose total substance is a form will be capable of acting by its total substance. Of no body can it be said that its whole substance consists of form; every body possesses matter because every body is mutable. Therefore, no body can produce a thing according to its total substance; and this pertains to the very essence of creation.

[5] Furthermore, creation is the act of an infinite power alone. For the greater the power of an agent, the greater is its capacity for actualizing a potentiality more and more remote

2. See above, ch. 19.
3. SCG, I, ch. 17.
4. Aristotle, *Metaphysics*, VI, 8 (1033b 25).

from actual existence; a power able to produce fire from water is greater than one that can make fire from air; so that where pre-existing potentiality is altogether eliminated, every relation of a determinate distance is transcended; and thus the power of an agent which produces something from no pre-existing potentiality whatever must immeasurably surpass the power of an agent which produces something from matter. Now, no power possessed by a body is infinite as Aristotle proved in *Physics* VIII.[5] Hence, no bodily thing is capable of creating— of making something from nothing.

[6]   Again, as Aristotle proves in *Physics* VII,[6] there is nothing intermediate between this mover moving and this thing moved by it; this thing making and this thing made by it; mover and moved, maker and made must exist together. But a bodily agent can be present to its effect only by contact, whereby the extremities of contiguous things come together. No bodily thing, then, can act except by contact. Now, contact involves the relation of one thing to another. Consequently, where there is nothing pre-existent besides the agent, there can be no contact; and this is the case in creation. Hence, no body can act by creating.

[7]   Patently false, therefore, is the position of those who said that the substance of the heavenly bodies causes the matter of the elements; matter can have no other cause than an agent which acts by creating, for matter is the first subject of motion and change.

Chapter 21.

THAT THE ACT OF CREATING BELONGS TO GOD ALONE

[1]   In the light of what has been said, it can be shown further that creation is an action proper to God, and that He alone can create.

5. Aristotle, *Physics*, VIII, 10 (266a 25).
6. Aristotle, *Physics*, VII, 2 (243a 4).

[2] Corresponding to the order of agents is the order of actions; for the nobler the agent, the nobler is its action; so that the first action must belong to the first agent. But creation is the first action because it presupposes no other action, whereas all others presuppose it. Therefore, creation is exclusively proper to God, who is the first agent.

[3] Moreover, it was proved that God creates things, from the fact that there can be nothing besides Himself that is not caused by Him. But of nothing else can this be said, for only He is the universal cause of being. Hence, creation belongs to God alone, as His proper action.

[4] Furthermore, effects correspond proportionally to their causes, so that we attribute actual effects to actual causes, potential effects to potential causes, and, similarly, particular effects to particular causes and universal effects to universal causes, as Aristotle teaches in *Physics* II.[1] Now, the act of being is the first effect, and this is evident by reason of the universal presence of this act. It follows that the proper cause of the act of being is the first and universal agent, namely, God. Other agents, indeed, are not the cause of the act of being as such, but of being *this*—of being a man or being white, for example. On the contrary, the act of being, as such, is caused by creation, which presupposes nothing; because nothing can pre-exist that is outside being as such. By makings other than creation, *this* being or *such* being is produced; for out of pre-existent being is made this being or such a being. It remains that creation is the proper action of God.

[5] Again, whatever is caused as regards some particular nature cannot be the first cause of that nature, but only a second and instrumental cause; for example, since the human nature of Socrates has a cause, he cannot be the first cause of human nature; if so, since his human nature is caused by someone, it would follow that he was the cause of himself, since he is what he is by virtue of human nature. Thus, a univocal generator must have the status of an instrumental agent in respect to that which is the primary cause of the whole species. Accordingly, all lower efficient causes must be

1. Aristotle, *Physics*, II, 3 (195b 25).

referred to higher ones, as instrumental to principal agents. The existence of every substance other than God is caused, as we proved above.[2] No such substance, then, could possibly be the cause of existence otherwise than as instrumental and as acting by virtue of another agent. But it is only in order to cause something by way of motion that an instrument is ever employed; for to be a moved mover is the very essence of an instrument. We have already shown,[3] however, that creation is not a motion. Hence, no substance besides God can create anything.

[6]   An instrument, moreover, is used because it is adapted to a certain effect, and can therefore mediate between the first cause and the effect, being in contact with both; the influence of the first cause thus reaches the effect through the instrument. Hence, there must be a recipient of the influx of the first cause upon that which is caused by the instrument. But this is contrary to the notion of creation, which presupposes nothing whatever. It therefore remains that nothing besides God can create, either as principal agent or as instrument.

[7]   Furthermore, it is by an action proper and connatural to itself that every instrumental agent carries out the action of the principal agent; thus, by processes of dissolving and dividing, natural heat generates flesh, and a saw, by cutting, plays its part in completing the work of making a stool. If, therefore, there exists a creature which participates in the work of creation as an instrument of the first creator, it must do so by an action due and proper to its own nature. Now, the effect answering to an instrument's proper action is prior, in the order of productive process, to the effect corresponding to the principal agent. So it is that the ultimate end corresponds to the first agent; thus, the cutting of the wood precedes the form of the stool, and the digestion of food, the production of flesh. Hence, by the proper operation of the creating instrument, something will have to be produced that is prior, in the order of production, to being—which is the effect corresponding to the action of the first agent. But this is impossible, because, the more universal a thing is, the greater its priority in the order of production; so, as Aristotle

2. See above, ch. 15.   3. See above, ch. 17.

says in his book *On the Generation of Animals*,[4] animal precedes man in the generation of man. That any creature should exercise creative action, either as principal agent, or instrumentally, is, therefore, impossible.

[8] Again, that which is caused with respect to some nature cannot be the cause of that nature simply, for then it would be the cause of itself. It can, however, be the cause of that nature in *this* individual; if Plato is the cause of human nature in Socrates, he is not so absolutely speaking, for Plato is himself caused with respect to human nature. Now, that which is the cause of something in *this* individual is the communicator of a common nature to some particular thing whereby that nature is specified or individuated. Such communication cannot be effected by creation, which presupposes nothing to which anything can be communicated by action. That a created being should be the creative cause of anything else is thus impossible.

[9] And again, since every agent acts so far as it is in act, the mode of action must follow the mode of a thing's actual being; the hotter a thing actually is, the more heat it gives. Therefore, anything whose actuality is subject to generic, specific, and accidental determinations must have a power that is limited to effects similar to the agent as such; for every agent produces its like. But nothing whose being is finite can be like another of the same genus or species, except as regards the nature of the genus or the species; for each single being, so far as it is this particular thing, is distinct from every other one. Therefore, nothing whose being is finite can be the efficient cause of another, except as regards its possession of a genus or species, not as regards its subsisting as distinct from others. Hence, that by which the effect of a finite agent subsists as an individual is the necessary pre-condition of such an agent's action. Therefore, it does not create. Rather, the act of creation belongs solely to that agent whose being is infinite, and which, as we proved in Book I, embraces in itself the likeness of all being.[5]

4. Aristotle, *De generatione animalium*, II, 3 (736b 3).
5. SCG, I, ch. 49ff.

[10]   Moreover, since the reason why anything is made is that it may be, if a thing is said to be made which existed before, it follows that it is made not through itself, but by accident; whereas that is made through itself which was not before. Thus, if from white a thing is made black, it indeed is made both black and colored; but black through itself, because it is made from not-black, and colored by accident, since it was colored before. So, in the production of a being of some particular kind, what is made through itself is *that particular being*; what is made by accident is simply a *being*; when a human being is born, it is a *man* that comes to be in an unqualified sense, a *being* that comes to be in a qualified sense, because a man is made, not from non-being as such, but from this particular non-being, as Aristotle says in *Physics* I.[6] Therefore, when a thing comes to be from non-being unqualifiedly speaking, what it made through itself is a *being*. In that case it must derive from that which is, through itself, the cause of being, for effects are referred to their proportionate causes. Now, it is the first being alone which is the cause of being as being; other things are the cause of being, by accident, and of this particular being, through themselves. Since to create is to produce being from nothing pre-existing, it follows that this act is exclusively God's own.

[11]   The authority of Sacred Scripture bears witness to this truth, affirming that God created all things: "In the beginning God created heaven and earth" (Gen. 1:1). Damascene, also, in the second part of his work writes: "All those who say that the angels are creators of any substance whatever have the devil as their father, for no creatures in existence are creators."[7]

[12]   Thus is destroyed the error of certain philosophers who said that God created the first separate substance, which in turn created the second, and so on in orderly fashion to the last one.[8]

6. Aristotle, *Physics*, I, 8 (191b 15).
7. St. John Damascene, *De fide orthodoxa*, II, 3 (PG, 94, col. 874).
8. Cf. St. Thomas Aquinas, *Summa Theologiae*, I, 14, 5.

Chapter 22.

THAT GOD IS OMNIPOTENT

[1] It is evident, then, that God's power is not determined to some single effect.

[2] For, if God alone can create, then anything that can be brought into being only by creative causality must necessarily be produced by Him. In this category fall all separate substances—which are not composed of matter and form, and whose existence we now suppose,[1] as well as the totality of corporeal matter. These diverse existents, then, are the immediate effects of God's power. Now, no power which produces immediately a number of effects, but not from matter, is determined to one particular effect. I say *immediately*, because, if it produced them through intermediaries, the diversity might result from the latter. And I say *not from matter*, because the same agent by the same action causes diverse effects in accordance with the diversity of the matter involved; the heat of fire hardens clay and melts wax. God's power, therefore, is not determined to one effect.

[3] Again, every perfect power reaches out to all those things to which the effect possessed by it through itself and proper to it can extend; whatever can have the character of a dwelling falls within the range of the art of building, if it is perfect. Now, God's power is through itself the cause of being, and the act of being is His proper effect, as was made clear above.[2] Hence, His power reaches out to all things with which the notion of being is not incompatible; for, if God's power were limited to some particular effect, He would not be through Himself the cause of a being as such, but of this particular being. Now, the opposite of being, namely, non-being, is incompatible with the notion of being. Hence, God can do all things which do not essentially include the notion of non-

1. See below, ch. 46.
2. See above, ch. 21.

being, and such are those which involve a contradiction. It follows that God can do whatever does not imply a contradiction.

[4] Furthermore, every agent acts so far as it is in act. Hence, the mode of an agent's power in acting accords with its mode of act; man begets man, and fire begets fire. Now, God is perfect act, possessing in Himself the perfections of all things, as we have already shown.[3] His active power, therefore, is perfect, extending to everything not repugnant to the notion of that which is being in act; namely, to everything except that which implies a contradiction. God, then, is omnipotent as regards all but this.

[5] Corresponding to every passive power, moreover, there is an active one; because potency is for the sake of act, as is matter for the sake of form. Now, it is only by the power of a thing existing actually that a potentially existent being can be made actual. A potency would thus be without purpose unless there existed the active power of an agent which could actualize it. And yet, in the real world, there is nothing purposeless. Thus, we see that all things potentially existent in the matter of generable and corruptible entities can be actualized by the active power present in the heavenly body, which is the primary active force in nature. Now, just as the heavenly body is the first agent in respect to lower bodies, so God is the first agent as regards the totality of created being. Therefore, by His active power God is able to do everything whatsoever that lies within the potency of the created being. But in the potency of the created being is everything that is not opposed to itself; just as human nature is patient of everything except that which would destroy it. Therefore, God can do all things.

[6] Furthermore, there are three reasons why some particular effect may escape the power of some particular agent. *First*, because the effect has no likeness or affinity to the agent—for every agent produces its like in some fashion. Thus, the power in human seed cannot produce an irrational animal or a plant, yet it can produce a man—a being superior to those things.

3. *SCG*, I, ch. 28.

Secondly, because of the excellence of the effect, which is disproportionate to the agent's power; thus, an active corporeal power cannot produce a separate substance. *Thirdly,* because the effect requires a matter upon which the agent cannot act; a carpenter cannot make a saw, since his art does not enable him to act upon iron, from which a saw is made.

[7]   But for none of these reasons can any effect be withdrawn from God's power. For, first, not because of its dissimilarity to Him can any effect be impossible to Him, since every being, so far as it has being, is similar to Him, as was shown above.[4] Nor, secondly, because of the excellence of the effect, since it has been shown already[5] that God transcends all things in goodness and perfection. Nor, thirdly, because of any material deficiency, since God is Himself the cause of matter, which cannot be produced except by creation. Moreover, in acting, God needs no matter, because He brings a thing into being where nothing whatever existed before; hence, His action cannot be hindered from producing its effect because of any lack of matter.

[8]   We therefore conclude that God's power is not limited to some particular effect, but that He is able to do absolutely all things; in other words, He is *omnipotent.*

[9]   So too, Divine Scripture teaches this as a matter of faith. For in the person of God Himself it is said: "I am the almighty God: walk before me and be perfect" (Gen. 17:1); and Job (42:2) says: "I know that Thou canst do all things"; and in the person of the angel: "No word shall be impossible with God" (Luke 1:37).

[10]   Thus is eliminated the error of certain philosophers who asserted that God produced immediately one effect only, as if His power were limited to the production of it, and that God can produce another only by acting in accordance with the natural train of events. Of such persons it is written: "Who looked upon the Almighty as if He could do nothing" (Job 22:17).

4. See above, ch. 6 and 15.
5. SCG, I, ch. 27 and 41.

Chapter 23.

THAT GOD DOES NOT ACT BY NATURAL NECESSITY

[1]   From what has been said it follows that God acts, in the realm of created things, not by necessity of His nature, but by the free choice of His will.

[2]   For the power of every agent which acts by natural necessity is determined to one effect; that is why all natural things invariablly happen in the same way, unless there be an obstacle; while voluntary things do not. God's power, however, is not ordered to one effect only, as we have just shown.[1] Therefore, God acts, not out of natural necessity, but by His will.

[3]   Also, as we have demonstrated,[2] whatever does not imply a contradiction is subject to the divine power. Now, there are many entities which do not exist in the realm of created things, but which, if they did so exist, would imply no contradiction; particularly obvious examples are the number, quantities, and distances of the stars and of other bodies, wherein, if the order of things were different, no contradiction would be implied. Thus, numerous entities, non-existent in the order of reality, are subject to the divine power. Now, whoever does some of the things that he can do, leaving others undone, acts by choice of his will, not by necessity of his nature. Therefore, God acts by His will, not by necessity of His nature.

[4]   Then, too, the mode of any agent's action is in keeping with the way in which the likeness of its effect exists in it; for every agent produces its like. Now, whatever is present in something else exists in it conformably to the latter's mode. But God is intelligent by His essence, as we have shown,[3] so

1. See above, ch. 22.
2. *Ibid.*
3. *SCG,* I, ch. 45.

that the likeness of His effect must exist in Him in an intelligible mode. Therefore, He acts by His intellect. But the intellect does not produce an effect except by means of the will, whose object is a good apprehended by the intellect and which moves the agent as an end. God, therefore, acts by His will, not of natural necessity.

[5] Moreover, there are two modes of action distinguished by Aristotle in *Metaphysics* IX:[4] a kind of action which remains in the agent and is a perfection of that agent—for example, seeing; another, which passes into things outside the agent, and is a perfection of the thing made as a result of that action, as burning in the case of fire. Now, God's action cannot belong to the class of actions which are not immanent in the agent, because His action is His substance, as was shown above.[5] Hence, it must be of the order of actions which are present in the agent, as actualities perfecting its own being. Such actions, however, are exclusively proper to a being endowed with knowledge and appetite. So, God acts by knowing and by willing—not by necessity of His nature, therefore, but by the decision of His will.

[6] That God acts for an end can also be evident from the fact that the universe is not the result of chance, but is ordered to a good, as Aristotle makes clear in *Metaphysics* XI.[6] Now, the first agent acting for an end must act by intellect and will, for things devoid of intellect act for an end as directed thereto by another. This is obviously true in the world of things made by art; it is the archer that directs the flight of the arrow to a definite mark. This must be the case also in the realm of natural things; the right ordering of a thing to a due end requires knowledge of that end and of the means to it, and of the due proportion between both; and this knowledge is found only in an agent endowed with intelligence. But God is the first agent; therefore, He acts, not by a necessity of His nature, but by His intellect and will.

[7] Moreover, that which acts by itself is prior to that which

4. Aristotle, *Metaphysics*, IX, 8 (1050a 18).
5. See above, ch. 9.
6. Aristotle, *Metaphysics*, XI, 10 (1075a 12).

acts by another, for whatever is by another must be referred to that which is by itself; otherwise, we fall into an infinite regress. A thing that is not master of its own action, however, does not act by itself; it acts as directed by something else, not as directing itself. Hence, the first agent must act as master of His own action. But it is only by will that one is master of his own action. It follows, therefore, that God, who is the first agent, acts by His will, not by necessity of His nature.

[8]   A further argument. To the first agent belongs the first action, even as the first motion pertains to the first thing movable. But the will's action is naturally prior to that of nature. For that which is more perfect is prior in nature, though in one and the same particular thing it be temporally posterior. Now, voluntary action is more perfect than natural action; in the realm of our own experience, agents which act by will are obviously more perfect than those whose actions are determined by natural necessity. Action by way of the will is, therefore, proper to God, the first agent.

[9]   This is likewise evident from the fact that when both actions are found together, the power which acts by will is superior to that which acts by nature, and uses the latter as an instrument; thus in man the intellect, which acts by means of the will, is superior to the vegetative soul, which acts by natural necessity. The power of God, however, is supreme over all things. It therefore acts on all things by will, not by natural necessity.

[10]   Again, the will has for its object a good considered precisely as such, whereas nature does not attain to goodness in its universal aspect, but only to this particular good which is its perfection. Now, every agent acts inasmuch as it aims at a good, because the end moves the agent; so that the agent acting by will must be compared to the agent acting by natural necessity as universal agent to particular agent. But a particular agent is related to a universal one as posterior to it and as its instrument. Therefore, the primary agent must be a voluntary one, and not an agent by natural necessity.

[11]   Divine Scripture teaches us this truth, too, declaring: "Whatsoever the Lord pleased He hath done" (Ps. 134:6),

and: "Who worketh all things according to the counsel of His will" (Eph. 1:11).

[12] And Hilary, too, in his work *De synodis* writes: "God's will gave substance to all creatures." And he adds: "For the whole universe of things were created such as God willed them to be."⁷

[13] This also abolishes the error of those philosophers who maintain that God's action is determined by natural necessity.

Chapter 24.

THAT GOD ACTS CONFORMABLY TO HIS WISDOM

[1] Now, it evidently follows from the foregoing that God produces His effects according to His wisdom.

[2] For the will is moved to act as the result of some sort of apprehension; the apprehended good is indeed the object of will. But, as was just shown,¹ God is a voluntary agent. Since in Him there exists intellectual apprehension—no other kind —and since He understands nothing except in the very act of understanding Himself,² and since this act is itself an act of wisdom, it follows that God produces all things according to His wisdom.

[3] Moreover, because every agent produces its like, it necessarily acts in keeping with the way in which the likeness of its effect exists in it; fire heats according to the measure of heat present in it. But the likeness of the effect produced by any voluntary agent, as such, is present in that agent according to the apprehension of his intellect, and not only according to the disposition of the agent's nature; for in the latter case, the agent would produce but one effect, because the natural principal of that which is one is itself one. Thus, every voluntary agent produces its effect according to the nature of his

7. St. Hilary, *De synodis*, 58 (*PL*, 10, col. 510).
1. See above, ch. 23.
2. *SCG*, I, ch. 46.

intellect. But in the preceding chapter we proved that God acts by His will. It is by the wisdom of His intellect, therefore, that God brings things into being.

[4] Moreover, according to the Philosopher, "it is the office of a wise man to set things in order."[3] For things can be ordered only by knowing their relation and proportion to one another, and to something higher, which is their end; for the order of certain things to one another is for the sake of their order to an end. But only a being endowed with intellect is capable of knowing the mutual relations and proportions of things; and to judge of certain things by the highest cause is the prerogative of wisdom. All ordering, therefore, is necessarily effected by means of the wisdom of a being endowed with intelligence. Even so, in the world of the mechanical arts, the planners of buildings are called the *wise men* of their craft. Now, the things produced by God have a mutual order among themselves which is not fortuitous, since this order is observed always or for the most part. That God brought things into being by ordering them is thus evident. Therefore, God brought things into being by His wisdom.

[5] Then, too, things which proceed from the will are either *things-to-be-done*, such as acts of the virtues, which are perfections of the doer, or *things-to-be-made*, which pass into matter outside the agent. So it is clear that creatures proceed from God as things *made*. Now, as Aristotle says, "art is the reason concerned with things to be made."[4] All created things, therefore, stand in relation to God as products of art to the artist. But the artist brings his works into being by the ordering of his wisdom and intellect. So, too, did God make all things by the ordering of His intellect.

[6] This truth is confirmed by divine authority. For we read in a Psalm (103:24): "Thou has made all things in wisdom"; and in the Book of Proverbs (3:19): "The Lord by wisdom hath founded the earth."

[7] Excluded hereby is the error of those who said that all things depend on the simple will of God, without any reason.

3. Aristotle, *Metaphysics*, I, 2 (982a 18).
4. Aristotle, *Nicomachean Ethics*, VI, 4 (1140a 5).

Chapter 25.

HOW THE OMNIPOTENT GOD IS SAID TO BE INCAPABLE OF CERTAIN THINGS

[1]   Now, from what has been said already, we can see that, although God is omnipotent, He is nevertheless said to be incapable of some things.

[2]   For we proved above[1] that active power exists in God; that there is no passive potency in Him had already been demonstrated in Book I of this work.[2] (We, however, are said *to-be-able* as regards both active and passive potentiality.) Hence, God is unable to do those things whose possibility entails passive potency. What such things are is, then, the subject of this inquiry.

[3]   Let us observe, first of all, that active potency relates to *acting*; passive potency, to *existing*. Hence, there is potency with respect to being only in those things which have matter subject to contrariety. But, since there is no passive potency in God, His power does not extend to any thing pertaining to His own being. Therefore, God cannot be a body or anything of this kind.

[4]   Furthermore, motion is the act of this passive potency of which we are speaking. But, since there is no passive potency in God, He cannot be changed. It can be concluded further that He cannot be changed with respect to the various kinds of change: increase and diminution, or alteration, coming to be and passing away—all are foreign to Him.

[5]   Thirdly, since a deprivation is a certain loss of being, it follows that God can lack nothing.

[6]   Moreover, every failing follows upon some privation. But the subject of privation is the potency of matter. In no way, therefore, can God fail.

1. See above, ch. 7.
2. SCG, I, ch. 16.

[7]   Then, too, since weariness results from a defect of power, and forgetfulness from defect of knowledge, God cannot possibly be subject to either.

[8]   Nor can He be overcome or suffer violence, for these are found only in something having a movable nature.

[9]   Likewise, God can neither repent, nor be angry or sorrowful, because all these things bespeak passion and defect.

[10]   An additional argument is this. The object and effect of an active power is a *being made*, and no power is operative if the nature of its object is lacking; sight is inoperative in the absence of the actually visible. It must therefore be said that God is unable to do whatever is contrary to the nature of being as being, or of *made being* as made. We must now inquire what these things are.

[11]   First of all, that which destroys the nature of being is contrary to it. Now, the nature of being is destroyed by its opposite, just as the nature of man is destroyed by things opposite in nature to him or to his parts. But the opposite of being is non-being, with respect to which God is therefore inoperative, so that He cannot make one and the same thing to be and not to be; He can not make contradictories to exist simultaneously.

[12]   Contradiction, moreover, is implied in contraries and privative opposites: to be white and black is to be white and not white; to be seeing and blind is to be seeing and not seeing. For the same reason, God is unable to make opposites exist in the same subject at the same time and in the same respect.

[13]   Furthermore, to take away an essential principle of any thing is to take away the thing itself. Hence, if God cannot make a thing to be and not to be at the same time, neither can He make a thing to lack any of its essential principles while the thing itself remains in being; God cannot make a man to be without a soul.

[14]   Again, since the principles of certain sciences—of logic, geometry, and arithmetic, for instance—are derived exclu-

sively from the formal principles of things, upon which their essence depends, it follows that God cannot make the contraries of those principles; He cannot make the genus not to be predicable of the species, nor lines drawn from a circle's center to its circumference not to be equal, nor the three angles of a rectilinear triangle not to be equal to two right angles.

[15] It is obvious, moreover, that God cannot make the past not to have been, for this, too, would entail a contradiction; it is equally as necessary for a thing to be while it is as to have been while it was.

[16) Also, there are things incompatible with the nature of *thing made*, as such. And these God cannot make, because whatever He does make must be something *made*.

[17] And from this it is clear that God cannot make God. For it is of the essence of a *thing made* that its own being depends on another cause, and this is contrary to the nature of the being we call God, as is evident from things previously said.[3]

[18] For the same reason God cannot make a thing equal to Himself; for a thing whose being does not depend on another is superior in being, and in the other perfections, to that which depends on something else, such dependence pertaining to the nature of that which is made.

[19] Likewise, God cannot make a thing to be preserved in being without Himself. For the preservation of each and every thing depends on its cause, so that, if the cause is taken away, the effect is necessarily removed also. Hence, if there can be a thing which is not kept in being by God, it would not be His effect.

[20] Moreover, since God is a voluntary agent, that which He cannot will He cannot do. Now, we can see what He cannot will if we consider how there can be necessity in the divine will; for that which necessarily is cannot not-be, and what cannot be necessarily is not.

3. SCG, I, ch. 13, ¶34.

[21] It clearly follows that God cannot make Himself not to be, or not to be good or happy; because He necessarily wills Himself to be, to be good and happy, as we have shown in Book I of this work.[4]

[22] We proved also, in that same Book, that God cannot will any evil.[5] It is therefore evident that God cannot sin.

[23] And it has already been demonstrated[6] that the will of God cannot be mutable; so, what He wills He cannot cause to be not fulfilled.

[24] But observe that God is said to be *unable to do* this in a different sense than in the preceding instances, for in those cases God's inability either to will or to make is absolute, whereas in this case God can either make or will if His will or His power be considered in themselves, though not if they be considered on the supposition of His having willed the opposite. For the   divine will, as regards creatures, has only suppositional necessity, as was shown in Book I.[7] Thus, all such statements as that *God cannot do the contrary of what He has designed to do* are to be understood compositely, for so understood they presuppose the divine will as regards the opposite. But, if such expressions be understood in a *divided* sense, they are false, because they then refer to God's power and will absolutely.

[25] Now, as we have shown,[8] just as God acts by will, so also does He act by *intellect* and *knowledge*. It follows that He cannot do what He has foreseen that He will not do, or abstain from doing what He has foreseen that He will do, for the same reason that He cannot do what He wills not to do, or omit to do what He wills. That God is unable to do these things is both conceded and denied: conceded on a certain condition or supposition; denied with respect to His power or will considered absolutely.

4. *SCG*, I, ch. 80.
5. *SCG*, I, ch. 95.
6. *SCG*, I, ch. 82, ¶3, 7.
7. *SCG*, I, ch. 81–83.
8. See above, ch. 24.

Chapter 26.

THAT THE DIVINE INTELLECT IS NOT
CONFINED TO LIMITED EFFECTS

[1] We have shown above[1] that God's power is not limited to certain determinate effects, because He acts not by a necessity of His nature, but by His intellect and will. But, lest someone should think that His intellect or knowledge can only attain to certain effects, and thus that He acts by a necessity of His knowledge, though not of His nature, it must be shown that His knowledge or intellect is limitless in its effects.

[2] For it was demonstrated in Book I of this work[2] that all that can proceed from Him God comprehends in the act of understanding His own essence, wherein all such things must necessarily exist by some kind of likeness, even as effects exist virtually in their cause. So, if God's power is not limited to certain determinate effects, as we have shown,[3] a like judgment must be made concerning His intellect.

[3] We argue further from our proof of the infinity of the divine essence.[4] By no addition of finite things, even if their number were infinite, is it possible to equal the infinite, because the infinite exceeds the finite, however great. But it is certain that nothing besides God is infinite in essence; for, by the very nature of their essence, all other things are included under certain genera and species. Hence, no matter how many or how great divine effects be taken into account, the divine essence will always exceed them; it can be the *raison d'être* of more. Therefore, God's intellect, as we have shown,[5] which knows the divine essence perfectly, surpasses all finiteness in the realm of effects. Therefore, it is not necessarily confined to these or those effects.

[4] Also, we have proved[6] that the divine intellect is cognizant of infinite things. But God brings things into being by

1. See above, ch. 22 and 23.
3. See above, ch. 22.
5. *SCG*, I, ch. 47.

2. *SCG*, I, ch. 49ff.
4. *SCG*, I, ch. 43.
6. *SCG*, I, ch. 69.

way of intellectual knowledge. Consequently, the causality of the divine intellect is not restricted to the production of finite effects.

[5] If, moreover, the causality of God's intellect were confined to certain effects, as though it produced them of necessity, this would have to do with the things brought into being by it. But that is impossible, since, as we have shown before,[7] God knows even those things which never are, nor will be, nor have been. Hence, it is not by any necessity on the part of His intellect or His knowledge that God works.

[6] Again. God's knowledge is in relation to the things produced by it as the knowledge of the craftsman to his handiwork. Now, every art includes in its scope all the things that can be comprised under the generic subject of that art; the art of building, for example, extends to all houses. But the genus that is subject to the divine art is being, since, as we have shown,[8] God is by His intellect the universal source of being. Hence, the causality of the divine intellect extends to everything not incompatible with the notion of being; for it is the nature of all such things, considered in themselves, to be contained under being. The divine intellect, therefore, is not restricted to the production of certain determinate effects.

[7] So it is said in a Psalm (146:5): "Great is the Lord, and great is His power, and of His wisdom there is no number."

[8] Excluded hereby is the position of those philosophers who say that, because God understands Himself, this particular disposition of things flows from Him necessarily—as though He did not, by His own free choice, determine the limits of each single thing and the disposition of them all, as the Catholic faith declares.

[9] Bear in mind, however, that, although God's intellect is not restricted to these or those effects, He nevertheless decides on certain determinate effects to be produced in a definite order by His wisdom. Thus, we read in the Book of Wisdom (11:21): "Lord, Thou hast ordered all things in number, weight, and measure."

7. SCG, I, ch. 66.   8. See above, ch. 15.

Chapter 27.

THAT THE DIVINE WILL IS NOT RESTRICTED
TO CERTAIN EFFECTS

[1] From the preceding considerations, it can also be shown that God's will, by which He acts, is subject to no necessity as regards the production of certain determinate effects.

[2] For the will must be commensurate with its object. But the object of will is a good grasped by the intellect, as stated above.[1] Therefore, it is of the nature of will to reach out to whatever the intellect can propose to it under the aspect of goodness. Therefore, if, as we have proved,[2] God's intellect is not restricted to certain effects, it follows that neither is the divine will necessitated to produce certain determinate effects.

[3] Moreover, nothing acting by the will produces a thing by not willing. But it was previously shown[3] that, with respect to things other than Himself, God wills nothing by absolute necessity. Therefore, effects proceed from God's will, not of necessity, but as He freely ordains.

Chapters 28 and 29.

HOW DUENESS IS ENTAILED IN THE
PRODUCTION OF THINGS

[1] From the foregoing it must also be shown that in the creation of things God did not work of necessity, as though He brought things into being as a debt of justice.

[2] As Aristotle points out,[1] justice involves a relationship

1. See above, ch. 24, ¶2.
2. See above, ch. 26.
3. *SCG*, I, ch. 81.
1. Aristotle, *Nicomachean Ethics*, V, 1 (1130a 3).

to another, to whom it renders what is due. But, for the universal production of things, nothing is presupposed to which anything may be due. It follows that the universal production of things could not result from a debt of justice.

[3] Then too, since the act of justice consists in rendering to each that which is his own, the act by which a thing becomes one's own property is prior to the act of justice, as we see in human affairs; a man's work entitles him to possess as his own that which his employer, by an act of justice, pays to him. The act by which a person first acquires something of his own cannot, therefore, be an act of justice. But, by the act of creation, a created thing first possesses something of its own. It is not from a debt of justice, therefore, that creation proceeds.

[4] Furthermore, no one owes anything to another except because he depends on him in some way, or receives something either from him or from someone else, on whose account he is indebted to that other person; a son is a debtor to his father, because he receives being from him; a master to his servant, because he receives from him the services he requires; and every man is a debtor to his neighbor, on God's account, from whom we have received all good things. God, however, depends on nothing, nor does He stand in need of anything that He may receive from another, as things previously said make perfectly clear.[2] Hence, it was from no debt of justice that God brought things into being.

[5] Another argument is this. In every genus that which is for its own sake is prior to that which is for the sake of something else. Thus, that which is absolutely the first of all causes is a cause solely on its own account. But whatever acts by reason of a debt of justice acts not on its own account alone, but on account of that to which it is indebted. Now, since God is the first cause and the primal agent, He did not bring things into existence because of any debt of justice.

[6] Hence St. Paul says: "Who hath first given to him, and recompense shall be made him? For of Him, and by Him, and in Him, are all things" (Rom. 11:35–36); and in the Book

2. SCG, I, ch. 13, 28, 40, and 102.

of Job (41:2) we read: "Who hath given me before that I should repay him? All things that are under heaven are Mine."

[7] Thus is set aside the error of those who try to prove that God can do nothing except what He does, on the argument that He can do only that which He ought to do; on the contrary, as we have proved, God does not produce things from a debt of justice.

[8] True enough, prior to the universal production of things, nothing created exists to which anything can be due; nevertheless, it is preceded by something uncreated, namely, the principle of creation. And this precedence can be considered in two ways. For the divine goodness precedes as end and prime motivating principle of creation—as Augustine says, "because God is good, we are."[3] And God's knowledge and will precede as that by which things are brought into being.

[9] Therefore, if we consider God's goodness absolutely, we find nothing due in the creation of things. For *in one way* a thing is said to be a person's due by reason of the relation of another person to him, so that he is obliged to make a return to that person for what he has received from him; thanks are due a benefactor for his kindness because the recipient owes this to him. This sort of dueness, however, has no place in the creation of things, because there is nothing pre-existent that could owe anything to God, nor does any benefaction of His pre-exist. *In another way*, something is said to be due a thing according to itself; for whatever is required for a thing's completeness is necessarily due that thing; it is a man's due to possess hands or strength, since without these he cannot be complete. But for the fulfillment of His goodness God needs nothing outside Him. Therefore, the production of things is not due Him by way of necessity.

[10] Moreover, as we have shown,[4] God brings things into being by His will. Now, if God wills His own goodness to be, He is under no necessity of willing the production of anything else; the antecedent of this conditional proposition is neces-

3. St. Augustine, *De doctrina christiana*, I, 32 (PL, 34, col. 32).
4. See above, ch. 23.

sary, but not the consequent; for, as we proved in Book I,[5] God necessarily wills His goodness to be, but He does not necessarily will anything else. Therefore, the production of creatures is not something due the divine goodness of necessity.

[11]   Also, it has been shown[6] that God brings things into being neither by a necessity of His nature, nor of His knowledge, nor of His will, nor of His justice. By no mode of necessity, then, is it due the divine goodness that things be brought into being.

[12]   It may be said, however, that this is God's due by way of a certain fittingness. But justice, properly so called, requires a debt of necessity, for what is rendered to someone by an act of justice is owed to him by a necessity of right.

[13]   Therefore, it cannot be said that the production of creatures arose from a debt of justice by which God is the creature's debtor, nor from a debt of justice whereby He is a debtor to His own goodness, if justice be taken in its proper sense. But, if the term be taken broadly, we may speak of justice in the creation of things, meaning that creation befits the divine goodness.

[14]   If, however, we consider the plan which God by His intellect and His will laid down for the production of things, then the latter proceeds from the necessity of that plan. For it is impossible that God should plan to do a certain thing which afterwards He did not; otherwise, His decision would be either changeable or weak. The fulfillment of His ordinance is therefore something necessarily due. Nevertheless, this dueness does not suffice for introducing the notion of justice, properly so called, into the creative production of things, wherein nothing can be considered except the act of God creating. (And, as Aristotle explains in *Ethics* v,[7] there is no justice properly speaking between a man and himself.) Therefore, it cannot properly be said that God brought things into being from a debt of justice, on the grounds that by His knowledge and will He ordained Himself to their production.

5. *SCG*, I, ch. 8off.   6. See above, ch. 23, 26, and 27.
7. Aristotle, *Nicomachean Ethics*, V, 11 (1138a 1off.).

[15] [Chapter 29] On the other hand, considering the production of a particular creature, we can see a debt of justice in it by comparing a posterior creature to a prior one; and I say *prior*, not only in *time* but also in *nature*.

[16] Thus, in the effects to be produced first by God, we discover nothing due, whereas in the production of subsequent effects, dueness is found, yet in a different order. For, if things prior in nature are also prior in being, those which follow become due on account of those naturally prior; given the causes, the possession of actions by which to produce their effects is due them. On the other hand, if things prior in nature are posterior in being, then the prior become due on account of the posterior; for medicine to come first in order that health may follow, is something due. Both cases have this in common: the dueness or necessity is taken from that which is naturally prior in relation to that which is naturally posterior.

[17] Now, the necessity arising from that which is posterior in being, although prior in nature, is not absolute, but *conditional*; if *this* ought to come to pass, then *this* must precede. So, in accordance with this kind of necessity, dueness is found in the production of creatures in *three ways*. *First,* there is a conditional indebtedness on the part of the whole universe of things in relation to each part of it that is necessary for the perfection of the whole; for, if God willed the production of such an universe, it was due that He should make the sun and moon, and like things without which the universe cannot be. *Secondly,* something conditionally due is found in one creature in relation to another; if God willed the existence of animals and plants, then it was due that He should make the heavenly bodies by which those things are kept in being; and if He willed the existence of man, then He has to make plants and animals, and the other things which man requires for a complete existence. And yet God made both these and other things of His pure will. *Thirdly,* there is something conditionally due in each creature as regards its parts, properties, and accidents, upon which the creature depends either for its being or for some perfection proper to it. For example, given that God willed to make man, it was man's due, on this

supposition, that God should unite in him soul and body, and furnish him with senses, and other like aids, both intrinsic and extrinsic. Now, in all these cases, rightly considered, God is said to be a debtor, not to the creature, but to the fulfillment of His own purpose.

[18]   But there is also another mode of necessity in the nature of things whereby a thing is said to be necessary absolutely; and this necessity depends on causes which are prior in being—on essential principles, for instance, and on efficient or moving causes. But this kind of necessity can have no place in the first creation of things so far as efficient causes are concerned, since in that creation the sole efficient cause was God, who alone can create, as we have already shown.[8] But, as we have also proved,[9] it is not by any necessity of His nature, but by His will, that God works while creating; and things done by the will can have no necessity except only on the supposition of the end; for the existence of those things by which an end is attained is that end's due. As regards formal or material causes, on the other hand, nothing prevents our finding absolute necessity even in the primal creation of things; for just because certain bodies were composed of the elements it was necessary that they be hot or cold; and from the very fact that a surface was extended in the form of a triangle it was necessary for it to have three angles equal to two right angles. But this kind of necessity results from the relation of an effect to its created material, or formal, cause, so that God cannot be said to be a debtor from the point of view of such necessity; here the debt of necessity falls upon the creature. However, in the propagation of things, where the creature is already active, an absolute necessity can arise from the created efficient cause; the sun's motion, for example, necessarily gives rise to changes in terrestrial bodies.

[19]   According to the foregoing kinds of dueness, then, natural justice is found in things, both as regards the creation of things and as regards their propagation. And so it is that God is said to have formed and to govern all things justly and reasonably.

8. See above, ch. 21.
9. See above, ch. 23.

[20] By what has been said a double error is eliminated: the error of those who, setting limits to God's power, said that God can do only that which He does because He is bound to this; and the error of those who assert that all things follow from the sheer will of God, there being no other reason either to be sought in things, or to be assigned.

Chapter 30.

HOW ABSOLUTE NECESSITY CAN EXIST IN CREATED THINGS

[1] Although all things depend on the will of God as first cause, who is subject to no necessity in His operation except on the supposition of His intention, nevertheless absolute necessity is not on this account excluded from things, so as to compel us to say that all things are contingent. (One might infer this from the fact that things have with no absolute necessity proceeded from their cause, for usually, in things, an effect is contingent which does not proceed from its cause necessarily.) On the contrary, there are some things in the universe whose being is simply and absolutely necessary.

[2] Such is the being of things wherein there is no possibility of not-being. Now, some things are so created by God that there is in their nature a potentiality to non-being; and this results from the fact that the matter present in them is in potentiality with respect to another form. On the other hand, neither immaterial things, nor things whose matter is not receptive of another form, have potentiality to non-being, so that their being is absolutely and simply necessary.

[3] Now, if it be said that whatever is from nothing of itself tends toward nothing, so that in all creatures there is the power not to be—this clearly does not follow. For created things are said to tend to nothing in the same way in which they are from nothing, namely, not otherwise than according to the power of their efficient cause. In this sense, then, the power not to be does not exist in created things. But in the

Creator there is the power to give them being, or to cease pouring forth being into them, for He produces things not by a necessity of His nature, but by His will, as we have shown.[1]

[4]   Moreover, it is because created things come into being through the divine will that they are necessarily such as God willed them to be. Now, the fact that God is said to have produced things voluntarily, and not of necessity, does not preclude His having willed certain things to be which are of necessity and others which are contingently, so that there may be an ordered diversity in things. Therefore, nothing prevents certain things that are produced by the divine will from being necessary.

[5]   Then, too, it pertains to God's perfection to have placed the seal of His own likeness upon created things, excluding only entities incompatible with the nature of created being; for it belongs to the perfect agent to produce its like as far as possible. But to be simply necessary is not incompatible with the notion of created being; for nothing prevents a thing being necessary whose necessity nevertheless has a cause, as in the case of the conclusions of demonstrations. Hence, nothing prevents certain things being produced by God in such fashion that they exist in a simply necessary way; indeed, this is a proof of God's perfection.

[6]   Again. The more distant a thing is from that which is a being by virtue of itself, namely, God, the nearer it is to non-being; so that the closer a thing is to God, the further is it removed from non-being. Now, things which presently exist are near to non-being through having potentiality to non-being. Therefore, that the order of things be complete, those nearest to God, and hence the most remote from non-being, must be totally devoid of potentiality to non-being; and such things are necessary absolutely. Thus, some created things have being necessarily.

[7]   And so we must bear in mind that if the universe of created things be considered as deriving from their first principle, then they are seen to depend on a will, and on no

1. See above, ch. 23.

necessity of their principle, except a suppositional one, as we have said.[2] On the other hand, if created things be considered in relation to their proximate principles, they are found to have absolute necessity. For nothing prevents the non-necessary production of certain principles on the supposition of which such and such an effect nevertheless follows necessarily; the death of this animal is an absolutely necessary consequence of its being composed of contraries, although it was not absolutely necessary for it to be composed of contraries. Similarly, the production of such and such natures by God was voluntary; but, having been so constituted, something having absolute necessity comes forth from them or exists as a result.

[8] In created things, however, there are diverse modes of necessity arising from diverse causes. For, since a thing cannot be without its essential principles, which are matter and form, whatever belongs to a thing by reason of its essential principles must have absolute necessity in all cases.

[9] Now, from these principles, so far as they are principles of existing, there arises a threefold absolute necessity in things. *First*, through the relation of a thing's principles to its act of being. Since matter is by its nature a being in potentiality, and since that which can be can also not be, it follows that certain things, in relation to their matter, are necessarily corruptible— animals because they are composed of contraries; fire because its matter is receptive of contraries. On the other hand, form is by its nature act, and through it things exist in act; so that from it there results in some things a necessity to be. And this happens either because those things are forms not existing in matter, so that there is no potentiality to non-being in them, but rather by their forms they are always able to be, as in the case of separate substances; or because their forms equal in their perfection the total potentiality of their matter, so that there remains no potentiality to another form, nor consequently, to non-being; such is the case with the heavenly bodies. But in things whose form does not fulfill the total potentiality of the matter, there still remains in the matter potentiality to another form; and hence in such things there is no necessity to be; rather, the power to be is in them the result of the victory of

2. *Ibid.*; cf. *SCG*, I, ch. 83.

form over matter, as we see in the elements and things composed of them. The form of an element does not embrace the matter in its total potentiality, for matter receives the form of one element only by being made subject to one of two contraries; but the form of a mixed body embraces the matter according as it is disposed by a certain kind of mixture. Now, contraries, and all intermediaries resulting from the mixture of extremes, must have a common identical subject. The manifest consequence of this fact is that all things which either have contraries or are composed of contraries are corruptible, whereas things not of this sort are everlasting—unless they be corrupted accidentally, as forms which are not subsistent but which exist by being in matter.

[10]   *Secondly,* from essential principles of things absolute necessity arises in them from the order of the parts of their matter or of their form, if it happens that in certain things these principles are not simple. For, since man's proper matter is a mixed body, having a certain temperament and endowed with organs, it is absolutely necessary that a man have in himself each of the elements and humours and principal organs. Even so, if man is a rational mortal animal, and this is his nature or form, then it is necessary for him to be both animal and rational.

[11]   *Thirdly,* there is absolute necessity in things from the order of their essential principles to the properties flowing from their matter or form; a saw, because it is made of iron, must be hard; and a man is necessarily capable of learning.

[12]   However, the agent's necessity has reference both to the action itself and the resulting effect. Necessity in the former case is like the necessity that an accident derives from essential principles; just as other accidents result from the necessity of essential principles, so does action from the necessity of the form by which the agent actually exists; for as the agent actually is, so does it act. But this necessitation of action by form is different in the case of action that remains in the agent itself, as understanding and willing, and in action which passes into something else, as heating. In the first case, the necessity of the action itself results from the form by which the agent is made actual, because in order for this kind of action to exist,

nothing extrinsic, as a terminus for it, is required. Thus, when the sense power is actualized by the sensible species, it necessarily acts; and so, too, does the intellect when it is actualized by the intelligible species. But in the second case, the action's necessity results from the form, so far as the power to act is concerned; if fire is hot, it necessarily has the power of heating, yet it need not heat, for something extrinsic may prevent it. Nor in this question does it make any difference whether by its form one agent alone suffices to carry out an action, or whether many agents have to be assembled in order to perform a single action—as, for example, many men to pull a boat—because all are as one agent, who is put in act by their being united together in one action.

[13] Now, the necessity in the effect or thing moved, resulting from the efficient or moving cause, depends not only on the efficient cause, but also on the condition of the thing moved and of the recipient of the agent's action; for the recipient is either in no way receptive of the effect of such action —as wool to be made into a saw—or else its receptivity is impeded by contrary agents or by contrary dispositions in the movable or by contrary forms, to such an extent that the agent's power is ineffective; a feeble heat will not melt iron. In order that the effect follow, it is therefore necessary that receptivity exist in the patient, and that the patient be under the domination of the agent, so that the latter can transform it to a contrary disposition. And if the effect in the patient resulting from the agent's victory over it is contrary to the natural disposition of the patient, then there will be necessity by way of violence, as when a stone is thrown upwards. But if the effect is not contrary to the natural disposition of its subject, there will be necessity not of violence, but of natural order; the movement of the heaven, for example, results from an extrinsic active principle, and yet it is not contrary to the natural disposition of the movable subject, and hence is not a violent but a natural movement. This is true also in the alteration of lower bodies by the heavenly bodies, for there is a natural inclination in lower bodies to receive the influence of higher bodies. Such is the case, also, in the generation of the elements; for the form to be engendered is not contrary

to prime matter, which is the subject of generation, although it is contrary to the form that is to be cast aside; for matter existing under a contrary form is not the subject of generation.

[14]   It is therefore clear from what we have said that the necessity which arises from an efficient cause in some cases depends on the disposition of the agent alone; but in others, on the disposition of both agent and patient. Consequently, if this disposition, according to which the effect follows of necessity, be absolutely necessary both in the agent and in the patient, then there will be absolute necessity in the efficient cause, as with things that act necessarily and always. On the other hand, if this disposition be not absolutely necessary, but removable, then from the efficient cause no necessity will result, except on the supposition that both agent and patient possess the disposition necessary for acting. Thus, we find no absolute necessity in those things that are sometimes impeded in their activity either through lack of power or the violent action of a contrary; such things, then, do not act always and necessarily, but in the majority of cases.

[15]   The final cause is responsible for a twofold necessity in things. In one way, necessity results from that cause inasmuch as it is first in the intention of the agent. And in this regard, necessity derives from the end in the same way as from the agent; for it is precisely so far as an agent intends an end that an agent acts. This is true of natural as well as voluntary actions. For in natural things the intention of the end belongs to the agent in keeping with the latter's form, whereby the end is becoming to it; hence, the natural thing necessarily tends to its end in accordance with the power of its form; a heavy body tends toward the center according to the measure of its gravity. And in voluntary things the will inclines to act for the sake of an end only so far as it intends that end, although the will, as much as it desires the end, is not always inclined to do this or that as means to it, when the end can be obtained not only by this or that means, but in several ways. Now, in another way, necessity follows from the end as posterior in actual being; and such necessity is not absolute, but conditional. Thus, we say that a saw will have to be made of iron if it is to do the work of a saw.

Chapter 31.

THAT IT IS NOT NECESSARY FOR CREATURES TO HAVE ALWAYS EXISTED

[1] It remains for us to show from the foregoing that it is not necessary for created things to have existed from eternity.

[2] For, if the existence of the whole universe of creatures, or of any single creature, is necessary, then its necessity must be derived either from itself or from something else. But it cannot owe its necessity to itself; for we proved above[1] that every being must derive its existence from the first being. But anything whose being is not self-derived cannot possibly have necessary existence from itself, because that which necessarily is cannot not-be; so, whatever of itself has necessary existence is for that reason incapable of not being; and it follows that it is not a non-being, and hence is a being.

[3] But, if the creature's necessity of which we speak is derived from something other than itself, then this must be from some extrinsic cause; for whatever is received within a creature owes its being to another. An extrinsic cause, however, is either an efficient or a final one. Now, from the efficient cause it follows that the effect exists necessarily when the agent necessarily acts; for it is through the agent's action that the effect depends on the efficient cause. Consequently, if the agent need not act in order to produce the effect, then it is not absolutely necessary for the effect to be. God, however, acts out of no necessity in the production of creatures, as we have shown.[2] Therefore, it is not absolutely necessary for the creature to be, as concerns necessity dependent on the efficient cause. Nor is it necessary as regards dependence on the final cause. For the means to an end derive necessity from the end only so far as without them the end either cannot be—life cannot be preserved without food—or cannot well be—as a

1. See above, ch. 15.
2. See above, ch. 23.

journey without a horse. Now, as we have shown in Book I, the end of God's will, whereby things came into being, cannot be anything else than His own goodness.[3] But the divine goodness does not depend on creatures, either as to being, since it is necessarily existent in virtue of itself, or as to well-being, since it is by itself absolutely perfect. (All these points have been previously[4] demonstrated.) Therefore, it is not absolutely necessary for a creature to exist; nor, then, is it necessary to maintain that a creature always existed.

[4]   Consider, also, that nothing proceeding from a will is absolutely necessary, except when it chances to be necessary for the will to will it. But, as we have shown,[5] God brings creatures into being not through a necessity of His nature, but voluntarily. Nor, as proved in Book I, does He necessarily will the existence of creatures.[6] Hence, it is not absolutely necessary for the creature to be, and therefore neither is it necessary for creatures to have existed always.

[5]   Moreover, we proved above[7] that God's action is not outside Himself, as though passing from Him and terminating in the created thing, in the way in which heat issues from fire and terminates in wood. On the contrary, His act of will is identical with His action; and things are as God wills them to be. But it is not necessary that God will a creature to have existed always, for indeed, as we proved in Book I, it is not necessary that God will a creature to be at all.[8] Hence, it is not necessary for a creature to have always been.

[6]   Then, too, a thing does not proceed necessarily from a voluntary agent except because of something due. But, as we have shown above,[9] it is not by reason of any debt that God brings the creature into being, if the universal production of creatures be considered absolutely. Therefore, God does not

3. SCG, I, ch. 75–80.
4. SCG, I, ch. 13 and 28.
5. See above, ch. 23.
6. SCG, I, ch. 81.
7. See above, ch. 9 and 23.
8. SCG, I, ch. 81.
9. See above, ch. 28.

of necessity produce the creature. Nor, then, is it necessary that God should have produced the creature from eternity because He Himself is eternal.

[7] Also, we have just shown[10] that absolute necessity in created things results not from a relation to a first principle which is of itself necessarily existent, namely, God, but from a relation to other causes whose existence is not essentially necessary. But the necessity arising from a relation to that which is not of itself necessarily existent does not make it necessary for something to have always existed; if a thing runs, it follows that it is in motion, yet it is not necessary for it to have always been in motion, because the running itself is not essentially necessary. There is, therefore, no necessity that creatures should have existed always.

Chapter 32.

ARGUMENTS OF THOSE WHO WISH TO DEMON-STRATE THE WORLD'S ETERNITY FROM THE POINT OF VIEW OF GOD

[1] However, since many have held that the world has existed always and of necessity, and have attempted to demonstrate this, it remains for us to present their arguments, so as to show that they do not constitute a necessary demonstration of the world's eternity.[1] *First*, we give the arguments taken from God's side of the matter; *second*, those taken from the point of view of the creature;[2] *third*, those derived from a consideration of the mode of the production of things, according to which they are held to begin to exist anew.[3]

[2] On the part of God the following arguments are used in order to prove the eternity of the world.

[3] Every agent which does not always act is moved through

10. See above, ch. 30.
1. See below, ch. 35.   2. See below, ch. 33.
3. See below, ch. 34.

itself or by accident: through itself, as in the case of a fire which, not always burning, begins to burn either because it is newly lit or because it is for the first time placed in proximity to the fuel; by accident, as when an agent that moves an animal begins to move it by some new movement made in its regard, either from within, as an animal begins to be moved when it awakes after having digested its food, or from without, as when actions arise anew that lead to the initiation of some new action. Now, God is moved neither through Himself nor by accident, as we proved in Book I of this work.[4] Therefore, God acts always in the same way. And by His action created things take their place in being. Hence, creatures always have been.

[4]   Again, an effect proceeds from its efficient cause through the latter's action. But God's action is eternal; otherwise, from being an agent potentially He would become an agent actually; and He would have to be actualized by some prior agent—which is impossible. Therefore, the things created by God have existed from eternity.

[5]   And again. Given a sufficient cause, its effect must be granted. For if, given the cause, it were still unnecessary to grant its effect, it would then be possible that the effect should be and not be; the sequence from cause to effect will in that case be only possible. But that which is possible needs something to make it actual. Some cause, therefore, will have to be posited in order to do this; thus, the first cause was not sufficient. God, however, is the sufficient cause of the production of creatures; otherwise, He would not be a cause; rather, He would be in potentiality to a cause, since in that case He would become a cause by the addition of something. But this is clearly impossible. Since, then, God has existed from eternity, it seems to follow necessarily that the creature also has existed from eternity.

[6]   Also, a voluntary agent delays in carrying out its intention only because of something expected but not yet present, and this sometimes is in the agent itself, as when complete competency to do something, or the removal of an impediment

4. SCG, I, ch. 13, ¶24–27.

to one's power, is waited for; while sometimes this anticipated thing is outside the agent, as when one awaits a person in whose presence an action is to be done, or at any event when one looks forward to the presence of an opportune moment that has not yet arrived. For, if the will be perfectly equipped, the power acts at once, unless there be a defect in it; at the will's command the movement of a limb follows immediately, if no defect exists in the motive power carrying out the movement. And from this we see that when one wills to do something and it is not done at once, this failure must be due either to a defect in the power, of which defect one awaits the removal, or to the fact that the will is not perfectly equipped to do this thing. By the will being perfectly equipped I mean that it wills to do something absolutely, in every respect; whereas the will is imperfectly equipped when one does not will absolutely to do a thing, but on the condition that something exist which is not yet present or that a present obstacle be removed. It is certain however, that God has willed from eternity the existence of whatever He now wills to exist, for no new movement of will can possibly accrue to Him. Nor could any defect or obstacle stand in the way of His power, nor could anything else be looked for as cause of the universal production of creatures, since nothing besides Him is uncreated, as we have proved above.[5] Therefore, it seems necessary to conclude that God brought creatures into being from all eternity.

[7] Moreover, an intellectual agent chooses one thing in preference to another only because of the superiority of the one over the other. But, where there is no difference, there can be no superiority, so that in the absence of difference there is no choice of the one rather than of the other. And on this account, no action will proceed from an agent equally indifferent to each of two alternatives, any more than from matter; for a potentiality of this kind is like that of matter. Now, there can be no difference between non-being and non-being. Therefore, one non-being is not preferable to another non-being. But outside the total universe of created things nothing whatever exists except the divine eternity. In nothingness, how-

5. See above, ch. 15.

ever, no difference of moments can possibly be assigned, so that a thing should be made in one moment rather than in another. Nor is there any difference of moments in eternity, the whole of which is, as was shown in Book I, uniform and simple.[6] It therefore follows that God's will is indifferent as concerns the production of the creature throughout all eternity. Accordingly, His will is either that the creature should never be established within His eternity, or that it should always have been so. The former clearly is not the case, for it is evident that creatures were originated and established by His will. It follows with apparent necessity that the creature has always existed.

[8]   Furthermore, things directed to an end receive their necessity from that end; especially is this true of things done voluntarily. Therefore, if the end remains the same, it follows that the things ordered to it remain the same or are produced in the same way, unless there arises a new relation between them and the end. Now, the end of creatures issuing forth from the divine will is the divine goodness, which alone can be the end of the divine will. From the fact that the divine goodness, throughout all eternity, is unchangeable in itself and in relation to the divine will, it would seem to follow that creatures are in the same manner brought into being by God's will throughout all eternity. For it cannot be said that some new relation to the end accrued to them, if they are held to have been absolutely non-existent prior to a particular time from which they are supposed to have begun to be.

[9]   Since the divine goodness is maximally perfect, it is said that all things issued from God on account of His goodness, but not in such a way that something accrued to Him from creatures; rather, this is said because it is of the essence of goodness to communicate itself as far as possible, and by so doing goodness itself is manifested. Now, since all things partake of God's goodness so far as they have being, the more enduring they are, so much the more do they participate in His goodness. This is why the perpetual being of a species is called a divine being.[7] The divine goodness, however, is in-

6. SCG, I, ch. 15.
7. Cf. Aristotle, De anima, II, 4 (415b 5).

finite, so that it is proper to it to communicate itself in an infinite manner, not in some limited time only. Therefore, it seems to belong to the divine goodness that some created things should have existed from eternity.

[10] These, then, are the arguments, taken from God's side of the question, which seem to show that creatures have existed always.

Chapter 33.

ARGUMENTS OF THOSE WHO WISH TO PROVE
THE ETERNITY OF THE WORLD FROM
THE STANDPOINT OF CREATURES

[1] There are also the following arguments, taken from the point of view of creatures, which seemingly arrive at the same conclusion.

[2] Things having no potentiality to non-being cannot possibly fail to exist. Now, in certain created things there is no potentiality to non-being. For there can be potentiality to non-being only in those things which possess matter subject to contrariety; for potentiality to being and non-being is potentiality to privation and form, the subject of which is matter; and privation is always connected with the contrary form, since matter cannot possibly exist without any form at all. But some creatures, wherein there is no matter subject to contrariety, do exist, either because they are completely without matter, as intellectual substances are—this we will show later[1]—or because they have no contrary opposite, as with the heavenly bodies—and this is proved by their movement, which has no contrary. It is, then, impossible for certain creatures not to exist; therefore, they must always exist.

[3] Moreover, each and every thing continues in being in proportion to its power of being—except by accident, as in things caused to perish by violence. But there are some creatures endowed with the power of existing, not for any limited

1. See below, ch. 50.

time, but forever; the heavenly bodies, for instance, and intellectual substances, which are imperishable because they have no contrary. It is therefore proper to these things to exist always. On the other hand, that which begins to be does not exist always. Therefore, an existential beginning does not pertain to imperishable or incorruptible things.

[4]   Furthermore, whenever something begins to be moved for the first time, either the mover, or the moved, or both, must needs exist in a different state now, while there is movement, than before, when no movement existed. For there is a certain condition or relation in the mover to the thing moved, as a result of which it moves actually; and the new relation does not arise without a change either in both or at least in one or other of the extremes related. But that thing is moved whose condition of existence is different now than it was before. Therefore, prior to the newly initiated movement, another movement must take place either in the movable thing or in the mover; so that every movement is either eternal or is preceded by another movement. Therefore, motion has always existed, and so, also, have things movable. Hence, creatures have always existed. For God is wholly immutable, as we proved in Book I of this work.[2]

[5]   Again, every agent which engenders its like intends to preserve perpetual being in the species, for existence cannot be so maintained in the individual. Now, it is impossible that natural desire should be futile. The species of generable things, therefore, must be perpetual.

[6]   And again, if time is everlasting, so also must motion be; for time "is the number of motion."[3] And, consequently, things movable must be perpetual, since motion is the "act of the movable."[4] But time must be everlasting. For time cannot be known to exist without the *now*, any more than a line without a point. But the *now* is always "the end of the past and the beginning of the future,"[5] for this is the definition of

2. *SCG*, I, ch. 13.
3. Aristotle, *Physics*, IV, 11 (219b 1).
4. Aristotle, *Physics*, III, 2 (202a 15).
5. Aristotle, *Physics*, IV, 13 (222b 1).

the *now*. Thus, every given *now* has time preceding it and following it, so that no *now* can be either first or last. It remains that mobile things, which created substances are, exist from eternity.

[7] Also, it is necessary either to affirm or to deny. If, therefore, a thing's existence is affirmed as a result of denying it, then that thing must exist always. Now, time is such a thing. For to suppose that time did not always exist is to think of it as not existing prior to existing; and, similarly, if time will not exist always, its non-existence must succeed its existence. But if time does not exist, there can be no before and after in duration; for "the number of before and after is time."[6] And thus, time must have existed before it began to be and will continue to exist after it has ceased to be. Time is, therefore, necessarily eternal. But time is an accident, and an accident cannot be without a subject. Now, God, who is above time, is not the subject of this accident, for He is altogether immutable, as we proved in Book I of this work.[7] It remains that some created substance is eternal.

[8] Many propositions, moreover, are of such nature that he who denies them must posit them; for example, whoever denies that truth exists posits the existence of truth, for the denial which he puts forward he posits as true. The same is true of one who denies the principle that *contradictories are not simultaneous*; for, by denying this, he asserts that the negation which he posits is true and that the opposite affirmation is false, and thus that both are not true of the same thing. Therefore, if a thing that is affirmed by being denied must, as we have just shown, exist always, then the aforesaid propositions, and all that follow from them, are everlasting. But these propositions are not God. It is, therefore, necessary that something besides God be eternal.

[9] These arguments, then, and others of like nature, can be taken from the standpoint of created things in order to prove that the latter have existed always.

6. Aristotle, *Physics*, IV, 11 (220a 25).
7. SCG, I, ch. 13.

Chapter 34.

ARGUMENTS TO PROVE THE ETERNITY OF THE
WORLD FROM THE POINT OF VIEW OF
THE MAKING [OF THINGS]

[1]   In order to establish the same conclusion, this time from the side of the making itself, other arguments also can be adduced, such as the following.

[2]   That which is asserted universally, by everyone, cannot possibly be totally false. For a false opinion is a kind of infirmity of the understanding, just as a false judgment concerning a proper sensible happens as the result of a weakness of the sense power involved. But defects, being outside the intention of nature, are accidental. And nothing accidental can be always and in all things; the judgment about savors given by every tasting cannot be false. Thus, the judgment uttered by everyone concerning truth cannot be erroneous. "Now, it is the common opinion of all the philosophers that nothing arises from what is not."[1]
This opinion, therefore, must be true; so that if a thing is made it must needs be made from something; and if the latter, also, is made, then it, too, must be made from something else. But this process cannot go on to infinity, since in that case no generation of anything would be completed; it is impossible to pass through an infinite number of things. It is therefore necessary to arrive at a first thing that was not made. But any and every thing which has not always existed must be made. Consequently, that being from which all things were first made, must be everlasting. Yet this is not God, because He cannot be the matter of anything, as we proved in Book I of this work.[2] Thus, it follows that something besides God is eternal, namely, prime matter.

[3]   Moreover, if a thing does not exist in the same way now

1. Aristotle, *Physics*, I, 4 (187a 34).
2. SCG, I, ch. 17.

as it did before, then in some respect it must be changed, for to be moved [or changed] is not to exist in the same state now as before. But everything that begins to exist anew is not now as it was before; hence, the reason for this must be that some motion or change has occurred. But every motion or change is in a subject, for it is "the act of the movable."[3] Now, since motion precedes that which is made by it, for it terminates in the latter, it follows that a movable subject must exist prior to anything made. And since to proceed to infinity in this matter is impossible, we must come to a first subject not newly originated but always existent.

[4] Then, too, in the case of a thing that begins to be anew, it was possible, before it existed, that it would exist; otherwise, it was impossible for it to be, and necessary for it not to be; so that it would always have been a non-entity and would never have begun to be. But that which is possibly existent is potentially a subject of being. Therefore, antecedently to everything which begins to exist *de novo*, there must be a subject which is potentially a being. And since an infinite regress is here impossible, we must affirm the existence of a primary subject which did not begin to be *de novo*.

[5] Furthermore, no permanent substance exists while it is being made, for it is made in order that it may be; so, it would not be made if it existed already. But, while it is being made, something must exist which is the subject of the making; for, since making is an accident, there can be no making without a subject. Thus, whatever is made has some pre-existing subject. And since this cannot go on indefinitely, it follows that the first subject was not made, but is everlasting; and it follows, also, that something besides God is eternal, because He cannot be the subject of making or of movement.

[6] These, then, are the arguments through adhering to which, as though they were demonstrations, some people say that created things must always have existed; in so saying they contradict the Catholic faith, which affirms that nothing besides God has always existed, but that all things, save the one eternal God, have had a beginning.

3. Aristotle, *Physics*, III, 2 (202a 7).

Chapter 35.

SOLUTION OF THE FOREGOING ARGUMENTS, AND FIRST OF THOSE TAKEN FROM THE STANDPOINT OF GOD

[1]   It remains for us to show that the arguments proposed above issue in no necessary conclusions. First, let us consider those taken from the agent's point of view.[1]

[2]   God need not be moved either essentially or accidentally if His effects begin to exist anew, as the *first argument* would have it. For the newness of an effect can indicate change on the agent's part inasmuch as it does manifest newness of action; a new action cannot possibly be in the agent unless the latter is in some way moved, at least from inaction to action. But the newness of an effect produced by God does not demonstrate newness of action in Him, since His action is His essence, as we have proved above.[2] Neither, therefore, can newness of effect prove change in God the agent.

[3]   Nor, if the action of the first agent is eternal, does it follow that His effect is eternal, as the *second argument* concludes. For we have already shown in this Book[3] that God acts voluntarily in the production of things, but not in such fashion that there be some other intermediate action of His, as in us the action of the motive power intervenes between the act of the will and the effect, as we have also previously shown.[4] On the contrary, God's act of understanding and willing is, necessarily, His act of making. Now, an effect follows from the intellect and the will according to the determination of the intellect and the command of the will. Moreover, just as the intellect determines every other condition of the thing made, so does it prescribe the time of its

1. See above, ch. 32.
2. See above, ch. 9.
3. See above, ch. 23.
4. See above, ch. 9, ¶5.

making; for art determines not only that this thing is to be such and such, but that it is to be at this particular time, even as a physician determines that a dose of medicine is to be drunk at such and such a particular time, so that, if his act of will were of itself sufficient to produce the effect, the effect would follow anew from his previous decision, without any new action on his part. Nothing, therefore, prevents our saying that God's action existed from all eternity, whereas its effect was not present from eternity, but existed at that time when, from all eternity, He ordained it.

[4] From this we see also that, although God is the sufficient cause of bringing things into being, it is not necessary to hold that because He is eternal His effect is eternal, as the *third argument* maintained. Given a sufficient cause, its effect is given, too, but not an effect that does not belong to the cause; for this would result from the insufficiency of the cause, as if a hot thing, for example, failed to give heat. Now, the will's proper effect is the being of that which it wills; and if something else were to be than what the will determines, this would be an effect not proper to the cause but foreign to it. But, as we have said, just as the will wills this thing to be such and such, so does it will it to be at such and such a time. Hence, for the will to be a sufficient cause it is not necessary that the effect should exist when the will exists, but at that time when the will has ordained its existence. But with things that proceed from a cause acting naturally, the case is different. For, as nature is, so is its action; hence, given the existence of the cause, the effect must necessarily follow. On the other hand, the will acts in keeping not with the manner of its being, but of its intention. So, then, just as the effect of a natural agent follows the being of the agent, if the latter is sufficient, so the effect of a voluntary agent follows the mode of his purpose.

[5] Moreover, what has been said makes it clear that, contrary to the *fourth argument*, the effect of God's will was not delayed, although having been always willed, the effect was not itself always existent. For within the scope of God's will fall not only the existence of His effect but also the time of its existence. Therefore, this thing willed, namely, that a creature

should exist at a certain time, is not delayed, for the creature
began to exist at that time which God appointed from all
eternity.

[6] Prior to the initial existence of the totality of created
being there is no diversity of parts of any duration, as was
supposed in the fifth argument. For nothingness has neither
measure nor duration. Now, God's duration, which is eternity,
does not have parts, but is utterly simple, without before or
after; since God is immovable, as we have shown in Book I of
this work.[5] Therefore, the beginning of the whole of creation
is not to be thought of in comparison to any diverse parts
designated in some pre-existing measure, to which parts the
beginning of creatures can stand in similar or dissimilar relations, so that there would have to be a reason in the agent
why he brought the creature into being in this designated
part of that duration rather than at some other preceding or
subsequent point. Such a reason would be required if, beside
the totality of created being, there existed some duration
divisible into parts, as is the case in particular agents, which
produce their effects in time, but do not produce time itself.
God, however, brought into being both the creature and time
together. In this case, therefore, the reason why He produced
them now and not before does not have to be considered,
but only why He did not produce them always. A comparison
with place will make this point clear. Particular bodies are
brought into being not only at a definite time, but also in a
definite place; and since the time and the place in which they
are involved are extrinsic to them, there must be a reason why
they are produced in this place and time rather than in another.
On the other hand, outside the entire heaven[6] there is no
place, the universal place of all things being produced together with it; so that there is no reason for considering why
the heaven was established in being here and not there. And
because they thought that such a reason ought to be sought
for, some have fallen into the error of attributing infinity to
bodily things. Similarly, outside the entire universe of crea-

5. SCG, I, ch. 15.
6. Cf. St. Thomas Aquinas, *Summa Theologiae*, I, 68, 4.

tures there is no time, time having been produced simultaneously with that universe; hence, we do not have to look for the reason why it was produced now and not before, so as to be led to concede the infinity of time; we have only to ask why it was not always produced, or why it was produced after not being or with some beginning.

[7] Now, in order to inquire into this matter, the *sixth argument* was adduced from the point of view of the end, which alone can introduce necessity into things done voluntarily. But the only possible end of God's will is His own goodness; and He does not act for the sake of bringing this end into being, as the craftsman acts in order to produce his handiwork. For God's goodness is eternal and immutable, so that nothing can accrue to Him. Nor can it be said that God acts for His own betterment. Nor does He act in order to obtain this end for Himself, as a king fights in order to gain possession of a city; for God is His own goodness. We therefore conclude that God acts for an end inasmuch as He produces an effect so that it may participate in His end. Therefore, in producing a thing for the sake of an end, in this sense, the uniform relation of the end to the agent is not to be thought of as the reason for His work being eternal; on the contrary, the thing to be attended to is the relation of the end to the effect brought forth on account of the end in order that the effect be produced in such a manner as to be most fittingly ordained to that end. Hence, from the fact that the relation of the end to the agent is uniform, we cannot conclude that the effect is eternal.

[8] Nor, as the *seventh argument* seemed to imply, is it necessary that God's effect should have always existed because it would then be more fittingly directed to its end. On the contrary, by not having existed always, it is more fittingly directed to its end. For every agent that produces an effect in participation of its own form intends to produce its own likeness in that effect. Thus, to produce the creature in participation of His own goodness was becoming to God's will, for by its likeness to Him the creature might show forth His goodness. But this representation cannot be in terms of equality,

in the manner in which a univocal effect represents its cause—
so that eternal effects would have to be produced by the divine
goodness. Rather, this representation is in keeping with the
way in which the transcendent is manifested by that which is
transcended. Now, the transcendence of God's goodness over
the creature is shown most of all by the fact that creatures
have not always existed. For this makes it perfectly clear that
all things other than God have Him as the author of their
being; and that His power is not fettered to the production of
those effects, as nature is to natural effects; and, consequently,
that He is a voluntary and intelligent agent. (Some, assuming
the eternity of creatures, have asserted views contrary to
these.)

[9]   There is, then, nothing from the agent's side of the question that compels us to maintain the eternity of creatures.

Chapter 36.

SOLUTION OF THE ARGUMENTS PROPOSED
FROM THE POINT OF VIEW OF THE
THINGS MADE

[1]   Likewise, there is nothing on the part of creatures that
induces us necessarily to affirm their eternity.[1]

[2]   The necessity of being that we find in creatures, whence
the first argument about this question is drawn, is a necessity
of order, as we have previously shown.[2] But, as we proved
above,[3] a necessity of order does not compel the subject in
which a necessity of this kind is present to exist always. For,
although the substance of the heaven has necessity with respect to being, in virtue of the fact that it lacks potentiality
to non-being, this necessity nevertheless is consequent upon
its substance. Hence, once its substance has been established
in being, this necessity entails the impossibility of not-being;

1. See above, ch. 33.
2. See above, ch. 30.
3. See above, ch. 31.

but if we consider the production of its very substance, it does not entail the impossibility of the heaven's not being at all.

[3] Likewise, the power of existing always, whereon the *second argument* is based, presupposes the production of the substance; so that, where the point at issue is the production of the substance of the heaven, this power cannot be a sufficient proof of the eternity of that substance.

[4] Nor does the argument brought up next compel us to assert the eternity of motion. For what we have said already[4] makes it clear that, without any change in God the agent, He can enact something new that is not eternal. But, if something can be done by Him anew, it is evidently possible, also, for something to be moved by Him anew. For newness of motion follows upon the decision of the eternal will of God, that motion be not always in existence.

[5] Then, too, the intention of natural agents to perpetuate the species—this was the starting point of the *fourth argument*—presupposes that natural agents already exist. Hence, this argument is relevant only to natural things already brought into being; where it is a question of the production of things, it has no place. But the question, whether it is necessary to hold that the engendering of things will go on for ever, will be dealt with later.[5]

[6] Furthermore, the *fifth argument*, drawn from a consideration of time, supposes the eternity of motion rather than proves it. For, as Aristotle teaches,[6] the before and after and the continuity of time follow upon the before and after and the continuity of motion. Clearly, then, the same instant is the beginning of the future and the end of the past because some assigned point in motion is the beginning and the end of the diverse parts of motion. So, not every instant need be of this kind unless we think of every assignable point in time as existing between a before and an after in movement; and this is to suppose that movement is eternal. On the other hand, if we held that motion is not eternal, we can say that

4. See above, ch. 35.
5. *SCG*, IV, ch. 97.
6. Aristotle, *Physics*, IV, 5 (219a 17).

the first instant of time is the beginning of the future and the terminus of no time past. Nor, simply because a line, wherein some point is a beginning and not an end, is fixed and not flowing, is it incompatible with time's successiveness if we suppose a *now* that is a beginning and not an end; for even in some particular movement, which is not stationary either, but transitory, it is possible to designate a point which is a beginning only and not an end; otherwise, all movement would be perpetual; and this is impossible.

[7]   True, if time had a beginning, we are supposing its non-existence to precede its existence. But the supposition of time's non-existence does not compel us to assert its existence, as the *sixth argument* would have it. For the *before* that we speak of as preceding time implies nothing temporal in reality, but only in our imagination. Indeed, when we say that time exists *after not existing*, we mean that there was no time at all prior to this designated *now*; even so, when we declare that *above the heaven there is nothing*, we are not implying the existence of a place outside the heaven which can be said to be above in relation to it, but that there is no place at all above it. In either case, the imagination can add a certain dimension to the already existing thing; and just as this is no reason for attributing infinite quantity to a body, as is said in *Physics* III,[7] so neither does it justify the supposition that time is eternal.

[8]   The truth of propositions whose denial entails their affirmation—and this was the starting point of the *seventh argument*—possesses the necessity of that order which obtains between predicate and subject. By such necessity, therefore, a thing is not compelled to exist everlastingly, except perhaps the divine intellect, in whom all truth is rooted, as was shown in Book I of this work.[8]

[9]   It is therefore clear that the arguments adduced from the point of view of creatures do not oblige us to maintain that the world is eternal.

7. Aristotle, *Physics*, III, 6 (206b 20).
8. *SCG*, I, ch. 62.

Chapter 37.

SOLUTION OF THE ARGUMENTS TAKEN FROM
THE POINT OF VIEW OF THE MAKING
OF THINGS

[1] Lastly, we must show that no argument drawn from the standpoint of the making of things can necessitate that same conclusion.[1]

[2] The common opinion of the philosophers, on which the *first argument* was based, namely, that from nothing comes nothing, is true as regards that particular making which they had in mind. Since our knowledge originates in sense perception, which is concerned with singular things, the progress of human thought has been from particular to universal considerations. That is why those who sought the principle of things considered only particular makings of things, inquiring how this particular fire or stone comes to be. And so those who came first, considering the making of things in a more extrinsic fashion than they needed to, claimed that a thing is made only as concerns certain accidental dispositions, such as rarity, density, and the like, and consequently they said that to be made was nothing else than *to be altered*; and this they held because it was their understanding that each and every thing was made from a being actually existing. But later thinkers, considering the making of things from a more intrinsic point of view, advanced to the problem of the making of things in terms of their substance; and they maintained that from an actually existing being a thing need be made only in an accidental respect, but that from a being potentially existent it is made in essential fashion. But this making, namely, of a being from any being whatever, is that of a particular being: one that is made inasmuch as it is *this* being, a man or a fire, for example, but not inasmuch as it is, uni-

1. See above, ch. 34.

versally,[2] because there was previously existent being that is transformed into this being.[3] Entering more deeply into the problem of the origin of things, philosophers came at last to consider the procession of all created being from one first cause: a truth made evident by arguments previously proposed.[4] Now, in this procession of all being from God it is impossible for anything to be made from some other preexisting thing; otherwise, this procession would not consist in the making of all created being.

[3]   Now, the first philosophers of nature, who shared the commonly received opinion that nothing is made from nothing, did not attain to the idea of such a making as this. Or, if any of them conceived of it, they did not consider it making properly speaking, since the word *making* implies motion or change, whereas in the origination of all being from one first being, the transmutation of one being into another is, as we have shown,[5] inconceivable. And on this account it is the business not of the philosopher of nature to consider that origination, but of the metaphysician, who considers universal being and things existing apart from motion. Nevertheless, in virtue of a certain likeness we transfer the word *making* even to that origination of things, saying that anything at all whose essence or nature originates from something else is *made*.[6]

[4]   From this we see that the *second argument*, based on the concept of motion, is also inconclusive. For creation can be called a change only in a metaphorical sense, that is, only so far as the created thing is thought of as having being after not being, even as with things not mutually transformed we say that one comes to be from another simply because one succeeds the other; for instance, that *day comes from night*.[7] Now, since that which in no way exists is not in any particular

2. See above, ch. 21.
3. See above, ch. 17.
4. See, for example, ch. 16, above, with St. Thomas Aquinas, *Summa Theologiae*, I, 44, 2.
5. See above, ch. 17.
6. St. Thomas Aquinas, *Summa Theologiae*, I, 45, 2, ad 2.
7. St. Thomas Aquinas, *Summa Theologiae*, I, 45, 1, ad 3.

state, the idea of motion used in the argument does not warrant the conclusion that, when a thing begins to be, it is *in another state now than it was before.*

[5] Whence it is also clear that, contrary to the *third argument,* no passive potentiality need precede the existence of all created being. Such a necessity obtains in the case of things that come into being by way of motion, for motion is *the act of a thing existing potentially.*[8] But before a created thing existed, its existence was possible, in virtue of the power of its agent, by which also it began to be. Or that thing was possible on account of the relationship between the terms involved, wherein no incompatibility is found; and this is possibility "according to no potentiality," as Aristotle states in *Metaphysics* v.[9] For the predicate, *act of being,* is not incompatible with the subject, *world* or *man,* as *commensurable* is incompatible with *diameter.* It therefore follows that the existence of the world or of man is not impossible, and, consequently, that before they actually existed their existence was possible, even in the absence of all potentiality. On the other hand, things produced by way of motion must be previously possible by virtue of a passive potentiality; and when Aristotle uses this argument in *Metaphysics* vii it is to these things that he refers.[10]

[6] Moreover, from what has been said it is clear that the *fourth argument* likewise misses the mark. For, in things made by way of motion, *to be made* and *to be* are not simultaneous, because the production of such things involves succession. But in things that are not made by way of motion, the making does not precede the being.

[7] In the light of all this, then, it is clear that nothing stands in the way of one's holding that the world has not always existed—a truth which the Catholic faith affirms: "In the beginning God created heaven and earth" (Gen. 1:1); and in the Book of Proverbs (8:22) it is said of God: "Before He made anything from the beginning," etc.

8. Aristotle, *Physics,* III, 1 (201a 10).
9. Aristotle, *Metaphysics,* V, 12 (1019b 12).
10. Aristotle, *Metaphysics,* VII, 7 (1032a 12).

Chapter 38.

ARGUMENTS BY WHICH SOME TRY TO SHOW
THAT THE WORLD IS NOT ETERNAL

[1] We now note a number of arguments introduced by certain persons with the intention of proving that the world did not always exist.

[2] It has been demonstrated that God is the cause of all things. But a cause must precede in duration the things produced by its action.

[3] Moreover, since all being is created by God, it cannot be said to be made from some being. It follows that it is made from nothing and, consequently, that it has being after not-being.

[4] Also, an infinite number of things cannot be traversed. But, if the world had always existed, an infinite number of things would have now been traversed, for what is past is passed by; and if the world always existed, then there are an infinite number of past days or revolutions of the sun.

[5] Moreover, in that case it follows that an addition is made to the infinite; to the [infinite number of] past days or revolutions every day brings another addition.

[6] Then, too, it follows that it is possible to proceed to infinity in the line of efficient causes, if the engendering of things has gone on perpetually—and this in turn follows necessarily on the hypothesis that the world always existed; the father is the cause of his son, and another person the cause of that father, and so on endlessly.

[7] Furthermore, if the world always existed, it will follow that there exists an infinite number of things, namely, the immortal souls of an infinite number of human beings who died in the past.[1]

1. See St. Thomas Aquinas: II Sententiis, I, 5, ad 6 (second set of objections); Opusculum, De aeternitate mundi, in fine; Summa Theologiae, I, 46, 2, ad 8.

[8] Now, these arguments, though not devoid of probability, lack absolute and necessary conclusiveness. Hence, it is sufficient to deal with them quite briefly, lest the Catholic faith might appear to be founded on ineffectual reasonings, and not, as it is, on the most solid teaching of God. It would seem fitting, then, to state how these arguments are countered by the partisans of the doctrine of the world's eternity.

[9] The *first statement*, that the agent necessarily precedes the effect resulting from its operation, is true of things which produce something by way of motion, because the effect does not exist until the motion is ended, but the agent must exist even when the motion begins. No such necessity obtains, however, in the case of things that act instantaneously. For instance, when the sun is at the point of the east, it immediately illuminates our hemisphere.

[10] The *second argument* also is ineffectual. If the proposition (a) *something is made from something* be not admitted, then the contradictory of it which must be given is: (b) *something is not made from something*, and not (c) *something is made from nothing*, except in the sense of proposition (b). And from this it cannot be concluded that something is made after not-being.

[11] Nor is the *third argument* cogent. For, although the infinite does not exist actually and all at once, it can exist successively.[2] For, so considered, any infinite is finite. Therefore, being finite, any single one of the preceding solar revolutions could be completed; but if, on the assumption of the world's eternity, all of them are thought of as existing simultaneously, then there would be no question of a first one, nor, therefore, of a passing through them, for, unless there are two extremes, no transition is possible.

[12] The *fourth argument* is weak. For there is no reason why an addition should not be made to the infinite on that side of it which is finite. Now, from the supposition of the eternity of time it follows that time is infinite in relation to the prior but finite in relation to the posterior; for the present is the terminal point of the past.

2. See, for example, St. Thomas, *II Sententiis*, I, 1, 5, ad 3; *De veritate*, II, 10; *Quodlibet*, IX, 1, 1; SCG, I, 69.

[13] Nor does the objection to the theory of the world's eternity that is raised in the *fifth argument* have compelling force. For, according to the philosophers, it is impossible to proceed to infinity in the order of efficient causes which act together at the same time, because in that case the effect would have to depend on an infinite number of actions simultaneously existing. And such causes are essentially infinite, because their infinity is required for the effect caused by them. On the other hand, in the sphere of non-simultaneously acting causes, it is not, according to the partisans of the perpetual generation theory, impossible to proceed to infinity. And the infinity here is accidental to the causes; thus, it is accidental to Socrates' father that he is another man's son or not. But it is not accidental to the stick, in moving the stone, that it be moved by the hand; for the stick moves just so far as it is moved.

[14] The objection concerning the souls, however, is more difficult. Yet the argument is not very useful, because it supposes many things.[3] For those who maintained that the world is eternal also held that human souls do not survive the body; and it was asserted that of all souls there remains only the separated intellect—either the agent intellect, according to some, or also the possible intellect, according to others. On the other hand, some have supposed a sort of circular movement in souls, saying that, after several ages have passed, the same souls return to bodies. And indeed there are those who do not consider it incongruous that, in the realm of things devoid of order, actual infinities should be found.

[15] However, a more effective approach toward proving the non-eternity of the world can be made from the point of view of the end of the divine will, as we have previously indicated.[4] For in the production of things the end of God's will is His own goodness as it is manifested in His effects. Now, His power and goodness are made manifest above all by the fact that things other than Himself were not always in existence. For this fact shows clearly that these things owe their existence to Him, and also is proof that God does not act by a necessity

3. See below, ch. 81, ¶9.
4. See above, ch. 35.

of His nature, and that His power of acting is infinite. Respecting the divine goodness, therefore, it was entirely fitting that God should have given created things a temporal beginning.[5]

[16] The preceding considerations enable us to avoid various errors made by the pagan philosophers: the assertion of the world's eternity; the assertion of the eternity of the world's matter, out of which at a certain time the world began to be formed, either by chance, or by some intellect, or even by love or by strive. For in all these cases something beside God is claimed to be eternal; and this is incompatible with the Catholic faith.

Chapter 39.

THAT THE DISTINCTION OF THINGS IS NOT THE RESULT OF CHANCE

[1] Having settled the problems concerning the production of things, it remains for us to deal with those that need to be taken into account as regards the distinction of things.[1] And in this connection what we must do first is show that the distinction of things is not fortuitous.

[2] For chance occurs only in things which can be otherwise; we do not say that things that exist necessarily and always are the result of chance. Now, it was shown above[2] that certain things have been created in whose nature there is no possibility of not being; in this category belong immaterial substances and those in which no contrariety is found. It is therefore impossible that their substances be from chance. But it is by their substance that they are distinct from one another. Consequently, their distinction is not the result of chance.

[3] Moreover, chance is found only in things that are possibly otherwise; and the source of this possibility is matter and not the form, which indeed determines the matter,

5. See St. Thomas Aquinas, *De potentia*, III, 14, ad 8.
1. See above, ch. 5.
2. See above, ch. 30.

reservoir of multiple possibilities, to one. It follows that those things whose distinction from one another is derived from their forms are not distinct by chance, although this is perhaps the case with things whose distinction stems from matter. Now, the distinction of species is derived from the form, and the distinction of singulars of the same species is from matter. Therefore, the distinction of things in terms of species cannot be the result of chance; but perhaps the distinction of certain individuals can be the result of chance.

[4] Again, since matter is the principle and cause of fortuitous things, as we have shown, in the making of things that are generated from matter there can be chance. Now, we proved above[3] that the first production of things into being was not from matter. Therefore, chance can have had no place in it. Nevertheless, that production necessarily involved the distinction of the things produced. For in the world of creation there are many things which are neither generated from one another nor from some one common source, because they are not united in the possession of a common matter. It is impossible, therefore, that the distinction of things should be the result of chance.

[5] Then, too, a thing that is a cause through itself is prior to one that is by accident. If, therefore, posterior things are from a cause determinate through itself, it would be incongruous to attribute things prior in nature to an indeterminate cause by accident. But the distinction of things is naturally prior to their movements and operations, because determinate movements and operations belong to things determinate and distinct. Now, the movements and operations of things are from causes that are determinate and are causes through themselves, since they proceed from their causes in the same manner either always, it is found, or in most cases. Consequently, the distinction of things is also the result of that kind of cause, and not of chance, which is an indeterminate cause by accident.

[6] And again, the form of any thing proceeding from an intellectual and voluntary agent is intended by that agent.

3. See above, ch. 16.

But, as we have already seen,[4] the universe of creatures has as its author God, who is a voluntary and intellectual agent. Nor can there be any defect in His power so that He might fail in accomplishing His intention; for, as we proved in Book I of this work,[5] His power is infinite. It therefore follows of necessity that the form of the universe is intended and willed by God, and for that reason it is not the result of chance. For it is things outside the scope of the agent's intention that we say are fortuitous. Now, the form of the universe consists in the distinction and order of its parts. The distinction of things, therefore, is not the result of chance.

[7] That which is good and best in the effect, furthermore, is the final cause of its production. But the good and the best in the universe consists in the mutual order of its parts, which is impossible without their distinction from one another; for by this order the universe is established in its wholeness, and in this does its optimum good consist. Therefore, it is this very order of the parts of the universe and of their distinction which is the end of the production of the universe. It remains that the distinction of things is not fortuitous.

[8] Sacred Scripture bears witness to this truth, as the Book of Genesis (1:1) makes clear; for, after the words, "In the beginning God created heaven and earth" we read: "God divided the light from the darkness," etc., so that not only the creation of things, but also their distinction, is shown to be from God, and not the result of chance; and as constituting the good and the highest good of the universe. Hence, it is added: "God saw all the things that He had made, and they were very good" (Gen. 1:34).

[9] Eliminated hereby is the opinion of the ancient natural philosophers who held that there was but one cause, a material one, from which all things were made by rarity and density.[6] For these thinkers were obliged to say that the distinction of things which we observe in the universe resulted not from the ordering intention of some principle, but from the fortuitous movement of matter.

4. See above, ch. 23 and 24.   5. *SCG*, I, ch. 43.
6. Aristotle, *Metaphysics*, I, 4 (985b 12).

[10]   Set aside, likewise, is the opinion of Democritus and Leucippus, who posited an infinite number of material principles, namely, indivisible bodies of the same nature but differing in shape, order, and position, whose coming together —which was necessarily fortuitous, since they denied the existence of an efficient cause—they attributed to the diversity in things, by reason of the three differentiating characters of the atoms just mentioned, namely, figure, order, and position. Thus, it followed that the distinction of things was the result of chance. And in the light of what has been said this is clearly false.

Chapter 40.

THAT MATTER IS NOT THE FIRST CAUSE OF
THE DISTINCTION OF THINGS

[1]   Moreover, it plainly follows that the distinction of things is not to be attributed primarily to diversity of matter.

[2]   For it is only by chance that anything determinate can proceed from matter, because matter is in potentiality to many things, of which, if but one were to issue forth, this could not possibly happen except in the minority of instances; and such a thing it is that comes about by chance—and especially is this so in the absence of an agent's intention. Now, we have shown[1] that the distinction of things is not the result of chance. It therefore follows that the primary reason why things are distinct from one another does not lie in the diversity of their matter.

[3]   Moreover, things that result from the intention of an agent do so not primarily on account of matter. For an efficient cause is prior in causal operation to matter, because it is only so far as it is moved by such a cause that matter itself becomes causally operative. Hence, if an effect follows upon a disposition of matter and the intention of an agent, it does not result from matter as its first cause. And on this account we observe

1. See above, ch. 39.

that things referred to matter as their primary cause fall outside the intention of the agent concerned—monsters, for instance, and other failures of nature. The form, however, results
from the agent's intention. This is evident from the fact that
the agent produces its like according to its form, and if it
sometimes fails to do so, the failure is fortuitous and is due
to the matter involved. Hence, forms are not consequent upon
the disposition of matter as their first cause; on the contrary,
the reason why matters are disposed in such and such ways is
that there might be forms of such and such kinds. Now, it is
by their forms that things are distinguished into species.
Therefore, it is not in the diversity of matter that the first
cause of the distinction of things is to be found.

[4] Then, too, the distinction of things cannot result from
matter except in the case of things made from pre-existing
matter. But there are many things distinct from one another
that cannot be made from pre-existing matter: the celestial
bodies, for example, which have no contrary, as their motion
shows. It follows that the diversity of matter cannot be the
first cause of the distinction of things.

[5] Again. There is a cause of the distinction that obtains
between all things whose existence is caused and which, therefore, are distinct from one another. For each and every thing is
made a being according as it is made one, undivided in itself
and distinct from others. But, if matter is by virtue of its
diversity the cause of the distinction of things, we shall then
have to maintain that matters are in themselves distinct. It
is, however, certain that every matter owes its existence to
something else, for it was shown above[2] that every thing which
is in any way whatever owes its being to God. So the cause of
distinction in matters is something other than matter itself.
Therefore, the first cause of the distinction of things cannot
be the diversity of matter.

[6] Furthermore, since every intellect acts for the sake of a
good, it does not produce a better thing for the sake of a thing
of less worth, but vice versa; and the same is true of nature.
Now, as we see from what has been said above,[3] all things

2. See above, ch. 15.   3. See above, ch. 40.

proceed from God acting by His intellect. Inferior things, therefore, proceed from God for the sake of better things, and not vice versa. Form, however, is nobler than matter, since it is its perfection and act. Hence, God does not produce such and such forms of things for the sake of such and such matters; rather, He produced such and such matters that there might be such and such forms. Therefore, the distinction of species in things, following as it does upon their form, is not on account of their matter. On the contrary, diverse matters were created in order that they might befit diverse forms.

[7]   Excluded hereby is the opinion of Anaxagoras, who asserted that there were an infinite number of material principles which in the beginning were mixed together in one confused whole, but which an intellect later separated, thus establishing the distinction of things from one another. Eliminated, likewise, is the opinion of any other thinkers who postulate various material principles as the cause of the distinction of things.

Chapter 41.

THAT A CONTRARIETY OF AGENTS DOES NOT ACCOUNT FOR THE DISTINCTION OF THINGS

[1]   From what has been said it can be shown, also, that the cause of the distinction of things is not a diversity or even a contrariety of agents.

[2]   For, if the diverse agents that cause the diversity of things are ordered to one another, there must be some single cause of this order; for many things are not united save by some one thing. And thus the ordering principle of this unity is the first and sole cause of the distinction of things. But, if these diverse agents are not ordered to one another, their unified action in producing the diversity of things will be accidental. The distinction of things, therefore, will be fortuitous. But we have already proved[1] that the contrary is true.

1. See above, ch. 39.

[3] Ordered effects, moreover, do not proceed from diverse causes devoid of order, except perhaps accidentally; for the diverse, as such, do not produce the one. Now, things mutually distinct are found to have a mutual order, and not fortuitously, since in the majority of cases one is served by another. Hence, the distinction of things thus ordered cannot possibly be accounted for by a diversity of agents without order.

[4] And let us add that the first cause of the distinction of things cannot be things whose distinction from one another itself is caused. Yet, if we consider several agents of the same order, their distinction from one another must necessarily have a cause; for their being itself is caused, since, as we have shown,[2] all beings are from one first being. But we have just proved[3] that the cause of a thing's being, and of its distinction from other things, is the same. Diversity of agents, therefore, cannot possibly be the first cause of the distinction among things.

[5] Furthermore, if the diversity of things results from the diversity or contrariety of diverse agents, this would seem especially true, as many say, of the contrariety of good and evil, such that all good things proceed from a good principle and evils from an evil principle—good and evil being found in every genus. It is, however, impossible that there should be one first principle of all evils. For, since things that exist through another are referred to those that exist of themselves, the first active cause of evils would necessarily be evil of itself. Now, we say that a thing is such *of itself* which is such by its essence. Therefore, the essence of a thing evil of itself will not be good. But this is impossible. For every thing that is must necessarily be good so far as it is being. For every thing loves its own being and desires its preservation, an indication of which is the fact that every thing resists its own dissolution; and *the good is that which all things desire*.[4] It is, therefore, impossible for the distinction among things to proceed from two contrary principles, the one good, the other evil.

[6] Again, every agent acts so far as it is in act; and so far as

2. See above, ch. 15.   3. See above, ch. 24.
4. Aristotle, *Nicomachean Ethics*, I, 1 (1094a 3).

it is in act, each and every thing is perfect; while every thing that is perfect, as such, is said to be good. It follows that every agent, as such, is good. If, then, a thing were evil of itself, it could not be an agent. But, if a thing is the first principle of evils, it must of necessity be evil of itself, as we have just shown. Therefore, the distinction in things cannot possibly proceed from two principles, one good, the other evil.

[7]   What is more, if every being, as such, is good, then evil, as such, is a non-being. But there can be no efficient cause of non-being as such. For every agent acts so far as it is a being in act; and every agent produces its like. Therefore, no cause that is of itself active in character can be assigned to evil as such. Evils cannot, then, be referred to one first cause that is of itself the cause of all evils.

[8]   Consider, too, that anything brought into being outside the scope of the agent's intention has no essential cause, but happens accidentally, as when a person finds a treasure while digging with the object of planting things. But evil in an effect cannot arise except beside the agent's intention; every agent intends good, for good is "that which all desire."[5] Evil, therefore, has no essential cause, but occurs accidentally in the effects of causes. Hence, there is no question of maintaining the existence of one first principle of all evils.

[9]   Bear in mind, also, that contrary agents have contrary actions, so that contrary principles are not to be attributed to things produced by one action. Now, good and evil are produced by the same action; for instance, by one and the same action water is corrupted and air generated. Hence, there is no reason for postulating contrary principles in order to explain the difference of good and evil that we find in things.

[10]   Another argument is this. That which has no being at all is neither good nor evil. And, as we have shown, whatever is, so far as it is, is good. Hence, a thing must be evil so far as it is a non-being. But this is a being deprived of being; so that evil, as such, is a being deprived of being; indeed, evil is itself this very privation. Now, privation has no efficient cause that is such through itself. For every agent acts so far as it

5. *Ibid.*

has form; that which is through itself the effect of an agent, then, must be something having form, since an agent produces its like, except by accident. It remains, therefore, that evil has no cause efficient through itself, but occurs by accident in the effects of such causes.

[11] There is, then, no single primary and essential principle of evils; rather, the first principle of all things is the one first good, in whose effects evil results accidentally.

[12] Hence, in the Book of Isaias (45:6–7) it is said: "I am the Lord and there is none other God: I form the light and create darkness, I make peace and create evil: I am the Lord that do all these things"; and we read also that "Good things and evil, life and death, poverty and riches, are from God," and that "Good is set against evil. So also is the sinner against a just man. And so look upon all the works of the Most High. Two and two, and one against another" (Eccli. 11:14; 33:15).

[13] Now, God is said to *make* or *create evils*, so far as He creates things which in themselves are good, yet are injurious to others; the wolf, though in its own kind a good of nature, is nevertheless evil to the sheep; so, too, is fire in relation to water, being dissolutive of the latter. And, likewise, God is the cause of those evils among men which are called penal. That is why it is said: "Shall there be evil in a city, which the Lord hath not done?" (Amos 3:6). And in this connection Gregory remarks: "Even evils, which have no subsistent nature of their own, are created by the Lord: but He is said to create evils when He uses created things, which in themselves are good, to punish us for our evil doings."[6]

[14] This cancels the error of those who postulated contrary first principles—an error originated by Empedocles, who laid down two primary efficient principles, *friendship* and *strife*, declaring the former to be the cause of generation, the latter of corruption, so that, as Aristotle remarks in *Metaphysics* I,[7] it would appear that Empedocles was the first to posit two contrary principles, good and evil.

6. St. Gregory the Great, *Moralia*, III, 9 (*PL*, 75, col. 607).
7. Aristotle, *Metaphysics*, I, 4 (985a 7).

[15] Pythagoras also postulated two primary principles, good and evil, not as efficient principles, however, but as formal ones. For, as Aristotle points out, Pythagoras held that these two are the genera under which all other things are contained.

[16] Now, although these errors of the earliest philosophers were sufficiently disposed of by thinkers of later times, certain men of perverse mind have presumed to link them up with Christian doctrine. The first of these was Marchius[8]—from whom the Marchians are named, who under the Christian label founded a heresy, holding the existence of two opposing principles. Following after him were the Cerdonians,[9] then later the Marchianists,[10] and at last came the Manicheans, who spread this error abroad most of all.

Chapter 42.

THAT THE FIRST CAUSE OF THE DISTINCTION
OF THINGS IS NOT THE WORLD OF
SECONDARY AGENTS

[1] From the same principles it can be shown, also, that the distinction of things is not caused by the order of secondary agents. And this contrary to the opinion of those who supposed that since God is one and simple He produces but one effect, which is the first caused substance, and that this effect, since it cannot possibly be on a par with the simplicity of the first cause (not being pure act, it contains some admixture of potentiality), possesses a certain multiple character, making it possible for some kind of plurality to issue from it; so that, with the effects perpetually falling short of the simplicity of their causes, the diversity of the things of which the universe

8. Perhaps Marcion (born c. 110). On the history and doctrine of Gnosticism, see the bibliography in E. Gilson, *History of Christian Philosophy in the Middle Ages* (New York, 1954), p. 562, note 57.
9. Named from Cerdo, a leading Gnostic of the second-century Syrian School of Gnosticism.
10. Possibly those Gnostics usually called Marcosians, after their leader, a certain Marcus, who flourished c. 175.

consists is being established while the effects are being multiplied.

[2] This position, then, does not assign one cause to the entire diversity of things, but different causes to different effects, while maintaining that the total diversity of things results from the concurrence of all causes. Now, we say that those things happen fortuitously which result from the concurrence of diverse causes, and not from one determinate cause. So, it will follow that the distinction of things and the order of the universe are the products of chance.

[3] Moreover, that which is best in things caused is referred, as to its first cause, to that which is best in causes; for effects must be proportionate to their causes. Now, among all caused beings what is best is the order of the universe, and in this does its good consist; even as in human affairs "the good of a people is more godlike than the good of one individual."[1] Therefore, the order of the universe must be referred to god as its proper cause, whom we have proved above[2] to be the highest good. Therefore, the distinction of things, wherein the order of the universe consists, proceeds not from secondary causes, but from the intention of the first cause.

[4] Then, too, it seems absurd to assign a defect in things as the cause of what is best in them. But, as we have just now shown, the best in things caused is their distinction and order. So, it would be incongruous to say that this distinction of things is the result of secondary causes falling short of the simplicity of the first cause.

[5] Moreover, in all ordered efficient causes, where action is done for the sake of an end, the ends of the secondary causes must be pursued for the sake of the end of the first cause; the ends of the art of war, of horsemanship, and of bridle-making, for example, are ordained to the end of the political art.[3] Now, the issuance of beings from the first being is brought about by an action ordained to an end, since, as we have shown,[4] it is

1. Aristotle, *Nicomachean Ethics*, I, 2 (1094b 9).
2. *SCG*, I, ch. 41.
3. Aristotle, *Nicomachean Ethics*, I, 1 (1094a 10–15, 30).
4. See above, ch. 24.

accomplished by the causality of an intellect; and every intellect acts for an end. So, if there are secondary causes at work in the production of things, the ends and actions of those causes are necessarily directed to the end of the first cause, which is the last end in things caused. Now, this is the distinction and order of the parts of the universe, which, as it were, constitute its ultimate form. Therefore, it is not on account of the actions of secondary agents that the distinction of things and their order exist; on the contrary, the actions of secondary causes are for the sake of the order and distinction to be established in things.

[6]   If the distinction of the parts of the universe and their order, furthermore, is the proper effect of the first cause, being the ultimate form and greatest good in the universe, then the distinction and order of things must needs be in the intellect of the first cause; for in things brought into being through the causality of an intellect, the form engendered in the things made proceeds from a like form in that intellect; the house existing in matter proceeds from the house existing in an intellect. But the form of distinction and order cannot exist in an agent intellect unless the forms of the distinct and ordered things are present there. Present in God's intellect, therefore, are the forms of diverse things mutually distinct and ordered. Nor, as we have shown above,[5] is this multiplicity incompatible with God's simplicity. Hence, if things outside the mind proceed from forms that are in it, it will be possible, in the case of things brought about by intellectual causation, for many and diverse things to be produced immediately by the first cause without detriment to the divine simplicity, on whose account some fell into the position referred to above.[6]

[7]   Also, the action of an intellectual agent terminates in the form which the agent apprehends, and in no other, except accidentally and by chance. But, as we have shown,[7] God is such an agent. Nor can His action be of a fortuitous character, since He cannot fail in its performance. It therefore necessarily

5. SCG, I, ch. 51–54.
6. In the first paragraph of this chapter.
7. See above, ch. 24.

follows that He produces His effect by the very fact that He knows it and intends it. But through the same idea whereby He apprehends one effect, He can grasp many effects other than Himself. Accordingly, without any intermediary He can cause many things all at once.

[8] Moreover, as we have previously shown,[8] the power of God is not limited to the production of one effect; and this accords with His simplicity, because, the more unified a power is, the more unlimited is its scope since it is able to extend itself to so many more things. But, except in the case of the agent's being determined to one effect, there is no necessary reason why only one thing should be made by one cause. Therefore, it is not necessary to say that, because God is one and absolutely simple, no multiplicity can proceed from Him unless it be through the mediation of certain things lacking in the simplicity proper to Himself.

[9] Then, too, it was shown above[9] that God alone can create. Now, there are numerous things that can come into being only by creation, such as all those which are not composed of form and matter subject to contrariety; for things of this kind are necessarily incapable of being generated, since it is from a contrary and from matter that every process of generation takes place.[10] Now, in this category belong all intellectual substances, and all heavenly bodies, and even prime matter itself. It must therefore be maintained that all such things originated immediately from God.

[10] Hence it is said: "In the beginning God created heaven and earth" (Gen. 1:1); and, in the Book of Job (37:18): "Thou perhaps hast made the heavens with Him, which are most strong as if they were of molten brass."

[11] Excluded by the preceding considerations is the opinion of Avicenna,[11] who says that God, by knowing Himself, produced one first intelligence, wherein there already exist potentiality and act; that this intelligence, by knowing God, pro-

8. See above, ch. 22.
9. See above, ch. 21.
10. Cf. Aristotle, *Physics*, I, 7 (190b 10ff.).
11. Avicenna, *Metaphysics*, IX, 4 (foll. 104rb–105ra).

duces the second intelligence; by knowing itself as it is in act, produces the soul of the sphere; and by knowing itself as being in potentiality, produces the substance of the first sphere. And thus, proceeding from this point, he teaches that the diversity of things is the effect of secondary causes.

[12] Excluded, also, is the opinion of certain heretics of early times who said that the angels, and not God, created the world. It is said that Simon Magus was the originator of this error.

Chapter 43.

THAT THE DISTINCTION OF THINGS IS NOT CAUSED BY SOME SECONDARY AGENT INTRO-DUCING DIVERSE FORMS INTO MATTER

[1]   Certain modern heretics say that God created the matter of all visible things, but that an angel diversified it by various forms. This opinion is clearly false.

[2]   For the heavenly bodies, in which no contrariety is found, cannot have been formed from any matter, because whatever is made from pre-existing matter must be made from a contrary. Therefore, no angel could possibly have formed the heavenly bodies from matter antecedently created by God.

[3]   The heavenly bodies, moreover, either have no matter in common with the lower bodies, or they have only prime matter in common with them; for the heaven neither is composed of elements nor is of an elemental nature—a fact shown by its motion, which is of another kind than that of all the elements. And prime matter could not have existed by itself prior to all formed bodies, since its being is purely potential, whereas everything actually existent is from some form. There is, then, no possibility of an angel's having formed all visible bodies from matter antecedently created by God.

[4]   Again, everything made is made in order that it may be, for making is the way to being. It befits every caused thing to

be made, even as it befits it to be. The act of being, however, does not belong to the form only, nor to the matter only, but to the composite. For matter exists only in potency, while form is that by which something is, since it is act. It remains, therefore, that it is the composite which, properly speaking, *is*. Hence, it belongs to the composite alone to be made, and not to matter without form. So, there is not one agent that creates the matter alone and another that introduces the form.

[5] And again, the first induction of forms into matter cannot have originated from an agent acting by means of movement only. All motion directed to a form is from a determinate form toward a determinate form, for matter cannot exist in the absence of all form; the existence of some form in matter is presupposed. But every agent whose action is directed only toward material forms is necessarily an agent that acts by means of motion. For, since material forms are not self-subsistent, and since, in their case, to be is to be in matter, there are but two possible ways in which they can be brought into being: either by the creation of the whole composite, or by the transmutation of matter to this or that form. The first induction of forms into matter, therefore, cannot possibly be from an agent that creates the form alone; rather, this is the work of Him who is the Creator of the whole composite.

[6] Then, too, motion in respect of form is naturally posterior to local motion, since the former is the act of that which is more imperfect, as Aristotle proves.[1] Now, in the natural order, things posterior are caused by things prior. Therefore, motion with respect to form is caused by local motion. The first local motion, however, is that of the heaven. Hence, all motion toward form is brought about through the mediation of the heavenly motion. Consequently, things that cannot be produced in that way cannot be made by an agent capable of acting only by means of movement; and, as we have just shown, the agent that can act only by inducing form into matter must be that kind of agent. There are, however, many sensible forms which cannot be produced by the motion of the heaven except through the intermediate agency of certain determinate principles pre-supposed to their production; cer-

1. Aristotle, *Physics*, VIII, 7 (261a 13).

tain animals, for example, are generated only from seed.
Therefore, the primary establishment of these forms, for producing which the motion of the heaven does not suffice without their pre-existence in the species, must of necessity proceed
from the Creator alone.

[7]   Furthermore, just as the local motion of part and whole
is the same—the motion of the whole earth and of one piece
of it, for example—so the change in which generation consists
is the same in the part and in the whole. Now, the parts of
generable and corruptible things are generated by acquiring
actual forms from forms present in matter, and not from forms
existing outside matter, since the generator must be like the
generated, as Aristotle proves in *Metaphysics* VII.[2] Neither,
then, is it possible that the total acquisition of forms by
matter should be brought about through motion proceeding
from some separate substance such as an angel; rather, this
must be effected either by the intermediation of a corporeal
agent, or by the Creator, who acts without motion.

[8]   Also, just as the act of being is first among effects, so,
correspondingly, is it the proper effect of the first cause. But
it is by virtue of form and not of matter that this act exists.
Therefore, the first causation of forms is to be attributed
above all to the first cause.

[9]   Furthermore, since every agent produces its like, the
effect obtains its form from that reality to which it is made
like through the form acquired by it; the material house
acquires its form from the art which is the likeness of the
house present in the mind. But all things are like God, who
is pure act, so far as they have forms, through which they
become actual; and so far as they desire forms, they are said
to desire the divine likeness. It is therefore absurd to say that
the formation of things is the work of anything other than
God the Creator of all.

[10]   So it is that in order to cast out this error, Moses, after
saying that God "in the beginning created heaven and earth"
(Gen. 1:1), went on to explain how God distinguished all
things by forming them in their proper species. And St. Paul

2. Aristotle, *Metaphysics*, VII, 8 (1033b 33).

says that "in Christ were all things created in heaven and on earth, visible and invisible" (Col. 1:16).

Chapter 44.

THAT THE DISTINCTION OF THINGS DOES NOT HAVE ITS SOURCE IN THE DIVERSITY OF MERITS OR DEMERITS

[1] We now have to show that the distinction among things did not result from diverse movements of free choice in rational creatures, as Origen maintained in his *Peri Archon*.[1] For he wished to oppose the objections and errors of the early heretics who endeavored to prove that the heterogeneous character of good and evil in things has its origin in contrary agents. Now, there are, as Origen saw, great differences in natural as well as human things which seemingly are not preceded by any merits; some bodies are luminous, some dark, some men are born of pagans, others of Christians, etc. And having observed this fact, Origen was impelled to assert that all diversity found in things resulted from a diversity of merits, in accordance with the justice of God. For he says that God, of His goodness alone, first made all creatures equal, and all of them spiritual and rational; and these by their free choice were moved in various ways, some adhering to God more, and some less, some withdrawing from Him more, and some less; and as a result of this, diverse grades in spiritual substances were established by the divine justice, so that some were angels of diverse orders, some human souls in various conditions, some demons in their differing states. And because of the diversity among rational creatures, Origen stated that God had instituted diversity in the realm of corporeal creatures so that the higher spiritual substances were united to the higher bodies, and thus the bodily creature would subserve, in whatever other various ways, the diversity of spiritual substances.

[2] This opinion, however, is demonstrably false. For in the

1. Origen, *Peri Archon*, II (PG, 11, col. 230).

order of effects, the better a thing is, so much the more is it prior in the intention of the agent. But the greatest good in things created is the perfection of the universe, consisting in the order of distinct things; for always the perfection of the whole has precedence of the perfection of the individual parts. Therefore, the diversity of things results from the original intention of the first agent, not from a diversity of merits.

[3]   Then, too, if all rational creatures were created equal from the beginning, it must be said that one of them would not depend, in its action, upon another. But that which results from the concurrence of diverse causes, one of which does not depend on another, is fortuitous. In accordance with the opinion just cited, therefore, this distinction and order of things is fortuitous. Yet this, as we have proved above,[2] is impossible.

[4]   Moreover, what is natural to a person is not acquired by him through the exercise of his will; for the movement of the will, or of free choice, presupposes the existence of the willer, and his existence presupposes the things proper to his nature. If the diverse grades of rational creatures result from a movement of free choice, then the grade of none of them will be natural, but every grade will be accidental. Now, this is impossible. For, since the specific difference is natural to each thing, it would follow, on that theory, that all created rational substances—angels, demons, human souls, the souls of the heavenly bodies (Origen attributed animation to these bodies)—are of one species. The diversity of natural actions proves the falsity of this position. For the natural mode of understanding proper to the human intellect is not the same as that which sense and imagination, the angelic intellect, and the soul of the sun, require—unless, perhaps, we picture the angels and heavenly bodies with flesh and bones and like parts, so that they may be endowed with organs of sense; which is absurd. It therefore remains that the diversity of intellectual substances is not the consequence of a diversity of merits, resulting from movements of free choice.

[5]   Again, if natural things are not acquired by a movement

2. See above, ch. 39.

of free choice, whereas a rational soul owes its union with a certain body to preceding merit or demerit in keeping with the movement of free choice, then it would follow that the union of this soul with this body is not natural. Neither, then, is the resulting composite natural. Nevertheless, according to Origen, man and the sun and the stars are composed of rational substances and such and such bodies. Therefore, all these things—which are the noblest among corporeal substances—are unnatural.

[6] Moreover, if the union of a particular rational substance with a particular body befits that substance, not so far as it is such a substance, but so far as it has merited that union, then it is not united to that body through itself, but by accident. Now, no species results from the accidental union of things; for from such a union there does not arise a thing one through itself; thus, *white man* is not a species, nor is *clothed man*. From the hypothesis in question, therefore, it would follow that man is not a species, nor is the sun a species, nor the moon, nor anything of the kind.

[7] Again, things resulting from merit may be changed for better or for worse; for merits and demerits may increase and diminish—a point particularly stressed by Origen, who said that the free choice of every creature can always be turned to either side. Hence, if a rational soul has obtained this body on account of preceding merit or demerit, then it is possible for it to be united again to another body; and it will follow not only that the human soul may take to itself another human body, but also that it may sometimes assume a sidereal body— a notion "in keeping with the Pythagorean fables according to which any soul could enter any body."[3] Obviously, this idea is both erroneous as regards philosophy, according to which determinate matters and determinate movable things are assigned to determinate forms and determinate movers, and heretical according to faith, which declares that in the resurrection the soul resumes the same body that it has left.

[8] Also, since multitude without diversity cannot exist, if from the beginning any multitude at all of rational creatures

3. Cf. Aristotle, *De anima*, I, 3 (407b 22).

existed, then there must have been some diversity among them. And this means that one of those creatures had something which another had not. And if this was not the consequence of a diversity in merit, for the same reason neither was it necessary that the diversity of grades should result from a diversity of merits.

[9] Every distinction, furthermore, is either in terms of a division of quantity, which exists only in bodies—so that, according to Origen, such distinctness could not exist in the substances first created; or in terms of formal division. But without a diversity of grades there can be no formal division, since division of this kind is reduced to privation and form. Necessarily, then, one of the reciprocally divided forms is better and the other less good. Hence, as Aristotle remarks,[4] the species of things are like numbers, one number being in addition to or in subtraction from the other. Therefore, if there were many rational substances created from the beginning, there must have been a diversity of grades among them.

[10] Then, too, if rational creatures can subsist without bodies, there was no need to have introduced distinctness in the realm of corporeal nature on account of the different merits of rational creatures; because, even in the absence of a diversity of bodies, diverse grades in rational substances could be found. If, however, rational creatures cannot subsist without bodies, then the corporeal creature also was produced from the beginning simultaneously with the rational creature. Now, the corporeal creature is more remote from the spiritual than spiritual creatures are from one another. So, if God from the beginning established such a great distance among His creatures without any antecedent merits, it was unnecessary for a diversity of merits to have been acquired previously in order that rational creatures might be constituted in diverse grades.

[11] Again, if, corresponding to the multiformity of rational creatures there is multiformity in corporeal creatures, then, for the same reason, corresponding to the uniformity of rational creatures, there would be uniformity in the corporeal

4. Aristotle, *Metaphysics*, VII, 3 (1043b 32).

nature. Consequently the corporeal nature would have been created, even if multifarious merits of rational creatures had not preceded, but a corporeal nature uniform in character. Hence, prime matter would have been created—a principle common to all bodies—but it would have been created under one form only. But prime matter contains potentially a multiplicity of forms. On the hypothesis under consideration, prime matter would therefore have remained unfulfilled, its one form alone being actualized; and this is at variance with the divine goodness.

[12] Moreover, if the heterogeneity of corporeal creatures arises from the various movements of the rational creature's free choice, it will have to be said that the reason why there is only one sun in the world is that only one rational creature was moved by its free choice in such a way as to deserve being joined to such a body as the sun. But, that only one rational creature sinned in this way was a matter of chance. Therefore, the existence of only one sun in the world is the result of chance; it does not answer to a need of corporeal nature.

[13] The spiritual creature, furthermore, does not deserve reduction to a lower status except for sin; and yet, by being united to visible bodies, it is brought down from its lofty state of being, wherein it is invisible. Now, from this it would seem to follow that visible bodies are joined to spiritual creatures because of sin—a notion seemingly akin to the error of the Manicheans who asserted that these visible things originated from the evil principle.

[14] This opinion is clearly contradicted by the authority of sacred Scripture, for in regard to each production of visible creatures, Moses says: "God saw that it was good," etc. (Gen. 1); and afterwards, concerning the totality of His creatures, Moses adds: "God saw all the things that He had made, and they were very good." By this we are clearly given to understand that the corporeal and visible creatures were made because it is good for them to be; and that this is in keeping with God's goodness, and not because of any merits or sins of rational creatures.

[15] Now, Origen seems not to have taken into considera-

tion the fact that when we give something, not in payment of a debt, but as a free gift, it is not contrary to justice if we give unequal things, without having weighed the difference of merits; although payment is due to those who merit. But, as we have shown above,[5] God brought things into being, not because He was in any way obliged to do so, but out of pure generosity. Therefore, the diversity of creatures does not presuppose a diversity of merits.

[16]   And again, since the good of the whole is better than the good of each part, the best maker is not he who diminishes the good of the whole in order to increase the goodness of some of the parts; a builder does not give the same relative value to the foundation that he gives to the roof, lest he ruin the house. Therefore, God, the maker of all things, would not make the whole universe the best of its kind, if He made all the parts equal, because many grades of goodness would then be lacking in the universe, and thus it would be imperfect.

Chapter 45.

THE TRUE FIRST CAUSE OF THE DISTINCTION OF THINGS

[1]   From the foregoing it can be shown what is truly the first cause of the distinction of things.

[2]   Since every agent intends to introduce its likeness into its effect, in the measure that its effect can receive it, the agent does this the more perfectly as it is the more perfect itself; obviously, the hotter a thing is, the hotter its effect, and the better the craftsman, the more perfectly does he put into matter the form of his art. Now, God is the most perfect agent. It was His prerogative, therefore, to induce His likeness into created things most perfectly, to a degree consonant with the nature of created being. But created things cannot attain to a perfect likeness to God according to only one species of creature. For, since the cause transcends the effect, that which is in the cause, simply and unitedly, exists in the effect in com-

5. See above, ch. 28.

posite and multiple fashion—unless the effect attain to the species of the cause; which cannot be said in this case, because no creature can be equal to God. The presence of multiplicity and variety among created things was therefore necessary that a perfect likeness to God be found in them according to their manner of being.

[3]   Moreover, just as things made from matter lie in the passive potentiality of matter, so things made by an agent must exist in the active power of the agent. The passive potentiality of matter, however, would not be completely actualized if only one of the things to which matter is in potentiality were made from it. Therefore, if an agent whose power extends to a number of effects were to produce only one of them, its power would not be as fully actualized as when it produces several. Now, by the fact that the active power is actualized the effect receives the likeness of the agent. Hence, there would not be a perfect likeness of God in the universe if all things were of one grade of being. For this reason, then, is there distinction among created things: that, by being many, they may receive God's likeness more perfectly than by being one.

[4]   Then, too, a thing approaches to God's likeness the more perfectly as it resembles Him in more things. Now, goodness is in God, and the outpouring of goodness into other things. Hence, the creature approaches more perfectly to God's likeness if it is not only good, but can also act for the good of other things, than if it were good only in itself; that which both shines and casts light is more like the sun than that which only shines. But no creature could act for the benefit of another creature unless plurality and inequality existed in created things. For the agent is distinct from the patient and superior to it. In order that there might be in created things a perfect representation of God, the existence of diverse grades among them was therefore necessary.

[5]   Furthermore, a plurality of goods is better than a single finite good, since they contain the latter and more besides. But all goodness possessed by creatures is finite, falling short of the infinite goodness of God. Hence, the universe of creatures is more perfect if there are many grades of things than

if there were but one. Now, it befits the supreme good to make what is best. It was therefore fitting that God should make many grades of creatures.

[6]   Again, the good of the species is greater than the good of the individual, just as the formal exceeds that which is material. Hence, a multiplicity of species adds more to the goodness of the universe than a multiplicity of individuals in one species. It therefore pertains to the perfection of the universe that there be not only many individuals, but that there be also diverse species of things, and, consequently, diverse grades in things.

[7]   Whatever acts by intellect, moreover, represents in the thing made the species present in its intellect, for thus does an agent that causes things by art produce his like. Now, as we have already shown,[1] God, acting as an intellectual agent and not by natural necessity, made the creature. Hence, the species present in God's intellect is represented in the creature made by Him. But an intellect which understands many things is not adequately represented in only one thing. Therefore, since the divine intellect knows many things, as was proved in Book I,[2] it represents itself more perfectly if it produces many creatures of all grades than if it had produced only one.

[8]   But there is more. The highest degree of perfection should not be lacking in a work made by the supremely good workman. But the good of order among diverse things is better than any of the members of an order, taken by itself. For the good of order is formal in respect to each member of it, as the perfection of the whole in relation to the parts. It was not fitting, therefore, that God's work should lack the good of order. And yet, without the diversity and inequality of created things, this good could not exist.

[9]   To sum up: The diversity and inequality in created things are not the result of chance,[3] nor of a diversity of matter,[4] nor of the intervention of certain causes[5] or merits,[6]

1. See above, ch. 23.   2. SCG, I, ch. 49ff.
3. See above, ch. 39.   4. See above, ch. 40.
5. See above, ch. 41–43.   6. See above, ch. 44.

but of the intention of God Himself, who wills to give the creature such perfection as it is possible for it to have. '

[10] Accordingly, in the Book of Genesis (1:31) it is said: "God saw all the things that He had made, and they were very good," each one of them having been previously said to be good. For each thing in its nature is good, but all things together are *very good*, by reason of the order of the universe, which is the ultimate and noblest perfection in things.

Chapter 46.

THAT THE PERFECTION OF THE UNIVERSE REQUIRED THE EXISTENCE OF SOME INTELLECTUAL CREATURES

[1] Having determined the actual cause of the diversity among things, it remains for us to tackle the third problem that we proposed,[1] namely, to inquire into those things themselves, as far as this concerns the truth of faith. And first we shall show that, as a result of the order established by God's assigning to creatures the optimum perfection consonant with their manner of being, certain creatures were endowed with an intellectual nature, thus being given the highest rank in the universe.

[2] An effect is most perfect when it returns to its source; thus, the circle is the most perfect of all figures, and circular motion the most perfect of all motions, because in their case a return is made to the starting point. It is therefore necessary that creatures return to their principle in order that the universe of creatures may attain its ultimate perfection. Now, each and every creature returns to its source so far as it bears a likeness to its source, according to its being and its nature, wherein it enjoys a certain perfection. Indeed, all effects are most perfect when they are most like their efficient causes— a house when it most closely resembles the art by which it was produced, and fire when its intensity most fully approximates

1. See above, ch. 5.

that of its generator. Since God's intellect is the principle of the production of creatures, as we have shown above,[2] the existence of some creatures endowed with intelligence was necessary in order that the universe of created things might be perfect.

[3] A thing's second perfection, moreover, constitutes an addition to its first perfection. Now, just as the act of being and the nature of a thing are considered as belonging to its first perfection, so operation is referred to its second perfection. Hence, the complete perfection of the universe required the existence of some creatures which return to God not only as regards likeness of nature, but also by their action. And such a return to God cannot be made except by the act of the intellect and will, because God Himself has no other operation in His own regard than these. The greatest perfection of the universe therefore demanded the existence of some intellectual creatures.

[4] Moreover, in order that creatures might perfectly represent the divine goodness, it was necessary, as we have shown,[3] not only that good things should be made, but also that they should by their actions contribute to the goodness of other things. But a thing is perfectly likened to another in its operation when not only the action is of the same specific nature, but also the mode of acting is the same. Consequently, the highest perfection of things required the existence of some creatures that act in the same way as God. But it has already been shown[4] that God acts by intellect and will. It was therefore necessary for some creatures to have intellect and will.

[5] Again. It is according to the form of the effect pre-existing in the agent that the effect attains likeness to the agent, for an agent produces its like with respect to the form by which it acts. Now, in some cases the form of the agent is received in the effect according to the same mode of being that it has in the agent; the form of the fire generated has the same mode of being as the form of the generating fire. But in other cases the form of the agent is received in the effect according to

another mode of being; the form of the house that exists in an intelligible manner in the builder's mind is received, in a material mode, in the house that exists outside the mind. And the former likeness clearly is more perfect than the latter. Now, the perfection of the universe of creatures consists in its likeness to God, just as the perfection of any effect whatever consists in its likeness to its efficient cause. Therefore, the highest perfection of the universe requires not only the second mode in which the creature is likened to God, but also the first, as far as possible. But the form through which God produces the creature is an intelligible form in Him, since, as we have shown above,[5] God is an intellectual agent. Therefore, the highest perfection of the universe demands the existence of some creatures in which the form of the divine intellect is represented according to intelligible being; that is to say, it requires the existence of creatures of an intellectual nature.

[6] Likewise, the only thing that moves God to produce creatures is His own goodness, which He wished to communicate to other things by likening them to Himself, as was shown in Book I of this work.[6] Now, the likeness of one thing is found in another thing in two ways: first, as regards natural being—the likeness of heat produced by fire is in the thing heated by fire; second, cognitively, as the likeness of fire is in sight or touch. Hence, that the likeness of God might exist in things perfectly, in the ways possible, it was necessary that the divine goodness be communicated to things by likeness not only in existing, but also in knowing. But only an intellect is capable of knowing the divine goodness. Accordingly, it was necessary that there should be intellectual creatures.

[7] Again, in all things becomingly ordered, the relation to the last term of the things intermediate between it and the first imitates the relation of the first to all the others, both intermediate and last, though sometimes deficiently. Now, it has been shown in Book I that God embraces in Himself all creatures.[7] And in corporeal creatures there is a representation of this, although in an other mode. For we find that the higher body always comprises and contains the lower, yet according

5. See above, ch. 23 and 24.   6. *SCG*, I, ch. 74–81.
7. *SCG*, I, ch. 54.

to quantitative extension, whereas God contains all creatures in a simple mode, and not by extension of quantity. Hence, in order that the imitation of God, in this mode of containing, might not be lacking to creatures, intellectual creatures were made which contain corporeal creatures, not by quantitative extension, but in simple fashion, intelligibly; for what is intellectually known exists in the knowing subject, and is contained by his intellectual operation.

Chapter 47.

THAT INTELLECTUAL SUBSTANCES ARE ENDOWED WITH WILL

[1]   Now, these intellectual substances must be capable of willing.

[2]   There is in all things appetite for the good, since, as the philosophers teach,[1] *the good is what all desire.* In things devoid of knowledge this desire is called *natural appetite;* thus it is said that a stone desires to be below. In things having sense knowledge this desire is called *animal appetite,* which is divided into concupiscible and irascible. In things possessed of understanding it is called intellectual or rational appetite, and this is *will.* Created intellectual substances, therefore, are endowed with will.

[3]   Moreover, that which exists through another is referred to that which exists through itself, as being prior to the former. That is why, according to Aristotle,[2] things moved by another are referred to the first self-movers. Likewise, in syllogisms, the conclusions, which are known from other things, are referred to first principles, which are known through themselves. Now, there are some created substances that do not activate themselves, but are by force of nature moved to act; such is the case with inanimate things, plants, and brute animals; for to act or not to act does not lie in their power. It is therefore necessary to go back to some first things that move them-

1. Cf. Aristotle, *Nicomachean Ethics,* I, 1 (1094a 3).
2. Aristotle, *Physics,* VIII, 5 (257a 30); 6 (259a 7).

selves to action. But, as we have just shown,[3] intellectual substances hold the first rank in created things. These substances, then, are self-activating. Now, to move itself to act is the property of the will, and by the will a substance is master of its action, since within such a substance lies the power of acting or not acting. Hence, created intellectual substances are possessed of will.

[4] The principle of every operation, furthermore, is the form by which a thing is in act, since every agent acts so far as it is in act. So, the mode of operation consequent upon a form must be in accordance with the mode of that form. Hence, a form not proceeding from the agent that acts by it causes an operation of which that agent is not master. But, if there be a form which proceeds from the agent acting by it, then the consequent operation also will be in the power of that agent. Now, natural forms, from which natural motions and operations derive, do not proceed from the things whose forms they are, but wholly from extrinsic agents. For by a natural form each thing has being in its own nature, and nothing can be the cause of its own act of being. So it is that things which are moved naturally do not move themselves; a heavy body does not move itself downwards; its generator, which gave it its form, does so. Likewise, in brute animals the forms sensed or imagined, which move them, are not discovered by them, but are received by them from extrinsic sensible things, which act upon their senses and are judged of by their natural estimative faculty. Hence, though brutes are in a sense said to move themselves, inasmuch as one part of them moves and another is moved, yet they are not themselves the source of the actual moving, which, rather, derives partly from external things sensed and partly from nature. For, so far as their appetite moves their members, they are said to move themselves, and in this they surpass inanimate things and plants; but, so far as appetition in them follows necessarily upon the reception of forms through their senses and from the judgment of their natural estimative power, they are not the cause of their own movement; and so they are not master of their own action. On the other hand, the

3. See above, ch. 46.

form understood, through which the intellectual substance acts, proceeds from the intellect itself as a thing conceived, and in a way contrived by it; as we see in the case of the artistic form, which the artificer conceives and contrives, and through which he performs his works. Intellectual substances, then, move themselves to act, as having mastery of their own action. It therefore follows that they are endowed with will.

[5]   The active, moreover, should be proportionate to the passive, and the moving to the movable. But in things having cognition the apprehending power is related to the appetitive power as mover to movable, for that which is apprehended by sense or imagination or intellect moves the intellectual or the animal appetite. Intellectual apprehension, however, is not limited to certain things, but reaches out to them all. And this is why Aristotle, in De anima III, says of the possible intellect that it is "that by which we become all things."[4] Hence, the appetite of an intellectual substance has relationship to all things; wherefore Aristotle remarks, in Ethics III,[5] that appetite extends to both possible and impossible things. Intellectual substances, then, are possessed of will.

Chapter 48.

THAT INTELLECTUAL SUBSTANCES HAVE
FREEDOM OF CHOICE IN ACTING

[1]   It is therefore clear that the aforesaid substances are endowed with freedom of choice in acting.

[2]   That they act by judgment is evident from the fact that through their intellectual cognition they judge of things to be done. And they must have freedom, if, as just shown,[1] they have control over their own action. Therefore, these substances in acting have freedom of choice.

[3]   Also, "the free is that which is its own cause."[2] Hence,

4. Aristotle, De anima, III, 5 (430a 15).
5. Aristotle, Nicomachean Ethics, III, 2 (1111b 23).
1. See above, ch. 47.
2. Cf. Aristotle, Metaphysics, I, 2 (982b 26).

that which is not the cause of its own acting is not free in acting. But things that do not move nor act unless they are moved by other things are not the cause of their own acting. So, only things that move themselves act freely. And these alone act by judgment. For the thing that moves itself is divided into mover and moved; and the mover is the appetite moved by intellect, imagination, or sense, to which faculties judgment belongs. Among these things, therefore, those alone judge freely which in judging move themselves. But no judging power moves itself to judge unless it reflects on its own action; for, if it moves itself to judge, it must know its own judgment; and this only an intellect can do. Thus, irrational animals have in a certain way freedom of movement or action, but not of judgment, whereas inanimate things, which are moved only by other things, have not even free action or movement. Intellectual beings, on the other hand, enjoy freedom not only of action, but also of judgment; and this is to have free choice.

[4] Then, too, the apprehended form is a moving principle according as it is apprehended under the aspect of the good or the fitting; for the outward action in things that move themselves proceeds from the judgment, made through that form, that something is good or fitting. Hence, if he who judges moves himself to judge, he must do so in the light of a higher form apprehended by him. And this form can be none other than the very intelligible essence of the good or the fitting, in the light of which judgment is made of any determinate good or fitting thing; so that only those beings move themselves to judge which apprehend the all-embracing essence of the good or the fitting. And these are intellectual beings alone. Hence, none but intellectual beings move themselves not only to act, but also to judge. They alone, therefore, are free in judging; and this is to have free choice.

[5] Movement and action, moreover, issue from a universal conception only through the intermediation of a particular apprehension. For movement and action have to do with particular things, whereas it is the nature of the intellect to grasp universals. Hence, for movement and action of any kind to result from the intellect's grasp of something, the universal

conception formed by it must be applied to particulars. But the universal contains many particulars potentially; so that the universal conception can be applied to many and diverse things. For this reason the judgment of the intellect concerning things to be done is not determined to one thing only. It follows, in short, that all intellectual beings have freedom of choice.

[6] Furthermore, certain things lack liberty of judgment, either because they have no judgment at all, as plants and stones, or because they have a judgment determined by nature to one thing, as do irrational animals; the sheep, by natural estimation, judges the wolf to be harmful to it, and in consequence of this judgment flees from the wolf; and so it is in other cases. Hence, so far as matters of action are concerned, whatever things possess judgment that is not determined to one thing by nature are of necessity endowed with freedom of choice. And such are all intellectual beings. For the intellect apprehends not only this or that good, but good itself, as common to all things. Now, the intellect, through the form apprehended, moves the will; and in all things mover and moved must be proportionate to one another. It follows that the will of an intellectual substance will not be determined by nature to anything except the good as common to all things. So it is possible for the will to be inclined toward anything whatever that is presented to it under the aspect of good, there being no natural determination to the contrary to prevent it. Therefore, all intellectual beings have a free will, resulting from the judgment of the intellect. And this means that they have freedom of choice, which is defined as *the free judgment of reason.*

Chapter 49.

THAT THE INTELLECTUAL SUBSTANCE IS NOT A BODY

[1] From the foregoing we proceed to show that no intellectual substance is a body.

[2] For it is only by quantitative commensuration that a body contains anything at all; so, too, if a thing contains a whole thing in the whole of itself, it contains also a part in a part of itself, a greater part in a greater part, a lesser part in a lesser part. But an intellect does not, in terms of any quantitative commensuration, comprehend a thing understood, since by its whole self it understands and encompasses both whole and part, things great in quantity and things small. Therefore, no intelligent substance is a body.

[3] Then, too, no body can receive the substantial form of another body, unless by corruption it lose its own form. But the intellect is not corrupted; rather, it is perfected by receiving the forms of all bodies; for it is perfected by understanding, and it understands by having in itself the forms of the things understood. Hence, no intellectual substance is a body.

[4] Again, the principle of diversity among individuals of the same species is the division of matter according to quantity; the form of this fire does not differ from the form of that fire, except by the fact of its presence in different parts into which the matter is divided; nor is this brought about in any other way than by the division of quantity—without which substance is indivisible. Now, that which is received into a body is received into it according to the division of quantity. Therefore, it is only as individuated that a form is received into a body. If, then, the intellect were a body, the intelligible forms of things would not be received into it except as individuated. But the intellect understands things by those forms of theirs which it has in its possession. So, if it were a body, it would not be cognizant of universals but only of particulars. But this is patently false. Therefore, no intellect is a body.

[5] Likewise, nothing acts except in keeping with its species, because in each and every thing the form is the principle of action; so that, if the intellect is a body, its action will not go beyond the order of bodies. It would then have no knowledge of anything except bodies. But this is clearly false, because we know many things that are not bodies. Therefore, the intellect is not a body.

[6]   Moreover, if an intelligent substance is a body, it is either finite or infinite. Now, it is impossible for a body to be actually infinite, as is proved in the *Physics*.[1] Therefore, if we suppose that such a substance is a body at all, it is a finite one. But this also is impossible, since, as was shown in Book I of this work,[2] infinite power can exist in no finite body. And yet the cognitive power of the intellect is in a certain way infinite; for by adding number to number its knowledge of the species of numbers is infinitely extended; and the same applies to its knowledge of the species of figures and proportions. Moreover, the intellect grasps the universal, which is virtually infinite in its scope, because it contains individuals which are potentially infinite. Therefore, the intellect is not a body.

[7]   It is impossible, furthermore, for two bodies to contain one another, since the container exceeds the contained. Yet, when one intellect has knowledge of another, the two intellects contain and encompass one another. Therefore, the intellect is not a body.

[8]   Also, the action of no body is self-reflexive. For it is proved in the *Physics*[3] that no body is moved by itself except with respect to a part, so that one part of it is the mover and the other the moved. But in acting the intellect reflects on itself, not only as to a part, but as to the whole of itself. Therefore, it is not a body.

[9]   A body's action, moreover, is not terminated in action, nor movement in movement—a point proved in the *Physics*.[4] But the action of an intelligent substance is terminated in action; for just as the intellect knows a thing, so does it know that it knows; and so on indefinitely. An intelligent substance, therefore, is not a body.

[10]   Hence it is that sacred Scripture calls intellectual substances *spirits*; and this term it customarily employs in reference to the incorporeal God; as St. John says: "God is a spirit" (John 4:24); and in the Book of Wisdom (7:22–23) we read:

1. Aristotle, *Physics*, III, 5 (206a 8).
2. *SCG*, I, ch. 20.
3. Aristotle, *Physics*, VIII, 5 (256a 2–33).
4. Aristotle, *Physics*, V, 2 (225b 12ff.).

"for in her" namely, divine Wisdom, "is the spirit of understanding, containing all intelligible spirits."

[11] This, then, does away with the error of the early natural philosophers, who supposed that no substance exists except the corporeal, and who therefore said that the soul is a body, either fire or air or water, or something of the kind[5]—an opinion which some have endeavored to introduce into the Christian faith by saying that the soul is the *effigy of the body*, like a body externally represented.

Chapter 50.

THAT INTELLECTUAL SUBSTANCES ARE IMMATERIAL

[1] It clearly follows that intellectual substances are immaterial.

[2] For everything composed of matter and form is a body, since matter cannot receive diverse forms except with respect to its various parts. And this diversity of parts can exist in matter only so far as one common matter is divided into several by dimensions existing in matter; for, without quantity, substance is indivisible. But it has just been shown,[1] that no intelligent substance is a body. It remains, therefore, that such a substance is not composed of matter and form.

[3] Furthermore, just as man does not exist apart from *this man*, so matter does not exist apart from *this matter*. Any subsistent thing that is composed of matter and form is, then, composed of individual form and individual matter. But the intellect cannot be composed of individual matter and form, because the species of things understood are made actually intelligible by being abstracted from individual matter. And as a result of being actually intelligible they become one with the intellect. That is why the intellect also must be without

5. Cf. Aristotle, *De anima*, I, 2 (403b 32–404a 15).
1. See above, ch. 49.

individual matter. Therefore, a substance endowed with intelligence is not composed of matter and form.

[4] Then, too, the action of anything composed of matter and form belongs not to the form alone, nor to the matter alone, but to the composite; for to act belongs to that which exists, and existence belongs to the composite through its form, so that the composite also acts through its form. So, if the intelligent substance is composed of matter and form, its act of understanding will be the act of the composite. Now, action terminates in a thing like the agent that produces it; that is why the composite, in generating, produces not a form but a composite. Hence, if the act of understanding is an action of the composite, neither the form nor the matter would be known, but only the composite. But this is patently false. Therefore, the intelligent substance is not composed of matter and form.

[5] Again. The forms of sensible things have a more perfect mode of existence in the intellect than in sensible things, for in the intellect they are simpler and extend to more things; thus, through the one intelligible form of man, the intellect knows all men. Now, a form existing perfectly in matter makes a thing to be actually such—to be fire or to be colored, for example; and if the form does not have that effect, then the form is in that thing imperfectly, as the form of heat in the air carrying it, and the power of the first agent in its instrument. So, if the intellect were composed of matter and form, the forms of the things known would make the intellect to be actually of the same nature as that which is known. And the consequence of this is the error of Empedocles, who said that "the soul knows fire by fire, and earth by earth";[2] and so with other things. But this is clearly incongruous. Therefore, the intelligent substance is not composed of matter and form.

[6] And since a thing's mode of presence in its recipient accords with the latter's mode of being, it would follow, were the intellect composed of matter and form, that the forms of things would exist in it materially, just as they exist outside the mind. Therefore, just as they are not actually intelligible

2. Cf. Aristotle, De anima, I, 2 (404b 15).

outside the mind, so they would not be actually intelligible when present in the intellect.

[7] Moreover, the forms of contraries, as they exist in matter, are contrary; hence, they exclude one another. But as they exist in the intellect the forms of contraries are not contrary; rather, one contrary is the intelligible ground of another, since one is understood through the other. They have, then, no material being in the intellect. Therefore, the intellect is not composed of matter and form.

[8] And again, matter does not receive a fresh form except through motion or change. But the intellect is not moved through receiving forms; rather, it is perfected and at rest while understanding, whereas movement is a hindrance to understanding.[3] Hence, forms are not received in the intellect as in matter or a material thing. Clearly, then, intelligent substances are immaterial, even as they are incorporeal, too.

[9] Hence, Dionysius says: "On account of the rays of God's goodness all intellectual substances, which are known to be incorporeal and immaterial, have remained immutably in existence."[4]

Chapter 51.

THAT THE INTELLECTUAL SUBSTANCE IS NOT A MATERIAL FORM

[1] From the same principles we proceed to show that intellectual natures are subsistent forms, and are not in matter as though their being depends on matter.

[2] Forms dependent in being upon matter do not themselves have being properly, but being properly belongs to the composites through their forms. Consequently, if intellectual substances were forms of this kind, it would follow that they have material being, just as they would if they were composed of matter and form.

3. Cf. Aristotle, *Physics*, VII, 3 (247b 8ff.).
4. Pseudo-Dionysius, *De divinis nominibus*, IV (PG 3, col. 694).

[3]   Moreover, forms that do not subsist through themselves cannot act through themselves; rather, the composites act through them. Hence, if intellectual natures were forms of this sort, it would follow that they do not themselves understand, but that it is the things composed of them and matter which understand. And thus, an intelligent being would be composed of matter and form; which is impossible, as we have just shown.[1]

[4]   Also, if the intellect were a form in matter and not self-subsistent, it would follow that what is received into the intellect would be received into matter, since forms whose being is bound to matter receive nothing that is not received into the matter. But the reception of forms into the intellect is not a reception of forms into matter. Therefore, the intellect cannot possibly be a material form.

[5]   Moreover, to say that the intellect is not a subsistent form, but a form embedded in matter, is the same in reality as to say that the intellect is composed of matter and form. The difference is purely nominal, for in the first way the intellect will be called the form itself of the composite; in the second way, the composite itself. So, if it is false that the intellect is composed of matter and form, it will be false that it is a form which does not subsist, but is material.

Chapter 52.

THAT IN CREATED INTELLECTUAL SUB-STANCES, BEING AND WHAT IS DIFFER

[1]   Although intellectual substances are not corporeal, nor composed of matter and form, nor existing in matter as material forms, it is not to be supposed that they therefore equal the divine simplicity. For a certain composition is found in them by the fact that in them *being* is not the same as *what is*.

[2]   For, if being is subsisting, nothing besides this act itself

1. See above, ch. 50.

is added to it. Because, even in things whose being is not subsistent, that which is in the existing thing in addition to its being is indeed united to the thing, but is not one with the thing's being, except by accident, so far as the thing is one subject having being and that which is other than being. Thus it is clear that in Socrates, beside his substantial being, there is white, which, indeed, is other than his substantial being; for to be Socrates and to be white are not the same except by accident. If, then, being is not in a subject, there will remain no way in which that which is other than being can be united to it. Now, being, as being, cannot be diverse; but it can be diversified by something beside itself; thus, the being of a stone is other than that of a man. Hence, that which is subsisting being can be one only. Now, we have shown in Book I that God is His own subsisting being.[1] Hence, nothing beside Him can be its own being. Of necessity, therefore, in every substance beside Him the substance itself is other than its being.

[3] Moreover, a common nature, if considered in separation from things, can be only one, although there can be a plurality of things possessing that nature. For, if the nature of *animal* subsisted as separate through itself, it would not have those things that are proper to a man or an ox; if it did have them, it would not be *animal* alone, but man or ox. Now, if the differences constitutive of species be removed, there remains the undivided nature of the genus, because the same differences which constitute the species divide the genus. Consequently, if this itself which is being is common as a genus, separate, self-subsisting being can be one only. But, if being is not divided by differences, as a genus is, but, as it is in truth, by the fact that it is the being of this or that, then it is all the more manifest that being existing through itself can only be one. Since God is subsisting being, it therefore remains that nothing other than He is its own being.

[4] Again, absolutely infinite being cannot be twofold, for being that is absolutely infinite comprises every perfection of being; hence, if infinity were present in two such things, in no respect would they be found to differ. Now, subsisting being

1. *SCG*, I, ch. 22.

must be infinite, because it is not terminated in some recipient. Therefore, there cannot be a subsisting being besides the first.

[5] Then, too, if there is a self-subsisting being, nothing belongs to it except that which is proper to a being inasmuch as it is a being, since what is said of a thing, not as such, appertains to it only accidentally, by reason of the subject. Consequently, if the thing so spoken of is held to be separated from the subject, it in no way belongs to it. Now, to be caused by another does not appertain to a being inasmuch as it is being; otherwise, every being would be caused by another, so that we should have to proceed to infinity in causes—an impossibility, as was shown in Book I of this work.[2] Therefore, that being which is subsisting must be uncaused. Therefore, no caused being is its own being.

[6] The substance of each and every thing, furthermore, belongs to it through itself and not through another; thus, it does not pertain to the substance of air to be actually luminous, since this quality it acquires through something else. But every created thing has its being through another; otherwise, it would not be caused. Therefore, the being of no created substance is that substance.

[7] Also, since every agent acts so far as it is in act, it belongs to the first agent, which is most perfect, to be most perfectly in act. Now, a thing is the more perfectly in act the more its act is posterior in the way of generation, for act is posterior in time to potentiality in one and the same thing that passes from potentiality to act. Further, act itself is more perfectly in act than that which has act, since the latter is in act because of the former. These things being posited, then, it is clear from what has been shown in Book I of this work[3] that God alone is the first agent. Therefore, it belongs to Him alone to be in act in the most perfect way, that is, to be Himself the most perfect act. Now, this act is being, wherein generation and all movement terminate, since every form and act is in potentiality before it acquires being. Therefore, it belongs to God alone to be His own being, just as it pertains to Him only to be the first agent.

2. SCG, I, ch. 13.   3. Ibid.

[8] Moreover, being itself belongs to the first agent according to His proper nature, for God's being is His substance, as was shown in Book I.[4] Now, that which belongs to a thing according to its proper nature does not belong to other things except by way of participation, as heat is in other bodies from fire. Therefore, being itself belongs to all other things from the first agent by a certain participation. That which belongs to a thing by participation, however, is not that thing's substance. Therefore, it is impossible that the substance of a thing other than the first agent should be being itself.

[9] Wherefore in Exodus (3:14) the proper name of God is stated to be "HE WHO IS," because it is proper to Him alone that His substance is not other than His being.

Chapter 53.

THAT IN CREATED INTELLECTUAL SUBSTANCES
THERE IS ACT AND POTENTIALITY

[1] Now, from the foregoing it is evident that in created intellectual substances there is composition of act and potentiality.

[2] For in whatever thing we find two, one of which is the complement of the other, the proportion of one of them to the other is as the proportion of potentiality to act; for nothing is completed except by its proper act. Now, in the created intellectual substance two principles are found: the substance itself and its being, which, as we have just shown,[1] is not the substance itself. Now, being itself is the complement of the existing substance, for each and every thing is in act through having being. It therefore remains that in each of the aforesaid substances there is composition of act and potentiality.

[3] There is also the consideration that what ever is present in a thing from an agent must be act, for it belongs to an agent

4. *SCG*, I, ch. 22.
1. See above, ch. 52.

to make something in act. Now, it was shown above[2] that all other substances have being from the first agent; and the substances themselves are caused by the fact that they have being from another. Therefore, being is present in caused substances as a certain act of their own. But that in which act is present is a potentiality, since act, as such, is referred to potentiality. Therefore, in every created substance there is potentiality and act.

[4]   Likewise, whatever participates in a thing is compared to the thing participated in as act to potentiality, since by that which is participated the participator is actualized in such and such a way. But it was shown above[3] that God alone is essentially a being, whereas all other things participate in being. Therefore, every created substance is compared to its own being as potentiality to act.

[5]   Furthermore, it is by act that a thing is made like its efficient cause, for the agent produces its like so far as it is in act. Now, as shown above[4] it is through being itself that every created substance is likened to God. Therefore, being itself is compared to all created substances as their act. Whence it follows that in every created substance there is composition of act and potentiality.

Chapter 54.

THAT THE COMPOSITION OF SUBSTANCE AND
BEING IS NOT THE SAME AS THE COMPOSITION
OF MATTER AND FORM

[1]   Now, these compositions are not of the same nature, although both are compositions of potentiality and act.

[2]   First, this is so because matter is not the very substance of a thing; for, if that were true, it would follow that all forms

2. See above, ch. 15.
3. See above, ch. 15.
4. See above, ch. 6.

are accidents, as the early natural philosophers supposed. But matter is not the substance; it is only part of the substance.

[3]   Secondly, because being itself is the proper act, not of the matter, but of the whole substance; for being is the act of that whereof we can say that it *is*. Now, this act is predicated not of the matter, but of the whole. Hence, matter cannot be called that which *is*; rather, the substance itself is that which is.

[4]   Thirdly, because neither is the form the being itself, but between them there is a relation of order, because form is compared to being itself as *light* to *illuminating*, or *whiteness* to *being white*.

[5]   Then, too, because being is compared even to the form itself as act. For in things composed of matter and form, the form is said to be the principle of being, for this reason: that it is the complement of the substance, whose act is being. Thus, transparency is in relation to the air the principle of illumination, in that it makes the air the proper subject of light.

[6]   Accordingly, in things composed of matter and form, neither the matter nor the form nor even being itself can be termed that which is. Yet the form can be called *that by which it is*, inasmuch as it is the principle of being; the whole substance itself, however, is *that which is*. And being itself is that by which the substance is called a *being*.

[7]   But, as we have shown,[1] intellectual substances are not composed of matter and form; rather, in them the form itself is a subsisting substance; so that form here is *that which is* and being itself is act and *that by which* the substance *is*.

[8]   And on this account there is in such substances but one composition of act and potentiality, namely, the composition of substance and being, which by some is said to be of *that which is* and being, or of *that which is* and *that by which a thing is*.

[9]   On the other hand, in substances composed of matter and form there is a twofold composition of act and poten-

1. See above, ch. 50 and 51.

tiality: the first, of the substance itself which is composed of matter and form; the second, of the substance thus composed, and being; and this composition also can be said to be of *that which is* and being, or of *that which is* and *that by which a thing is.*

[10] It is therefore clear that composition of act and potentiality has greater extension than that of form and matter. Thus, matter and form divide natural substance, while potentiality and act divide common being. Accordingly, whatever follows upon potentiality and act, as such, is common to both material and immaterial created substances, as *to receive* and *to be received, to perfect* and *to be perfected.* Yet all that is proper to matter and form, as such, as *to be generated* and *to be corrupted,* and the like, are proper to material substances, and in no way belong to immaterial created substances.

Chapter 55.

THAT INTELLECTUAL SUBSTANCES ARE INCORRUPTIBLE

[1] Now, from what has just been said it is clearly shown that every intellectual substance is incorruptible.

[2] For all corruption occurs through the separation of form from matter; absolute corruption, through the separation of the substantial form; relative corruption, through the separation of an accidental form. For, so long as the form remains, the thing must exist, since by the form the substance is made the proper recipient of the act of being. Now, where there is no composition of matter and form, there can be no separation of them; neither, then, can there be corruption. It has been shown,[1] however, that no intellectual substance is composed of matter and form. Therefore, no intellectual substance is corruptible.

[3] Moreover, that which belongs to a thing through itself

1. See above, ch. 50.

is necessarily in it always and inseparably; thus, roundness is in a circle through itself, but is by accident in a coin; so that the existence of a non-round coin is possible; whereas it is impossible for a circle not to be round. Now, being is consequent upon form through itself; for by *through itself* we mean according as *that thing is such;*[2] and each and every thing has being according as it has form. Therefore, substances which are not themselves forms can be deprived of being, so far as they lose form, even as a coin is deprived of roundness as a result of ceasing to be circular. But substances which are themselves forms can never be deprived of being; thus, if a substance were a circle, it could never be non-round. Now, we have already shown[3] that intellectual substances are themselves subsisting forms. Hence, they cannot possibly cease to be, and therefore they are incorruptible.

[4] In every instance of corruption, furthermore, potentiality remains after the removal of act. For when a thing is corrupted it does not dissolve into absolute non-entity, any more than a thing is generated from absolute non-entity. But, as we have proved,[4] in intellectual substances the act is being itself, while the substance is as potentiality. Therefore, if an intellectual substance is corrupted, it will remain after its corruption; which is simply impossibility. Therefore, every intellectual substance is incorruptible.

[5] Likewise, in every thing which is corrupted there must be potentiality to non-being. Hence, if there be a thing in which there is no potentiality to non-being, such a thing cannot be corruptible. Now, in the intellectual substance there is no potentiality to non-being. For it is clear from what we have said[5] that the complete substance is the proper recipient of being itself. But the proper recipient of an act is related to that act as potentiality, in such fashion that it is in no way in potentialilty to the opposite; thus, the relationship of fire to heat is such that fire is in no way in potentiality to cold. Hence, neither in the case of corruptible substances is there potentiality to non-being in the complete substance itself,

2. Cf. Aristotle, *Posterior Analytics*, I, 4 (73b 10).
3. See above, ch. 51.   4. See above, ch. 53. .
5. See above, ch. 54.

except by reason of the matter. But there is no matter in intellectual substances, for they are themselves complete simple substances. Consequently, there is no potentiality to non-being in them. Therefore, they are incorruptible.

[6] Then, too, in whatever things there is composition of potentiality and act, that which holds the place of first potentiality, or of first subject, is incorruptible; so that even in corruptible substances prime matter is incorruptible. But, with intellectual substances, that which holds the place of first potentiality and subject is itself the complete substance of those things. Hence, the substance itself is incorruptible. But nothing is corruptible except by the fact that its substance is corruptible. Therefore, all intellectual natures are incorruptible.

[7] Moreover, whatever is corrupted is corrupted either through itself or by accident. Now, intellectual substances cannot be corrupted through themselves, because all corruption is by a contrary. For the agent, since it acts according as it is a being in act, always by its acting brings something into actual being; so that if a thing is corrupted by its ceasing to be in act, this must result from the mutual contrariety of the terms involved; since things are contrary which exclude one another. And on this account whatever is corrupted through itself must either have a contrary or be composed of contraries. Yet neither the one nor the other is true of intellectual substances; and a sign of this is that in the intellect things even of contrary nature cease to be contraries. Thus, white and black are not contraries in the intellect, since they do not exclude one another; rather, they are co-implicative, since by grasping the one we understand the other. Therefore, intellectual substances are not corruptible through themselves. Likewise, neither are they corruptible by accident, for in this manner are accidents and non-subsistent forms corrupted. Now, it was shown above[6] that intellectual substances are subsistent. Therefore, they are altogether incorruptible.

[8] Again, corruption is a kind of change, and change must be the terminal point of a movement, as is proved in the

6. See above, ch. 51.

Physics.[7] Hence, whatever is corrupted must be moved. Now, it is shown in natural philosophy[8] that whatever is moved is a body. Hence, whatever is corrupted must be a body, if it is corrupted through itself, or a form or power of a body depending thereon, if it be corrupted by accident. Now, intellectual substances are not bodies, nor powers or forms dependent on a body. Consequently, they are corrupted neither through themselves nor by accident. They are, then, utterly incorruptible.

[9] And again. Whatever is corrupted is corrupted through being passive to something, for to be corrupted is itself to be passive in a certain way. Now, no intellectual substance can be passive in such a way as will lead to its corruption. For passivity is a kind of receptivity, and what is received into an intellectual substance must be received in it in a manner consonant with its mode, namely, intelligibly. What is thus received into an intellectual substance, however, perfects that substance and does not corrupt it, for the intelligible is the perfection of the intelligent. Therefore, an intelligent substance is incorruptible.

[10] Furthermore, just as the sensible is the object of sense, so the intelligible is the object of intellect. But sense is not corrupted by a corruption proper to itself except on account of the exceedingly high intensity of its object; thus, is sight corrupted by very brilliant objects, hearing by very loud sounds, etc. Now, I say by *corruption proper to the thing itself* because the sense is corrupted also accidentally through its subject being corrupted. But this mode of corruption cannot happen to the intellect, since it is not the act of any body, as depending thereon, as we have shown above.[9] And clearly it is not corrupted by the exceeding loftiness of its object, because he who understands very intelligible things understands things less intelligible not less but more. Therefore, the intellect is in no way corruptible.

[11] Also, the intelligible is the proper perfection of the

7. Aristotle, *Physics,* V, 1 (224b 7).
8. Cf. Aristotle, *Physics,* VI, 4 (234b 10).
9. See above, ch. 51.

intellect; so that "the intellect in act and the intelligible in act are one."[10] Hence, whatever appertains to the intelligible, as such, must appertain to the intellect, as such, because perfection and the perfectible are of one genus. Now, the intelligible, as such, is necessary and incorruptible; for necessary things are perfectly knowable by the intellect, whereas contingent things, as such, are only deficiently knowable, for concerning them we have not science but *opinion*. So it is that the intellect has scientific knowledge of corruptible things so far as they are incorruptible, that is, inasmuch as they are universal. The intellect, therefore, must be incorruptible.

[12]   Moreover, a thing is perfected according to the mode of its substance. Hence, the mode of a thing's substance can be learned from the mode of its perfection. Now, the intellect is not perfected by movement, but by the fact of its being outside movement; for, as concerns the intellective soul, we are perfected by science and prudence when bodily changes and alterations of the soul's passions are put at rest, as Aristotle points out in *Physics* VII.[11] Hence, the mode of an intelligent substance consists in the fact that its being is above movement and consequently above time; whereas the being of every corruptible thing is subject to motion and time. Therefore, an intelligent substance cannot possibly be corruptible.

[13]   A further argument. It is impossible for natural desire to be in vain, "since nature does nothing in vain."[12] But every intelligent being naturally desires to be forever; and to be forever not only in its species but also in the individual. This point is made clear as follows. Natural appetite is present in some things as the result of apprehension; the wolf naturally desires the killing of the animals on which it feeds, and man naturally desires happiness. But in some other things natural desires results without apprehension from the sole inclination of natural principles, and this inclination, in some, is called *natural appetite*; thus, a heavy body desires to be down. Now, in both ways there is in things a natural desire for being; and a sign of this is that not only things devoid of knowledge

10. Cf. Aristotle, *De anima*, III, 4–5 (430a 3, 20).
11. Aristotle, *Physics*, VII, 3 (247b 18).
12. Cf. Aristotle, *De caelo*, II, 11 (291b 14).

resist, according to the power of their natural principles, whatever is corruptive of them, but also things possessed of knowledge resist the same according to the mode of their knowledge. Hence, those things lacking knowledge, in whose principles there is a power of keeping themselves in existence forever so that they remain always the same numerically, naturally desire to exist everlastingly even in their numerical self-identity. But things whose principles have not the power to do this, but only the power of perpetuating their existence in the same species, also naturally desire to be perpetuated in this manner. Hence, this same difference must be found also in those things in which there is desire for being, together with knowledge, so that those things which have no knowledge of being except as *now* desire to be as *now*, but not to be always, because they do not apprehend everlasting being. Yet they desire the perpetual existence of the species, though without knowledge, because the generative power, which conduces to this effect, is a forerunner and not a subject of knowledge. Hence, those things which know and apprehend perpetual being desire it with natural desire. And this is true of all intelligent substances. Consequently, all intelligent substances, by their natural appetite, desire to be always. That they should cease to be is, therefore, impossible.

[14] Furthermore, all things that begin to be and cease to be do so in virtue of the same potency, for the same potency regards being and non-being. Now, intelligent substances could not begin to be except by the potency of the first agent, since, as we have shown,[13] they are not made out of a matter that could have existed antecedently to them. Hence, there is no potency with respect to their non-being except in the first agent, inasmuch as it lies within His power not to pour being into them. But nothing can be said to be corruptible with respect to this potency alone; and for two reasons: because things are said to be necessary and contingent according to a potentiality that is in them, and not according to the power of God, as we have already shown,[14] and also because God, who is the Author of nature, does not take from things

13. See above, ch. 49–56.
14. See above, ch. 30.

that which is proper to their natures; and we have just shown that it is proper to intellectual natures to exist forever, and that is why God will not take this property from them. Therefore, intellectual substances are in every way incorruptible.

[15] So it is that in the Psalm (148:1, 6): "Praise ye the Lord from the heavens," after speaking of the angels and the heavenly bodies together, it is added: "He hath established them for ever and for ages of ages," thus designating the everlastingness of those things.

[16] Dionysius also, in his work *On the Divine Names*, says that "it is because of the rays of God's goodness that intelligible and intellectual substances subsist and are and live; and they have life unfailing and undiminishable, being free from universal corruption, free from generation and death, lifted above the instability of this world in flux."[15]

Chapter 56.

IN WHAT WAY AN INTELLECTUAL SUBSTANCE
CAN BE UNITED TO THE BODY

[1] Having shown that an intellectual substance is not a body or a power dependent on a body,[1] it remains for us to inquire whether an intellectual substance can be united to a body.

[2] In the first place, it is evident that an intellectual substance cannot be united to a body by way of mixture.

[3] For things mixed together are necessarily altered in relation to one another. But such alteration occurs only in things whose matter is the same, and which can be active and passive in relation to one another.[2] But intellectual substances have no matter in common with bodies, since, as shown above,[3] they are immaterial. Hence, they are not combinable with bodies.

15. Pseudo-Dionysius, *De divinis nominibus*, IV, (PG, 3, col. 694).
1. See above, ch. 49–51.
2. Cf. Aristotle, *De generatione et corruptione*, I, 10 (328a 20).
3. See above, ch. 50.

[4] Moreover, the things that are combined with one another do not themselves, having been combined, remain actually, but only virtually; for, were they to remain actually, it would be not a mixture, but only a collection; that is why a body constituted by a mixture of elements is none of those elements.[4] But this cannot possibly occur in the case of intellectual substances, since, as we have just shown,[5] they are incorruptible.

[5] Therefore, an intellectual substance cannot be united to a body by way of mixture.

[6] It is likewise evident that an intellectual substance cannot be united to a body *by way of contact properly so called.* For there is contact only between bodies, since things are in contact when they come together at their extremities,[6] as the points or lines or surfaces which are the extremities of bodies. It is, therefore, impossible for an intellectual substance to be united to a body by way of contact.

[7] And from this it follows that neither by continuation nor composition or colligation can union of an intellectual substance with a body be effected. For without contact none of these is possible.

[8] There is, however, a certain kind of contact whereby an intellectual substance can be united to a body. For, when they are in contact, natural bodies alter one another, thus being mutually united not only by way of their quantitative extremities, but also by way of likeness in quality or form, as long as the altering body impresses its form upon the body altered. Now, if the quantitative extremities alone be considered, then in all cases contact must of necessity be mutual. On the other hand, if attention is given to activity and passivity, it will be found that certain things touch others and are not themselves touched, while certain things are themselves touched and touch nothing else. For, indeed, the heavenly bodies touch elemental bodies in this way, inasmuch as they alter them, but they are not touched by the elemental bodies, since they

4. Cf. Aristotle, *De generatione et corruptione,* I, 10 (328a 8).
5. See above, ch. 55.
6. Aristotle, *Physics,* V, 3 (226a 23).

are not acted upon by them. Consequently, if there are any agents not in contact by their quantitative extremities, they nevertheless will be said to touch, so far as they act; and in this sense we say that a person in sorrow touches us. Hence, it is possible for an intellectual substance to be united to a body by contact, by touching it in this way. For intellectual substances, being immaterial and enjoying a higher degree of actuality than bodies, act on the latter and move them.

[9]   This, however, is not contact of quantity, but of power. It therefore differs from bodily contact in three ways. First, because by this contact the indivisible can touch the divisible. Now, in bodily contact this cannot occur, since only an indivisible thing can be touched by a point. But an intellectual substance, though it is indivisible, can touch divisible quantity, so far as it acts upon it. For, indeed, a point is indivisible in one way and an intellectual substance in another. A point is indivisible as being the terminus of a quantity, and for this reason it occupies a determinate position in a continuous quantity, beyond which it cannot extend. But an intellectual substance is indivisible, as being outside the genus of quantity, and that is why no quantitative indivisible entity with which it can make contact is assigned to it. Contact of quantity differs from quantity of power, secondly, because the former obtains only with respect to the extremities, whereas the latter regards the whole thing touched. For by contact of power a thing is touched according as it is acted upon and is moved. And this comes about inasmuch as the thing is in potentiality. Now, potentiality regards the whole and not the extremities of the whole; so that it is the whole that is touched. And from this the third difference emerges, because in contact of quantity, which takes place in respect of extremities, that which touches must be extrinsic to that which is touched; and it cannot penetrate the thing touched, but is obstructed by it. But, since contact of power, which appertains to intellectual substances, extends to the innermost things, it makes the touching substance to be within the thing touched, and to penetrate it without hindrance.

[10]   The intellectual substance, then, can be united to a body by contact of power. Now, things united by contact of

this kind are not unqualifiedly one. For they are one with respect to acting and being acted upon, but this is not to be unqualifiedly one. Thus, indeed, *one* is predicated in the same mode as *being*.[7] But to be acting does not mean to be, without qualification, so that neither is to be one in action to be one without qualification.

[11] Now, *one*, in the unqualified sense of the term, has a threefold reference: to the *indivisible*, to the *continuous*, and to the *one in reason*. Now, from the union of an intellectual substance and a body there cannot result a thing indivisibly one, because such a union must consist in a composite of two things; nor a thing continuously one, because the parts of the continuous are parts of quantity. It therefore remains for us to inquire whether from an intellectual substance and a body there can be formed a thing one in reason.

[12] Now, from two permanent entities a thing one in reason does not result unless one of them has the character of substantial form and the other of matter. For the joining of subject and accident does not constitute a unity of this kind; the idea of *man*, for example, is not the same as the idea of *white*. So, it must be asked whether an intellectual substance can be the substantial form of a body.

[13] Now, to those who consider the question reasonably, such a union would seem to be impossible.[8]

[14] From two actually existing substances one thing cannot be made, because the act of each thing is that by which it is distinguished from another. Now, an intellectual substance is an actually existing substance, as is clear from what has been said.[9] And so, too, is a body. It therefore seems that from an intellectual substance and a body something one cannot be made.

[15] Also, form and matter are contained in the same genus, for every genus is divided by act and potentiality. But intel-

7. Cf. St. Thomas Aquinas, *Summa Theologiae*, I, 11, 1; *De veritate*, I, 1.
8. See below, ch. 68 and 69.
9. See above, ch. 51.

lectual substance and body are diverse genera. Hence, it does not seem possible for one to be the form of the other.

[16] Moreover, every thing whose being is in matter must be material. Now, if an intellectual substance is the form of a body, it must have its being in corporeal matter. For the form's act of being is not outside that of the matter. Hence, it will follow that an intellectual substance is not immaterial, as it was shown to be above.[10]

[17] Likewise, it is impossible for a thing that has its being in a body to be separate from the body. It is, however, proved by philosophers that the intellect is separate from the body, and that it is neither a body nor a power in a body. Therefore, an intellectual substance is not the form of a body; if it were, it would have its being in a body.

[18] Again a thing having its being in common with a body must have its operation in common with a body, for every thing acts in keeping with its being. Nor can the operative power of a thing be superior to its essence, since power is consequent upon principles of the essence of a thing. Now, if an intellectual substance is the form of a body, its being must be common to it and the body, since from form and matter there results a thing unqualifiedly one, which exists by one act of being. Therefore, an intellectual substance not only will have its operation in common with the body, but also its power will be a power in a body—a conclusion evidently impossible in the light of what has already been said.[11]

Chapter 57.

THE POSITION OF PLATO CONCERNING THE UNION OF THE INTELLECTUAL SOUL WITH THE BODY

[1] Moved by these and like reasons, some have said that no intellectual substance can be the form of a body. But, since

10. See above, ch. 50.   11. See above, ch. 49ff.

the very nature of man seemed to contradict this position, in that he appears to be composed of an intellectual soul and a body, they sought to save the nature of man by divising certain solutions.

[2]   Accordingly, Plato and his followers asserted that the intellectual soul is not united to the body as form to matter, but only as mover to movable, for Plato said that the soul is in the body "as a sailor in a ship."[1] Thus, the union of soul and body would only be by contact of power—which we have spoken of above.[2]

[3]   But this doctrine seems not to fit the facts. For, as a result of contact of power, a thing unqualifiedly one does not arise, as we have shown;[3] whereas from the union of soul and body there results a man. On Plato's theory, then, a man is not one unqualifiedly speaking, nor, consequently, is he a being unqualifiedly speaking, but a being by accident.

[4]   In order to avoid this, Plato asserted[4] that man is not a being composed of body and soul, but that *the soul itself using the body* is man; just as Peter is not a thing composed of man and clothes, but *a man using clothes.*

[5]   This, however, is shown to be impossible. For animal and man are sensible and natural realities. But this would not be the case if the body and its parts were not of the essence of man and animal; rather, the soul would be the entire essence of both, according to the aforesaid position; for the soul is neither a sensible nor a material thing. It is, therefore, impossible that man and animal should be *a soul using a body,* and not a thing composed of body and soul.

[6]   It is, moreover, impossible that things diverse in being should have one operation. Now, I speak of an operation being one, not with reference to that in which the action terminates, but to the manner of its issuance from the agent. For many men pulling a boat make one action on the part of the thing done, which is one, yet on the part of the haulers there are

1. Cf. Aristotle, *De anima,* I, 1 (413a 8).
2. See above, ch. 56.   3. *Ibid.*
4. Plato, *Alcibiades,* 129E, 130C.

many actions, since there are many acts of hauling. For, since action is consequent upon form and power, things having diverse forms and powers must likewise have diverse actions. Now, though the soul has an operation proper to itself, in which the body does not share, namely, understanding, there are nevertheless some operations common to it and the body, as fear, anger, sensation, and the like; for these operations occur through some transmutation in a determinate part of the body, and, therefore, obviously are operations of soul and body together. It necessarily follows that the soul and the body make up one single being, and that they have not each a distinct being.

[7]   Now, according to the opinion of Plato, this argument may be obviated by pointing out that there is nothing contradictory in the action of mover and moved being the same, though of things diverse in being; since the same act belongs to the mover as that *from which* it is and to the moved as that *in which* it is. Accordingly, Plato asserted that the aforesaid operations were common to soul and body, being operations of the soul as mover and of the body as moved.

[8]   But this cannot be, because, as Aristotle proves in *De anima* II, "sensation occurs as the result of one's being moved by external objects of sense."[5] Hence, man cannot sense without an external sensible object, any more than a thing can be moved without a mover. Therefore, the sense organ is moved and is passive in sensing—but in relation to an external sensible object. And that whereby it is passive [suffers] is the sense, for it is obviously the fact that things devoid of sense are not passive in relation to sensibles by the same kind of passivity. Therefore, sense is the passive power of the organ itself. Hence, the sensitive soul has not the function of mover and agent in sensing, but of that whereby the patient is passive; and this cannot possibly be diverse in being from the patient. Therefore, the sensible soul is not, in being, diverse from the animate body.

[9]   Furthermore, although motion is the common act of the mover and the moved, nevertheless to cause motion is one

5. Aristotle, *De anima*, II, 5 (416b 33ff.).

thing, to receive motion is another; that is why there are two categories, action and passion.[6] If, then, in sensing the sensitive soul plays the role of agent and the body of patient, the operation of the soul will be one thing and that of the body another. Therefore, the sensitive soul will have an operation proper to itself, and, consequently, will enjoy a subsistence of its own. It will therefore follow that, when the body is destroyed, the soul will not cease to be. Thus, the sensitive souls, even of irrational animals, will be immortal; which indeed seems improbable, though it is not inconsistent with Plato's opinion. But there will be an occasion later on to inquire into this matter.[7]

[10] Then, too, the movable does not derive its species from its mover. Therefore, if the soul is united to the body only as mover to thing movable, then the body and its parts do not owe to the soul that which they specifically are; so that, with the passing of the soul, the body and its parts will remain of the same species. But this is clearly false; for flesh and bones and hands, and like parts, after the soul's departure, are so called only in an equivocal sense, because none of these parts is then possessed of its proper operation, which stems from the specific nature of the thing whose parts they are. It remains that the soul is not united to the body only as mover to movable, or as a man to his clothes.

[11] Again, the movable does not owe its being to its mover, but only its movement. If, then, the soul were united to the body merely as its mover, the body would indeed be moved by the soul, but it would not owe its being to the soul. Now, in the living thing living is a certain being.[8] Therefore, the body would not live in virtue of the soul.

[12] Likewise, the movable is neither generated by the mover's being joined to it nor corrupted by its separation from it, because the movable does not depend on the mover for its being, but only for its being moved. Therefore, if the soul were united to the body only as its mover, it will follow that

6. Aristotle, *Categories*, IX (11b).
7. See below, ch. 82.
8. Cf. Aristotle, *De anima*, II, 4 (415b 13).

in the union of soul and body there will be no generation, nor will their separation mean corruption. And thus death, which consists in the separation of soul and body, will not be the corruption of the animal. And this is manifestly false.

[13] Furthermore, to be moved and not to be moved, to move and not to move, lie within the power of every self-mover. But the soul, according to the Platonic opinion, moves the body in the capacity of self-mover.[9] It is, therefore, in the soul's power to move the body and not to move it. Accordingly, if the soul is united to the body merely as mover to movable, it will be in the soul's power to be separated from the body at will and to be reunited to it at will. And this clearly is false.

[14] Now, that the soul is united to the body as its proper form is proved as follows. That by which something becomes a being in act from a being in potency is its form and act. But it is through the soul that the body becomes a being in act from being potentially existent, for living is the being of the living thing.[10] Now, the seed before animation is living only in potency, and, through the soul, becomes living in act. Therefore, the soul is the form of the animated body.

[15] In addition, since being as well as operating belong neither to the form alone, nor to the matter alone, but to the composite, to be and to act are attributed to two things, one of which is to the other as form to matter. For we say that a man is healthy in body and in health, and that he is knowing in knowledge and in his soul, knowledge being a form of the knower's soul and health a form of the healthy body. Now, life and sensation are ascribed to both soul and body, for we are said to live and to sense both in soul and body. But we live and sense by the soul as the principle of life and sensation. The soul is, therefore, the form of the body.

[16] The whole sensitive soul, moreover, is related to the whole body as a part to a part. And part is to part in such fashion that it is its form and act, for sight is the form and act of the eye. Therefore, the soul is the form and act of the body.

9. Cf. Plato, Phaedrus, 24D.
10. Aristotle, De anima, II, 4 (415b 13).

Chapter 58.

THAT IN MAN THERE ARE NOT THREE SOULS, NUTRITIVE, SENSITIVE, AND INTELLECTIVE

[1] Now, according to Plato's theory, the arguments proposed above can be met, so far as the present question is concerned. For Plato maintains[1] that in us the same soul is not intellective, nutritive, and sensitive. That is why, even if the sensitive soul were the form of the body, it would not be necessary to conclude that some intellectual substance can be the form of a body.

[2] That this opinion is impossible we must now show by the following arguments.

[3] Things attributed to the same thing according to diverse forms are predicated of one another by accident; a white thing is said to be musical by accident, because whiteness and music are accidental to Socrates, for example. Accordingly, if in us the intellective, sensitive, and nutritive soul are diverse powers or forms, then the things that appertain to us according to those forms will be predicated of one another by accident. Now, it is with respect to the intellective soul that we are said to be *men*; to the sensitive soul, *animals*; to the nutritive soul, *living beings*. It follows that the predication, *man is an animal*, or *an animal is a living thing*, will be by accident. But this predication is *through itself*, since man, as such, is an animal, and animal, as such, is a living thing. It is by the same principle, therefore, that one is a man, an animal, and a living thing.

[4] Now, it may be said that even if the aforesaid souls are diverse, it does not follow that the predications in question will be by accident, because these souls are mutually subordinate. But this, again, is ruled out. For the sensitive is subordinate to the intellective and the nutritive to the sensitive,

1. Plato, *Timaeus*, 69C–71A.

as potency is subordinate to act, since in the order of generation the intellective comes after the sensitive and the sensitive
after the nutritive; thus, animal is prior to man in that line.
Therefore, if this order makes the above mentioned predications to be *through themselves*, they will be so, not in that
mode of predication *through itself* which arises from the form,
but in that mode which arises from the matter and the subject; as a surface, for example, is said to be colored. But this
is impossible, because in this latter mode of predication
through itself that which is formal is predicated through itself
of the subject, as when we say: *The surface is white* or *the
number is even*. And again, in this kind of predication *through
itself* the subject is placed in the definition of the predicate,
as *number* in the definition of *even*. But, in the previous case,
the contrary is true; for man is not predicated of animal
through itself, but vice versa; nor is the subject placed in the
definition of the predicate, but vice versa. Therefore, such
things are not predicated through themselves by reason of
the order in question.

[5]   Moreover, the principle of a thing's unity is the same
as that of its being; for *one* is consequent upon *being*. Therefore, since each and every thing has being from its form, it
will also have unity from its form. Consequently, if several
souls, as so many distinct forms, are ascribed to man, he will
not be one being, but several. Nor will an order among forms
suffice to give man unity, because to be one in respect of order
is not to be one unqualifiedly speaking; since unity of order is
the least of unities.

[6]   Also, the impossibility noted above[2] will again arise,
namely, that from the intellective soul and the body there
results a thing that is one not unqualifiedly speaking but only
accidentally. For whatever comes to a thing after it is complete
in its being, comes to it accidentally, since it is outside that
thing's essence. Now, every substantial form makes a being
complete in the genus of substance, for it makes a being in act,
and this particular thing. Therefore, whatever accrues to a
thing after its first substantial form will accrue to it accidentally. Now, the nutritive soul is a substantial form, for *the*

2. See above, ch. 57.

living is predicated substantially of man and animal. It will then follow that the sensitive soul accrues to man accidentally, and likewise the intellective soul. Thus, neither *animal* nor *man* will signify one thing unqualifiedly speaking, nor will they denote a genus or a species in the category of *substance*.

[7] Again, if man, in Plato's theory, is not a thing composed of body and soul, but a soul using a body, this is to be understood either of the intellective soul only, or of the three souls, if there are three, or of two of them. If of three or two, it follows that man is not one being, but two or three, since he is then three souls or at least two. And if this is understood of the intellective soul only, so that the sensitive soul is thought to be the body's form, and the intellective soul, using the animated and sense-endowed body, to be the man, then this, again, will lead to absurd consequences, namely, that man is not an animal, but *uses an animal* (for through the sensitive soul a thing is an animal), and that man does not sense, but *uses a sentient thing*. These statements being contrary to the facts, it is impossible that there should be in us three souls differing in substance, the intellective, the sensitive, and the nutritive.

[8] And again, the one cannot be made from two or more, without something to unite them, unless one of them be related to the other as act to potentiality; for thus matter and form become one, without anything outside uniting them. Now, if there are several souls in man, they are not related to one another as matter and form, but they are all by hypothesis acts and principles of actions. So, if they are united in order to form one thing, say, a man or an animal, there must be something to unite them. But this cannot be the body, since it is precisely the body which is united together by the soul; a sign of which is the fact that, when the soul departs, the body is dissolved. It therefore remains that there must be something of a more formal character to make these several entities into one. And this will be the soul rather than those several entities which are united by this thing. Hence, if this latter, again, has diverse parts and is not one thing in itself, there will still be need of something to unite them. Since, then, it is impossible to go on to infinity, it is necessary to come to a

thing that is one in itself. And the soul, especially, is such a thing. Therefore, there must be but one soul in one man or in one animal.

[9]   Then, too, if that which belongs to the soul in man is an aggregate of several things, it follows that, as the totality of them is to the whole body, so each of them is to each part of the body. Nor does this idea conflict with Plato's position, for he located the rational soul in the brain, the nutritive in the liver, and the appetitive in the heart.[3] But this doctrine is evidently false, for two reasons. First, because there is a part of the soul which cannot be allocated to any part of the body, namely, the intellect; as we have already proved,[4] the intellect is not the act of some part of the body. Secondly, because it is manifest that the operations of different parts of the soul appear in the same part of the body, as we see in the case of animals that live after being cut in two, since the same part has the movement, sensation, and appetite by which it is moved; so too, the same part of a plant, after being cut off, is nourished, grows, and blossoms. And from this it is clear that the diverse parts of the soul are in one and the same part of the body. Therefore, there are not distinct souls in us which are allocated to various parts of the body.

[10]   Furthermore, diverse powers that are not rooted in one principle do not hinder one another in acting, unless, perhaps, their action be contrary; and this is not so in the present case. Now, we observe that the diverse actions of the soul hinder one another, for when one is intense another is remiss. Therefore, these actions and the powers that are their proximate principles must be referred to one principle. But this principle cannot be the body, both because there is an action in which the body does not share, namely, understanding, and because, if the body, as such, were the principle of these powers and actions, they would be found in all bodies; which is clearly false. It therefore remains that their principle is some one form, by which this body is such a body. And this principle is the soul. It follows, then, that all the actions of the soul which are in us proceed from the one soul. Thus, there are not several souls in us.

3. Plato, *Timaeus*, 69C–71A.   4. See above, ch. 51 and 56.

[11] Now, this conclusion accords with what is said in the book *On the Teachings of the Church:* "Nor do we believe that there are two souls in one man, as James and other Syrians write: one being the animal soul by which the body is animated and which is mingled with the blood; the other, a spiritual soul, which provides the reason. On the contrary, we say that it is one and the same soul in man which both gives life to the body by its union with it, and orders itself by its own reason."[5]

Chapter 59.

THAT MAN'S POSSIBLE INTELLECT IS NOT A SEPARATE SUBSTANCE

[1] There have been others who discovered an additional reason for holding that the intellectual soul cannot be united to the body as its form. For they say that the intellect, which Aristotle calls possible,[1] is a separate substance not united to us as a form.

[2] First, they endeavor to prove this from the words of Aristotle, who says that this intellect is "separate, not mixed with the body, simple, impassible"[2]—things that could not be said of the intellect if it were the body's form.

[3] Also, they try to prove this from the demonstration by which Aristotle shows[3] that, since the possible intellect receives all the species of sensible things through being in potentiality to them, it must be devoid of them all. Likewise, the pupil, which receives all the species of colors, lacks all color. For, if of itself it had any color, the latter would prevent it from seeing other colors; indeed, it would see nothing except under that color. And the same would be true of the possible intellect, if by itself it possessed any form or nature

5. Gennadius, *De ecclesiasticis dogmatibus,* XV (*PL,* 42, col. 1216).
1. Cf. Aristotle, *De anima,* III, 4 (429a 12 - 430a 9).
2. *Ibid.*
3. *Ibid.*

of sensible things. But this would necessarily be the case if the possible intellect were combined with the body, or if it were a form of some body. For, since one thing is made from form and matter, the form must share something of the nature of which it is the form. Therefore, the possible intellect cannot be combined with the body, or be the act or form of a body.

[4] If, moreover, the possible intellect were the form of a material body, its receptivity would be of the same kind as that of prime matter. For that which is the form of a body receives nothing without its matter. Now, prime matter receives individual forms, which in fact are individuated through being in matter. Hence, the possible intellect would receive forms as they are individual. And thus it would not be cognizant of universals; which is clearly false.

[5] Then, too, prime matter is not cognizant of the forms which it receives. If, then, the receptivity of the possible intellect were the same as that of prime matter, the possible intellect would not be cognizant of the forms received. And this is false.

[6] Again, as Aristotle proves in *Physics* VIII,[4] an infinite power cannot possibly exist in a body. But the possible intellect is endowed with a certain infinite power, since by it we judge of things infinite in number, inasmuch as by it we know universals, under which potentially infinite particulars are contained. Therefore, the possible intellect is not a power in a body.

[7] Now, for these reasons Averroes[5] was moved, and, as he himself says, some of the ancients, to hold that the possible intellect, by which the soul understands, has a separate existence from the body, and is not the form of the body.

[8] However, since such an intellect would in no way belong to us, nor would we understand by it, unless it were united to us in some manner, Averroes determines how it is brought

4. Aristotle, *Physics*, VIII, 10 (266a 25ff.).
5. Averroes, *Commentarium magnum in Aristotelis de Anima*, III, t.c. 5 (p. 389, lines 56–62).

into contact with us,[6] saying that the species understood in act is the form of the possible intellect, just as the visible in act is the form of the power of sight. Thus there arises one thing from the possible intellect and the form understood in act. The possible intellect, then, is united to anyone to whom that form is united. Now, it is united to us by means of the phantasm, which is a kind of subject of that understood form; and in this way the possible intellect also is brought into connection with us.

[9] But it is easy to see that these notions are worthless and impossible. For the one who understands is the one who has intellect. Now, the thing understood is the thing whose intelligible species is united to the intellect. Hence, simply because the intelligible species united to the intellect is present in a man in some way, it does not follow that it is the man who understands, but only that he is understood by [Averroes'] separate intellect.

[10] Moreover, the actually understood species is the form of the intellect, just as the actually visible species is the form of the power of sight, or of the eye itself. Now, the species understood is compared to the phantasm as the actually visible species to the colored thing outside the mind; indeed, Averroes himself uses this comparison, as does Aristotle.[7] Through the intelligible form, therefore, the possible intellect is in touch with the phantasm in us, even as the power of sight is in touch with the color present in the stone. But this contact does not make the stone to see, but only to be seen. So, too, the aforesaid contact of the possible intellect with us does not make us to understand, but only to be understood. Now, of course, it is properly and truly said that man understands, for we would not inquire into the nature of the intellect were it not for the fact that we understand ourselves. Therefore, the manner of contact in question is not sufficient.

[11] Furthermore, every knower by its cognitive power is united to its object, and not vice versa, just as every operator by its operative power is united to the thing operated. But

6. *Ibid.*, pp. 404 f., lines 500–522
7. Aristotle, *De anima*, III, 5 (430a 14).

man is intelligent by his intellect as by his cognitive power. Hence, he is not united to the intellect by the intelligible form; on the contrary, it is by the intellect that he is united to the intelligible.

[12]   Then, too, that by which a thing operates must be its form. For nothing acts except so far as it is in act; and nothing is in act except by its form. And that is why Aristotle proves that the soul is a form, from the fact that an animal lives and senses through its soul.[8] Now, man understands, and this by his intellect alone; and therefore Aristotle, when inquiring into the principle by which we understand, explains to us the nature of the possible intellect.[9] Consequently, the possible intellect must be united to us formally, and not merely by its object.

[13]   Again. "The intellect in act and the intelligible in act are one,"[10] "just as the sense in act and the sensible in act."[11] But the intellect in potentiality and the intelligible in potentiality are not one, any more than the sense in potentiality and the sensible in potentiality. Hence, the species of a thing, as present in phantasms, is not actually intelligible, since in this state it is not one with the intellect in act, but is one with it according as the species is abstracted from the phantasms. Just so, the species of color is not actually perceived as it exists in the stone, but only as it exists in the pupil. Now, according to the [Averroistic] doctrine stated above, the intelligible species is in contact with us only in respect of its existence in the phantasms; it is not, then, in contact with us according as it is one with the possible intellect as its form. Therefore, the intelligible species cannot be the means of bringing the possible intellect into contact with us; because, according as it is in contact with the possible intellect, it is not in contact with us, or vice versa.

[14]   Now, he who invented this doctrine was evidently deceived by an equivocation. For colors existing outside the soul

8. Cf. Aristotle, De anima, II, 2 (414a 4ff.).
9. Aristotle, De anima, III, 4.
10. Aristotle, De anima, III, 4 (430a 3).
11. Aristotle, De anima, II, 4 (425b 27).

are in the presence of light actually visible, as having the power to move the sight; but are not actually visible in the sense of being actually perceived as the result of becoming one with the sense power in act. And similarly, phantasms are made actually intelligible by the light of the agent intellect, so that they are able to move the possible intellect; but not so as to be actually understood, through union with the possible intellect actualized.

[15] Likewise, where the living thing has a higher operation, there is a higher kind of life corresponding to that operation. For in plants the only action we find is that which has to do with nutrition. But in animals we find a higher action, namely, sensation and locomotion; and that is why the animal lives by a higher kind of life. Now, in man we find a still higher vital operation than in the animal, namely, understanding. Therefore, man will have a higher kind of life. Now, life is through the soul. Therefore, the soul by which man lives will be of a higher sort than the sensible soul. But none is higher than the intellect. Therefore, the intellect is man's soul, and, consequently, his form.[12]

[16] And again. That which follows upon the operation of a thing does not give a thing its species, because operation is second act, whereas the form to which a thing owes its species is first act. But, according to the doctrine under consideration, the union of the possible intellect with man is the result of an operation of man, for it takes place by means of the imagination which, according to Aristotle, is "a movement resulting from the exercise of a sense power."[13] Therefore, man does not derive his species from that union. So it is not because of having an intellect that man differs specifically from brute animals.

[17] Furthermore, if man derives his species in virtue of his being rational and having an intellect, then whoever belongs to the human species is rational and endowed with an intellect. But a child, even before leaving the womb, is specifically human, although there are as yet no actually intelligible phan-

12. See above, ch. 57.
13. Aristotle, *De anima*, III, 3 (429a 2).

tasms present in it. Therefore, a man has not an intellect as the result of its being united to him by means of an intelligible species whose subject is a phantasm.

Chapter 60.

THAT MAN DERIVES HIS SPECIFIC NATURE, NOT FROM THE PASSIVE, BUT FROM THE POSSIBLE, INTELLECT

[1] These arguments are countered by others in keeping with the doctrine considered above.[1] For Averroes says[2] that man differs specifically from the brutes by the intellect which Aristotle calls *passive* and which is the same as the *cogitative power* that is proper to man, in place of which the other animals have a certain *natural estimative power*. Now, it is the function of this cogitative power to distinguish individual intentions and to compare them with one another, even as the intellect which is *separate* and *unmixed* compares and distinguishes universal intentions. And by this cogitative power, together with the imagination and memory, the phantasms are prepared to receive the action of the agent intellect, whereby they are made intelligible in act, just as there are certain arts which prepare the matter for the master artificer. Accordingly, this power is given the name of *intellect* or *reason*, which physicians declare to be seated in the middle cell of the head. And according to the disposition of this power, one man differs from another in genius and in other qualities pertaining to understanding. And by the use and exercise of this power a man acquires the habit [*habitus*[3]] of science. Hence, the habits of the sciences are in this passive intellect as their subject. Moreover, this passive intellect is in the child from the beginning, and through it the child receives its specific nature as a human being, before it actually understands.

1. See above, ch. 59.
2. Averroes, *Commentarium magnum in Aristotelis de Anima*, III, t.c. 20 (p. 454, lines 315–316; p. 449, lines 174–175).
3. Cf. St. Thomas Aquinas, *Summa Theologiae*, I-II, 49, 1–4.

[2] But it is quite obvious that these notions are false and involve an abuse of terms. For the vital operations are compared to the soul as second acts to the first act, as Aristotle makes clear in *De anima* II.[4] Now, in the same thing first act precedes the second in time, just as knowledge precedes reflection. Consequently, in whatever thing we find a vital operation we must place a part of the soul which will be related to that operation as first act to second act. But man has a proper operation higher than the other animals, namely, understanding and reasoning, which is the operation of man as man, as Aristotle says in *Ethics* I.[5] Hence, we must attribute to man a principle that properly gives him his specific nature and is related to the act of understanding as first act to second act. Now, this principle cannot be the aforesaid passive intellect, because the principle of man's proper operation must be *impassible* and *not mixed with the body*, as Aristotle proves;[6] whereas, the contrary is clearly true of the passive intellect. Therefore, it is impossible that man's specific nature, whereby he is distinguished from the other animals, should be given him by the cogitative power, which is called the passive intellect.

[3] Furthermore, an affection of the sensitive part of a thing cannot place it in a higher kind of life than the sensitive, just as an affection of the nutritive soul does not place it in a higher kind of life than the nutritive. Now, it is clear that the imagination, and like powers consequent upon it, such as the memory and so on, are affections of the sensitive part, as Aristotle proves in the *De memoria*.[7] Hence, an animal cannot be placed by these powers or by any one of them in a higher category of life than the sensitive. But man's life is of a higher kind—a point clearly explained in *De anima* II, where Aristotle, in distinguishing the kinds of life, places the intellective, which he attributes to man, above the sensitive, which he ascribes to all animals in general.[8] Therefore, it is

4. Aristotle, *De anima*, II, 1 (412a 23ff.).
5. Aristotle, *Nicomachean Ethics*, I, 7 (1098a 3).
6. Aristotle, *De anima*, III, 4 (429a 12 - 430a 9).
7. Aristotle, *De memoria et reminiscentia*, I (450a 12ff.).
8. Aristotle, *De anima*, II, 2 (413a 20ff.).

not by virtue of the aforesaid cogitative power that man is a living being with a life proper to himself.

[4] Then, too, every self-mover is composed of mover and moved, as Aristotle proves in *Physics* VIII.[9] Now, man, in common with the other animals, is a self-mover. Therefore, mover and moved are parts of him. And the first mover in man is the intellect, since the intellect by its intelligible object moves the will. Nor can it be said that the passive intellect alone is the mover, because the passive intellect has to do with particulars only; whereas, actual movement involves both the universal judgment, which belongs to the possible intellect, and the particular judgment, which can belong to the passive intellect, as Aristotle explains in *De anima* III,[10] and in *Ethics* VII.[11] Therefore, the possible intellect is a part of man. And it is the most noble and most formal thing in him. Hence, man derives his specific nature from it, and not from the passive intellect.

[5] The possible intellect, moreover, is demonstrably not the act of any body, because it is cognizant of all sensible forms universally.[12] Therefore, no power whose operation can extend to the universals of all sensible forms can be the act of a body. Now, such a power is the will, for our will can reach out to all the things that we can understand, at least our will to know them. And the act of the will is clearly directed to the universal; as Aristotle says in the *Rhetoric*, "we hate robbers in general, but are angry only with individual ones."[13] Therefore, the will cannot be the act of any part of the body, nor can it follow upon a power that is an act of the body. Now, every part of the soul is an act of the body, with the single exception of the intellect properly so called. Therefore, the will is in the intellective part; and that is why Aristotle says in *De anima* III: "Will is in the reason, but the irascible and concupiscible appetite are in the sensitive part."[14] So it is that acts

9. Aristotle, *Physics*, VIII, 5 (257a 15).
10. Aristotle, *De anima*, III, 11 (434a 17).
11. Aristotle, *Nicomachean Ethics*, VII, 3 (1147a 1).
12. Aristotle, *De anima*, III, 4 (420a 27).
13. Aristotle, *Rhetoric*, II, 4 (1382a 4).
14. Aristotle, *De anima*, III, 9 (432b 6).

of concupiscence and irascibility involve passion, but not the act of the will, which involves choice. Now, man's will is not outside him, as though it resided in some separate substance, but is within him. Otherwise, man would not be master of his own actions, since he would then be acted upon by the will of a separate substance, and in him there would be only the appetitive powers functioning in association with passion, namely, the irascible and concupiscible powers, which are in the sensitive part, as in other animals that are acted upon rather than act themselves. But this is impossible and would destroy all moral philosophy and sociality. It follows that there must exist in us the possible intellect, so that by it we differ from brute animals, and not only in terms of the passive intellect.

[6] Likewise, just as nothing is able to act except through an active potentiality in it, so nothing can be passive save through an inherent passive potentiality; the combustible is able to be burned not only because there is a thing capable of burning it, but also because it has in itself a potentiality to be burned. Now, *understanding is a kind of undergoing*, as is stated in *De anima* III.[15] Therefore, since the child is potentially understanding, even though he is not actually understanding, there must be in him a potentiality whereby he is able to understand. And this potentiality is the possible intellect. Hence, there must already be a union of the possible intellect to the child before he understands actually. Therefore, it is not through the actually understood form that the possible intellect is brought into connection with man; rather, the possible intellect itself is in man from the beginning as part of himself.

[7] Averroes, however, has an answer to this argument.[16] For he avers that a child is said to be understanding potentially for two reasons: first, because the phantasms in him are potentially intelligible; second, because the possible intellect is able to come in contact with him, and not because the intellect is already united to him.

[8] Now we have to show that neither of these reasons suf-

15. Aristotle, *De anima*, III, 4 (429a 13).
16. Averroes, *Commentarium magnum in Aristotelis de Anima*, III, t.c. 5 (p. 405, lines 520–527).

fices. Thus, the potentiality that enables the agent to act is distinct from the potentiality that enables the patient to receive action; and they differ as opposites. So, just because a thing is able to act, it does not follow that it is capable of receiving action. But ability to understand is ability to be passive; for as Aristotle remarks, "understanding is a kind of undergoing."[17] The child, therefore, is not said to be able to understand simply because the phantasms in him can be actually understood; this has to do with the ability to act, since the phantasms move the possible intellect.

[9]   Moreover, a potentiality derivative from the specific nature of a thing does not belong to it as a result of that which does not confer upon the thing its specific nature. Now, ability to understand is a consequence of the specific nature of man, for understanding is an operation of man as man. But phantasms do not give man his specific nature; rather, they are consequent upon his operation. Therefore, it cannot be said that the child is potentially understanding because of the phantasms.

[10]   And it is likewise impossible to say that a child is potentially understanding because the possible intellect can be in touch with him. For a person is said to be able to act or to be passive by active or passive potentiality, just as he is said to be white by whiteness. But he is not said to be white before whiteness is united to him. Therefore, neither is a person said to be able to act or to be passive before active or passive potentiality is present in him. Consequently, it cannot be said that a child is able to understand before the possible intellect, which is the power of understanding, is in contact with him.

[11]   Furthermore, a person is said in one way to be able to act before having the nature by which he acts, and in another way after he already has that nature, but is accidentally prevented from acting; thus, a body is in one sense said to be capable of being lifted upwards before it is light, and in another, after it is made light but is impeded in its movement. Now, a child is potentially understanding, not as though he

17. Aristotle, De anima, III, 4 (429a 13).

has not yet the nature enabling him to understand, but as having an obstacle to understanding, since he is prevented from understanding "because of the multiform movements in him," as is said in *Physics* VII.[18] Hence, he is not said to have the power of understanding because the possible intellect, which is the principle of understanding, can be joined to him, but because it is already in contact with him and is prevented from exercising its proper action; so that, upon the removal of the obstacle, he immediately understands.

[12] Likewise, "a habit is that by which one acts when he wills."[19] Therefore, a habit and the operation in keeping with it must exist in the same subject. Intellectual consideration, which is the act of the habit of science, cannot, however, be the function of the passive intellect, but belongs to the possible intellect itself; for a power must not be the act of a body if it is to be capable of understanding. Thus, the habit of science is not in the passive but in the possible intellect. Now, science is in us, and it is in accordance with this science that we are said to know scientifically. Therefore, the possible intellect also is in us, and has no being apart from us.

[13] Scientific knowledge, moreover, consists in the assimilation of the knower to the thing known. Now, the knower is assimilated to the thing known, as such, only with respect to universal species; for such are the objects of science. Now, universal species cannot be in the passive intellect, since it is a power using an organ, but only in the possible intellect. Therefore, scientific knowledge cannot reside in the passive intellect, but only in the possible intellect.

[14] Also, the intellect in the state of habit is, as the opponent admits,[20] the effect of the agent intellect. But it is the agent intellect which causes things to be actually intelligible, and the proper recipient of these things is the possible intellect, to which the agent intellect is compared as "art to its material," in Aristotle's phrase. Therefore, the intellect in habit, which is the habit of science, must have its locus in the possible, and not in the passive intellect.

18. Aristotle, *Physics,* VII, 3 (248a 1).
19. Averroes, *op. cit.,* III, t.c. 18 (p. 438, lines 26–28).
20. Averroes, *loc. cit.,* lines 30–34.

[15]   Then, too, the perfection of a higher substance cannot possibly depend upon a lower substance. Now, the perfection of the possible intellect depends on the operation of man, for it depends on the phantasms, which move the possible intellect. Therefore, the possible intellect is not a higher substance than man. Consequently, it must be part of man as his act and form.

[16]   Again, things separate in being also have separate operations, because things are for the sake of their operations, as first act for the sake of second act; that is why Aristotle says that, if any operation of the soul does not involve the body, then "it is possible for the soul to have a separate existence."[21] But the operation of the possible intellect requires the body, for Aristotle says in De anima III[22] that the intellect can act by itself, namely, it can understand, when it has been actuated by a species abstracted from phantasms—which have no existence apart from the body. Therefore, the possible intellect is not altogether separate from the body.

[17]   And again, every thing naturally endowed with a certain operation has by nature those attributes without which that operation cannot be carried out. Thus, Aristotle proves in De caelo II[23] that if the movement of the stars were progressive, like that of animals, nature would have given them organs of progressive movement. But the operation of the possible intellect is accomplished by bodily organs, in which there must be phantasms. Therefore, nature has united the possible intellect to bodily organs. Consequently, it has no being separate from the body.

[18]   Furthermore, if the possible intellect had being separate from the body, it would know substances that are separate from matter, rather than sensible forms, because such substances are more intelligible and more conformed to the intellect. But it cannot know substances that are altogether separate from matter, because there are not phantasms of them; and this intellect "in no case understands without a phan-

21. Aristotle, De anima, I, 1 (403a 10).
22. Aristotle, De anima, III, 4 (429a 15).
23. Aristotle, De caelo et mundo, II, 8 (290a 32).

tasm," as Aristotle says in *De anima* III,[24] because the phantasms are to it "as sensible objects to the senses," without which objects the sense power is inoperative. Therefore, the possible intellect is not a substance separate from the body in being.

[19] In every genus, moreover, the passive potentiality is equal in its scope to that of the correlative active potentiality, and so there does not exist in nature a passive potentiality without a corresponding natural active potentiality. But the agent intellect makes only the phantasms to be intelligible. Therefore, the possible intellect is moved by no other intelligible objects than the species abstracted from the phantasms. And thus, it is unable to understand separate substances.

[20] Then, too, the species of sensible things exist in separate substances in an intelligible mode, and it is through those species that such substances have knowledge of sensible things. If, then, the possible intellect understands separate substances, it would in knowing them receive knowledge of sensible things. It would not, therefore, receive this knowledge from phantasms, for *nature does not abound in superfluities.*

[21] Yet, if it be said that separate substances have no knowledge of sensible things, at least it will have to said that they enjoy a higher kind of knowledge: a knowledge which the possible intellect must not lack if it understands those substances. Accordingly, the possible intellect will have a twofold science: one, in the manner of separate substances; the other, received from the senses. And one of these would be superfluous.

[22] The possible intellect, furthermore, is that "by which the soul understands," as is said in *De anima* III.[25] Therefore, if the possible intellect understands separate substances, then we also understand them. And this is clearly false, because in relation to them we are "as the eye of the owl to the sun," as Aristotle remarks.[26]

24. Aristotle, *De anima*, III, 7 (431a 15).
25. Aristotle, *De anima*, III, 4 (429a 10).
26. Aristotle, *Metaphysics*, II, 1 (993b 10).

[23] Now, these arguments are answered as follows, along the lines of the doctrine we have been dealing with.[27] The possible intellect, as the result of being self-subsistent, knows separate substances, and is in potentiality to them as a transparent body to the light. But, so far as the possible intellect is in contact with us, it is from the beginning in potentiality to forms abstracted from phantasms. That is why we do not from the beginning know separate substances by its means.

[24] This answer, however, cannot stand. For the possible intellect, according to them, is said to be in contact with us as a result of being perfected by intelligible species abstracted from phantasms. Prior to its contact with us, therefore, the intellect is to be thought of as being in potentiality to these species; so that it is not in potentiality to them by its being in contact with us.

[25] Moreover, according to this view the possible intellect would owe not to itself, but to something else, the fact of its being in potentiality to the intelligible species in question. But a thing ought not to be defined in terms of things not belonging to it in itself. Therefore, the definition of the possible intellect is not derived from its being in potentiality to those species, as Aristotle defines it in *De anima* III.[28]

[26] Again, the possible intellect cannot understand several things at the same time unless it understands one through another, for a single power is not perfected by several acts at the same time except in keeping with a certain order. Consequently, if the possible intellect understands separate substances, and species abstracted from phantasms, it must either understand the substances through the species or the species through the substances. Now, in either case it follows that we do not understand separate substances. For, if we understand the natures of sensible things so far as the possible intellect understands them, and the possible intellect knows them through understanding separate substances, then we will understand them in the same way. And this also follows if the converse is true. But this is manifestly false. It remains that the

27. Averroes, *op. cit.*, III, t.c. 5 (p. 411, lines 693–703); t.c. 20 (p. 450, lines 193–198); t.c. 36 (p. 488, lines 251–257).
28. Aristotle, *De anima*, III, 4 (429a 17).

possible intellect does not understand separate substances, and, therefore, it is not a separate substance.

Chapter 61.

THAT THIS THEORY IS CONTRARY TO THE TEACHING OF ARISTOTLE

[1] Averroes, however, attempts to strengthen his position[1] by appealing to authority, saying, therefore,[2] that Aristotle was of the same opinion. We shall, then, show clearly that Averroes' doctrine is contrary to that af Aristotle.

[2] First, because Aristotle in *De anima* II defines the soul "as the first act of an organic physical body having life potentially";[3] and he adds that this definition "applies universally to every kind of soul";[4] nor, as Averroes imagines,[5] does Aristotle express any doubt concerning this definition. The Greek texts, as well as Boethius' translation, give clear proof of this.

[3] And afterwards in the same chapter, Aristotle remarks that "certain parts of the soul are separable."[6] But these are no other than intellective parts. Hence, it remains that these parts are acts of the body.

[4] Nor is this point contradicted by what Aristotle says later on, namely: "Nothing is clear as yet about the intellect and the power of insight, but it seems to be another kind of soul."[7] For Aristotle does not mean by this to exclude the intellect from the common definition of *soul*, but from the nature proper to the other parts of the soul; thus, he who

1. See above, ch. 60.
2. Averroes, *Commentarium magnum in Aristotelis de Anima*, III, t.c. 5, *passim*.
3. Aristotle, *De anima*, II, 1 (412a 29).
4. Aristotle, *De anima*, II, 1 (412b 4).
5. Averroes, *op. cit.*, II, t.c. 7 (p. 138, lines 15–22).
6. Aristotle, *De anima*, II, 1 (413a 7).
7. Aristotle, *De anima*, II, 1 (413b 24).

says that "the flying animal is of another kind than the walking" does not exclude the former from the common definition of animal. So, in order to explain what he meant by saying another, Aristotle immediately adds: "And this alone is capable of separate existence, as the everlasting apart from the perishable." Nor is it Aristotle's intention, as Averroes imagines,[8] to say that, in contrast with the clear knowledge which we have concerning the other parts of the soul, it is not yet clear whether the intellect is the soul. The genuine text does not read, *nothing has been declared*, or *nothing has been said*, but *nothing is clear*; and this must be taken to refer to that which is proper to the intellective soul, and not to the common definition. But if, as Averroes says,[9] *soul* is predicated equivocally of the intellect and of other souls, then Aristotle would first have pointed out the equivocation, and given the definition afterwards, in keeping with his usual procedure. Otherwise, his argument would have been based on an equivocation, and in demonstrative science there is no room for that sort of thing.

[5]   Moreover, Aristotle in *De anima* II[10] reckons the intellect among the powers of the soul; and in the text previously quoted[11] he calls it the *power of insight*. Therefore, the intellect is not outside the human soul, but is one of its powers.

[6]   And when in that same work Aristotle begins his discussion of the possible intellect by speaking of it as "the part of the soul with which the soul has knowledge and wisdom,"[12] he thus plainly indicates that the possible intellect is a part of the soul.

[7]   Aristotle indeed makes this point still more explicit when he explains later on what the nature of the possible intellect is: "By the intellect," he says, "I mean that by which the soul judges and understands."[13] This makes it perfectly clear that

8. Averroes, op. cit., II, t.c. 21 (p. 160, lines 6–27).
9. *Ibid*, line 27.
10. Aristotle, *De anima*, II, 3 (414a 32).
11. Aristotle, *De anima*, II, 3 (413b 24).
12. Aristotle, *De anima*, III, 4 (429a 10).
13. Aristotle, *De anima*, III, 4 (429a 23).

the intellect is that part of the human soul by which it understands.

[8] The Averroistic position in question is, then, contrary to the opinion of Aristotle and to the truth, and is to be rejected therefore as sheer fiction.

Chapter 62.

AGAINST ALEXANDER'S OPINION CONCERNING THE POSSIBLE INTELLECT

[1] Having considered these sayings of Aristotle, Alexander asserted that the possible intellect is a power in us,[1] so that the common definition of soul given by aristotle in *De anima* II[2] might apply to that intellect. But because he was unable to understand how an intellectual substance could be the form of a body, he held that the power of which we speak does not have its foundation in an intellectual substance, but that it is consequent upon a blending of elements in the human body. For the particular kind of blending found in the human body makes man to be in potentiality to receive the influx of the agent intellect, which is always in act, and according to him is a separate substance, the effect of that influx being that man is made to understand actually. Now, that which enables man to understand is the possible intellect. And thus, it seemed to follow that the possible intellect is in us the result of a particular blending.

[2] But this position seems at first glance to be contrary to both the words and the proof of Aristotle. For, as we have already pointed out,[3] Aristotle proves in *De anima* III that the possible intellect is "free from all admixture with the body."[4] And this could not possibly be said of a power resulting from a blending of elements, since such a power must be

1. Alexander of Aphrodisias, *De intellectu et intellecto* (pp. 74–77); cf. Averroes, *Commentarium magnum in Aristotelis de Anima*, III, t.c. 5 (p. 393, line 196ff.).
2. See above, ch. 61, ¶2.   3. See above, ch. 60, ¶2.
4. Aristotle, *De anima*, III, 4 (429a 20, 24).

rooted in that very blending of elements, as we see in the case
of taste, smell, and the like. Seemingly, then, this notion of
Alexander's is incompatible with the words and the proof of
Aristotle.

[3]   To this, however, Alexander replies that the possible
intellect is the very *preparedness* in human nature to receive
the influx of the agent intellect. And preparedness is not itself
a particular sensible nature, nor is it intermixed with the body;
rather, preparedness is a certain relation, and the order of one
thing to another.

[4]   But this notion also clearly clashes with Aristotle's meaning. For Aristotle proves that the reason why the possible
intellect does not itself have the nature of any particular sensible thing, and consequently is free from any admixture with
the body, is because it is receptive of all the forms of sensible
things, and cognizant of them. Now, preparedness cannot be
thought of in such terms, for it does not mean to receive, but
to be prepared to receive. So it is that Aristotle's demonstration proceeds not from preparedness, but from a prepared
recipient.

[5]   Moreover, if what Aristotle says about the possible intellect applies to it as a preparedness, and not by reason of the nature of the subject prepared, it will follow that it applies to
every preparedness. Now, in the senses there is a certain preparedness to receive sensibles in act. And so, the same thing
must be said of the senses as of the possible intellect. But Aristotle clearly says the contrary in explaining[5] the difference between the receptivity of the senses and of the intellect, from
the fact that the sense is corrupted by objects exceedingly high
or intense, but not the intellect.[6]

[6]   Likewise, Aristotle says that the possible intellect is
passive to the intelligible, *receives* intelligible species, *is in
potentiality* to them.[7] He even compares it to "a tablet on
which nothing is written."[8] Now, none of these things can be

5. Aristotle, *De anima*, III, 4 (429a 30).
6. Cf. Aristotle, *De anima*, III, 4 (429b 2).
7. Aristotle, *De anima*, III, 4.
8. Aristotle, *De anima*, III, 4 (430a 2).

said of preparedness, but they all apply to the subject prepared. The notion that the possible intellect is a mere preparedness is, therefore, contrary to Aristotle's meaning.

[7] "The agent is superior to the patient, and the maker to the thing made,"[9] as act to potentiality. Now, the more immaterial a thing is, the higher its level of being. Therefore, the effect cannot be more immaterial than its cause. But every cognitive power, as such, is immaterial. Thus, Aristotle says that the power of sense, which occupies the lowest place in the order of cognitive powers, is "receptive of sensible species without matter.'[10] It is therefore impossible for a cognitive power to be caused by a commingling of elements. Now, the possible intellect is the highest cognitive power in us; for Aristotle says that the possible intellect is "that by which the soul knows and understands."[11] Therefore, the possible intellect is not caused by a mixture of elements.

[8] If the principle of an operation proceeds from certain causes, that operation must not go beyond those causes, for the second cause acts by virtue of the first. But even the operation of the nutritive soul exceeds the power of the elemental qualities; for, in *De anima* II Aristotle proves that "fire is not the cause of growth, but in a sense its concurrent cause, the principal cause of growth being the soul,"[12] to which heat is compared as the instrument to the craftsman. It follows that the vegetative soul cannot be produced by an intermingling of the elements, and much less, therefore, the sense and possible intellect.

[9] Understanding is an operation in which no bodily organ can possibly take part. Now, this operation is attributed to the soul, or even to the man, for it is said that *the soul understands*, or *man, by the soul*. Hence, there must be in man a principle, independent of the body, which is the source of that operation. However, the preparedness that results from a blending of the elements clearly depends on the body; and,

9. Aristotle, *De anima*, III, 5 (430a 17).
10. Aristotle, *De anima*, II, 12 (424a 16).
11. Aristotle, *De anima*, III, 4 (429a 10).
12. Aristotle, *De anima*, II, 4 (416a 14).

consequently, it is not this principle. But the possible intellect is, for Aristotle says in *De anima* III that this intellect is "that by which the soul knows and understands."[13] Therefore, the possible intellect is not a preparedness.

[10]   Now, seemingly it is not enough to say that the principle of the operation of understanding in us is the intelligible species brought into act by the agent intellect. For man comes to understand actually after understanding potentially. So, it follows that he understands not only by the intelligible species, whereby he is made to understand actually, but also by an intellective power, which is the principle of this operation of understanding; and such is the case also with the senses. Now, Aristotle holds that this power is the possible intellect. Therefore, the possible intellect is independent of the body.

[11]   Moreover, a species is intelligible in act only so far as it is freed from its presence in matter. But this cannot be done so long as it remains in a material power, namely, a power which is caused by material principles, or is the act of a material organ. The presence in us of an intellective power that is immaterial must, therefore, be granted. And this power is the possible intellect.

[12]   Also, Aristotle speaks of the possible intellect as being *part of the soul.*[14] Now, the soul is not a preparedness, but an act, since preparedness is *the order of potentiality to act.* And yet an act is followed by a preparedness for a further act; the act of transparency is followed by an order to the act of light. Therefore, the possible intellect is not a preparedness itself, but is a certain act.

[13]   Man owes his specific essence and his human nature to that part of the soul which is proper to him, namely, the possible intellect.[15] Now, nothing receives its species and its nature so far as it is in potentiality, but so far as it is in act. And since preparedness simply consists in an *order of potentiality to act,* the possible intellect cannot be merely a preparedness existing in human nature.

13. Aristotle, *De anima,* III, 4 (429a 10).
14. Aristotle, *De anima,* III, 4 (429a 10).
15. See above, ch. 60.

Chapter 63.

THAT THE SOUL IS NOT A TEMPERAMENT, AS GALEN MAINTAINED

[1] The opinion of the physician Galen about the soul is similar to the previously discussed notion,[1] of Alexander concerning the possible intellect. For Galen says that the soul is a temperament.[2] Now, he was moved to say this because of our observation that diverse passions, ascribed to the soul, result from various temperaments in us: those possessed of a choleric temperament are easily angered; melancholics easily grow sad. And so we see that the same arguments which we used a moment ago against Alexander's theory can serve to disprove this notion of Galen's, as well as some arguments specifically relevant to that notion.

[2] For it was shown above[3] that the operation of the vegetative soul, sensitive knowledge, and, much more, the operation of the intellect transcend the power of the active and passive qualities. But temperament is caused by active and passive qualities. Therefore, it cannot be a principle of the soul's operations. It is, then, impossible for a soul to be a temperament.

[3] Moreover, temperament is something constituted by contrary qualities, as a kind of mean between them, and therefore it cannot possibly be a substantial form, since "substance has no contrary, and does not admit of variation of degree."[4] But the soul is a substantial, not an accidental, form; otherwise, a thing would not obtain genus or species through the soul. It follows that the soul is not a temperament.

[4] Again, temperament is not responsible for the local move-

1. See above, ch. 62.
2. Cf. St. Gregory of Nyssa, *De anima*, serm. 1 (PG, 45, col. 195); Nemesius, *De natura hominis*, (PG, 40, col. 553).
3. See above, ch. 62.
4. Aristotle, *Categories*, III (3b 24, 32).

ment of an animal's body; if it were, then that body would follow the movement of the preponderant element, and thus would always be moved downwards. But the soul moves the body in all directions; therefore, it is not the temperament.

[5] Then, too, the soul rules the body and resists the passions, which follow the temperament. For by temperament some are more prone than others to concupiscence or anger, yet refrain more from these things because something keeps them in check, as we see in continent persons. Now, it is not the temperament that does this. Therefore, the soul is not the temperament.

[6] It would seem that Galen was misled through not having considered that passions are attributed to the temperament in quite a different manner than to the soul. For passions are ascribed to the temperament as a dispositive cause in their regard, and as concerns that which is material in them, such as the heat of the blood and the like. On the other hand, passions are ascribed to the soul as their principal cause, and as regards that which is formal in them; for instance, the desire of vengeance in the passion of anger.

Chapter 64.

THAT THE SOUL IS NOT A HARMONY

[1] Along the lines of the foregoing theory is the view of those who say that the soul is a harmony. For these persons thought of the soul not as a harmony of sounds, but of the contraries of which they observed animate bodies to be composed. In the De anima[1] this notion seems to be attributed to Empedocles, although Gregory of Nyssa[2] ascribes it to Dinarchus. And it is disproved in the same way as Galen's theory, as well as by arguments that apply properly to itself.

[2] For every mixed body has harmony and temperament. Nor can harmony move a body or rule it or curb the passions,

1. Aristotle, De anima, I, 4 (407b 31; 408a 17).
2. St. Gregory of Nyssa, De anima, serm. 1 (PG, 45, col. 193; 40, cols. 537, 551).

any more than can temperament. Moreover, harmony is subject to intensification and remission; and so, too, is temperament. All these things show that the soul is not a harmony, even as it is not a temperament.

[3] Furthermore, the nature of harmony pertains to the qualities of the body rather than to those of the soul; thus, health consists in a kind of harmony of the humours; strength, in a certain harmony of sinews and bones; beauty, in harmony of limbs and colors. But it is impossible to assign the things of which sense or intellect or the other powers of the soul are the harmony. Therefore, the soul is not a harmony.

[4] Again, *harmony* has two senses; for it can be taken to signify the *composition itself*, or the *mode of composition*. Now, the soul is not a composition, since each part of the soul would have to consist in the composition of some of the parts of the body; and such an alloting of psychic part to corporeal part is impossible. Nor is the soul a mode of composition; for, since in the various parts of the body there are various modes or proportions of composition, each part of the body would have a distinct soul: since bone, flesh, and sinew are in each case composed according to a different proportion, each would possess a different soul. Now, this is patently false. Therefore, the soul is not a harmony.

Chapter 65.

THAT THE SOUL IS NOT A BODY

[1] There were also others whose thinking was even wider of the mark, since they asserted that the soul is a body. Although they held divergent and various opinions, it suffices to refute them here collectively.

[2] For, since living things are physical realities, they are composed of matter and form. Now, they are composed of a body and a soul, which makes them actually living. Therefore, one of these two must be the form and the other matter. But the body cannot be the form, because the body is not present in another thing as its matter and subject. The soul,

then, is the form, and consequently is not a body, since no body is a form.

[3] It is, moreover, impossible for two bodies to coincide. But, so long as the body lives, the soul is not apart from it. Therefore, the soul is not a body.

[4] Then, too, every body is divisible Now, whatever is divisible requires something to keep together and unite its parts, so that, if the soul is a body, it will have something else to preserve its integrity, and this yet more will be the soul; for we observe that, when the soul departs, the body disintegrates. And if this integrating principle again be divisible, we must at last either arrive at something indivisible and incorruptible, which will be the soul, or go on to infinity; which is impossible. Therefore, the soul is not a body.

[5] Again. It has been proved in Book I of this work,[1] and in *Physics* VIII,[2] that every self-mover is composed of two parts: one, the part that moves and is not moved; the other, the part that is moved. Now, the animal is a self-mover, and the mover in it is the soul, and the body is the moved. Therefore, the soul is an unmoved mover. But no body moves without being moved, as was shown in that same Book.[3] Therefore, the soul is not a body.

[6] Furthermore, we have already shown[4] that understanding cannot be the act of a body. But it is the act of a soul. Consequently, at least the intellective soul is not a body.

[7] Now the arguments by which some have tried to prove that the soul is a body are easily solved. They argue as follows: that the son is like the father even in accidents of the soul, despite the fact that the begetting of the one by the other involves the parting of body from body; that the soul suffers with the body; that the soul is separate from the body, and separation is between mutually contacting bodies.

[8] But against this argumentation it has already been

1. *SCG*, I, ch. 13.
2. Aristotle, *Physics*, VIII, 5 (257a 17).
3. *SCG*, I, ch. 20.   4. See above, ch. 49, ¶5, 8, 9.

pointed out[5] that the bodily temperament has a certain dispositive causality with respect to the passions of the soul. Moreover, it is only accidentally that the soul suffers with the body; for, since the soul is the form of the body, it is moved accidentally by the body's being moved. Also, the soul is separate from the body, not as a thing touching from a thing touched, but as form from matter, although, as we have shown,[6] that which is incorporeal does have a certain contact with the body.

[9] Indeed, what motivated many to adopt this position was their belief that there is nothing that is not a body, for they were unable to rise above the imagination, which is exclusively concerned with bodies. That is why this view is proposed in the person of the foolish, who say of the soul: "The breath in our nostrils is smoke, and speech a spark to move our heart" (Wis. 2:2).

Chapter 66.

AGAINST THOSE WHO MAINTAIN THAT
INTELLECT AND SENSE ARE THE SAME

[1] Thinking that there was no difference between intellect and sense, some of the early philosophers[1] were close to the persons referred to above. But that notion of theirs is impossible.

[2] For sense is found in all animals, whereas animals other than man have no intellect. This is evident from the fact that the latter perform diverse and opposite actions, not as though they possessed intellect, but as moved by nature, carrying out certain determinate operations of uniform character within the same species; every swallow builds its nest in the same way. Therefore, intellect is not the same as sense.

[3] Moreover, sense is cognizant only of singulars; for every sense power knows through individual species, since it receives the species of things in bodily organs. But the intellect is

5. See above, ch. 63.   6. See above, ch. 56, ¶8-9.
1. Aristotle, *De anima*, III, 3 (427a 22).

cognizant of universals, as experience proves. Therefore, intellect differs from sense.

[4]   Then, too, sense-cognition is limited to corporeal things. This is clear from the fact that sensible qualities, which are the proper objects of the senses, exist only in such things; and without them the senses know nothing. On the other hand, the intellect knows incorporeal things, such as wisdom, truth, and the relations of things. Therefore, intellect and sense are not the same.

[5]   Likewise, a sense knows neither itself nor its operation; for instance, sight neither sees itself nor sees that it sees. This self-reflexive power belongs to a higher faculty, as is proved in the *De anima*.[2] But the intellect knows itself, and knows that it knows. Therefore, intellect and sense are not the same.

[6]   Sense, furthermore, is corrupted by excess in the sensible object.[3] But intellect is not corrupted by the exceedingly high rank of an intelligible object; for, indeed, he who understands greater things is more able afterwards to understand lesser things.[4] The sensitive power therefore differs from the intellective.

Chapter 67.

AGAINST THOSE WHO HOLD THAT THE POSSIBLE INTELLECT IS THE IMAGINATION

[1]   The opinion of those who asserted that the possible intellect is not distinct from the imagination[1] was akin to the notion just discussed. And that opinion is evidently false.

[2]   For imagination is present in non-human animals as well as in man. This is indicated by the fact that in the absence of sensible things, such animals shun or seek them; which would

2. Aristotle, *De anima*, III, 2 (425b).
3. Aristotle, *De anima*, III, 2 (426a 30).
4. Aristotle, *De anima*, III, 4 (429b 4).
1. See, for example, Averroes, *Commentarium magnum in Aristotelis de Anima*, III, t.c. 5 (p. 397, lines 299–303). Averroes here refers to Abubacher.

not be the case unless they retained an imaginative apprehension of them. But non-human animals are devoid of intellect, since no work of intellect is evident in them. Therefore imagination and intellect are not the same.

[3] Moreover, imagination has to do with bodily and singular things only; as is said in the *De anima*,[2] imagination is *a movement caused by actual sensation*. The intellect, however, grasps objects universal and incorporeal. Therefore, the possible intellect is not the imagination.

[4] Again, it is impossible for the same thing to be mover and moved. But the phantasms move the possible intellect as sensibles move the senses, as Aristotle says in *De anima* III.[3] Therefore, the possible intellect cannot be the same as the imagination.

[5] And again. It is proved in *De anima* III[4] that the intellect is not the act of any part of the body. Now the imagination has a determinate bodily organ. Therefore, the imagination is not the same as the possible intellect.

[6] So it is that we read in the Book of Job (35:11): "Who teacheth us more than the beasts of the earth, and instructeth us more than the fowls of the air." And by this we are given to understand that man is possessed of a power of knowledge superior to sense and imagination, which are shared by the other animals.

Chapter 68.

HOW AN INTELLECTUAL SUBSTANCE CAN BE
THE FORM OF THE BODY

[1] From the preceding arguments,[1] then, we can conclude that an intellectual substance can be united to the body as its form.

2. Aristotle, *De anima*, III, 3 (429a 2).
3. Aristotle, *De anima*, III, 7 (431a 14).
4. Aristotle, *De anima*, III, 4 (429a 24).
1. See above, ch. 57–67.

[2]   For, if an intellectual substance is not united to the body merely as its mover, as Plato held that it is, nor is in contact with it merely by phantasms, as Averroes said, but as its form; and if the intellect whereby man understands is not a preparedness in human nature, as Alexander supposed it to be, nor the temperament, according to Galen, nor a harmony, as Empedocles imagined, nor a body, nor the senses or the imagination, as the early philosophers maintained, then it remains that the human soul is an intellectual substance united to the body as its form. This conclusion can be made evident as follows.

[3]   For one thing to be another's substantial form, two requirements must be met. *First*, the form must be the principle of the substantial being of the thing whose form it is; I speak not of the productive but of the formal principle whereby a thing exists and is called a *being*. The *second* requirement then follows from this, namely, that the form and the matter be joined together in the unity of one act of being; which is not true of the union of the efficient cause with that to which it gives being. And this single act of being is that in which the composite substance subsists: a thing one in being and made up of matter and form. Now, as we have shown,[2] the fact that an intellectual substance is subsistent does not stand in the way of its being the formal principle of the being of the matter, as communicating its own being to the matter. For it is not unfitting that the composite and its form should subsist in the same act of being, since the composite exists only by the form, and neither of them subsists apart from the other.

[4]   Nevertheless, it may be objected that an intellectual substance cannot communicate its being to corporeal matter in such fashion that the two will be united in the same act of being, because diverse genera have diverse modes of being, and to the nobler substance belongs a loftier being.

[5]   Now, this argument would be relevant if that single act of being belonged in the same way to the matter as to the intellectual substance. But it does not. For that act of being appertains to the corporeal matter as its recipient and its subject, raised to a higher level; it belongs to the intellectual sub-

2. See above, ch. 51 and 57, ¶14–16.

stance as its principle, and in keeping with its very own nature. Nothing, therefore, prevents an intellectual substance from being the human body's form, which is the human soul.

[6] Thus are we able to contemplate the marvelous connection of things. For it is always found that the lowest in the higher genus touches the highest of the lower species. Some of the lowest members of the animal kingdom, for instance, enjoy a form of life scarcely superior to that of plants; oysters, which are motionless, have only the sense of touch and are fixed to the earth like plants. That is why Blessed Dionysius says in his work *On the Divine Names* that "divine wisdom has united the ends of higher things with the beginnings of the lower."[3] We have, therefore, to consider the existence of something supreme in the genus of bodies, namely, the human body harmoniously tempered, which is in contact with the lowest of the higher genus, namely, the human soul, which holds the lowest rank in the genus of intellectual substances, as can be seen from its mode of understanding; so that the intellectual soul is said to be on the *horizon* and *confines* of things corporeal and incorporeal,[4] in that it is an incorporeal substance and yet the form of a body. Nor is a thing composed of an intellectual substance and corporeal matter less one than a thing made up of the form of fire and its matter, but perhaps it is more one; because the greater the mastery of form over matter, the greater is the unity of that which is made from it and matter.

[7] But, though the form and the matter are united in the one act of being, the matter need not always be commensurate with the form. Indeed, the higher the form, the more it surpasses matter in its being. This fact is clearly apparent to one who observes the operations of forms, from the study of which we know their natures; for, as a thing is, so does it act. That is why a form whose operation transcends the condition of matter, itself also surpasses matter in the rank of its being.

[8] For we find certain lowest-grade forms whose operations are limited to the class of those proper to the qualities which

3. Pseudo-Dionysius, *De divinis nominibus*, VII, (PG, 3, col. 871).
4. *Liber de causis*, II (p. 162).

are dispositions of matter; qualities such as heat, cold, moisture and dryness, rarity and density, gravity and levity, etc. And those forms are the forms of the elements: forms which therefore are altogether material and wholly embedded in matter.

[9]   Above these are found the forms of mixed bodies. Althought their operations are no greater in scope than those which can be effected through qualities of the aforesaid variety, nevertheless they sometimes produce those same effects by a higher power which they receive from the heavenly bodies, and which is consequent upon the latter's species. A case in point is that of the lodestone attracting iron.

[10]   One rung higher on the ladder of forms, we encounter those whose operations include some which exceed the power of the previously mentioned material qualities, although the latter assist organically in the operations of those forms. Such forms are the souls of plants, which likewise resemble not only the powers of the heavenly bodies, in surpassing the active and passive qualities, but also the movers of those bodies, the souls of plants being principles of movement in living things, which move themselves.

[11]   A step above, we find other forms resembling the higher substances, not only in moving, but even, somehow, in knowing, so that they are capable of operations to which the aforesaid qualities are of no assistance, even organically, although these operations are performed only by means of a bodily organ. Such forms are the souls of brute animals. For sensation and imagination are not brought about by heating and cooling, although these are necessary for the due disposition of the organ involved.

[12]   Above all these forms, however, is a form like to the higher substances even in respect of the kind of knowledge proper to it, namely, understanding. This form, then, is capable of an operation which is accomplished without any bodily organ at all. And this form is the intellective soul; for understanding is not effected through any bodily organ. That is why this principle, the intellective soul by which man understands and which transcends the condition of corporeal matter, must not be wholly encompassed by or imbedded in matter,

as material forms are. This is proved by its intellectual operation, wherein corporeal matter has no part. But since the human soul's act of understanding needs powers—namely, imagination and sense—which function through bodily organs, this itself shows that the soul is naturally united to the body in order to complete the human species.

Chapter 69.

SOLUTION OF THE ARGUMENTS ADVANCED ABOVE IN ORDER TO SHOW THAT AN INTELLECTUAL SUBSTANCE CANNOT BE UNITED TO THE BODY AS ITS FORM

[1] With the preceding points[1] in mind, it is not difficult to solve the arguments previously proposed[2] against the union in question.

[2] In the *first argument* a false supposition is made, because body and soul are not two actually existing substances; rather, the two of them together constitute one actually existing substance. For man's body is not actually the same while the soul is present and when it is absent; but the soul makes it to be actually.

[3] In the *second argument* the statement that form and matter are contained in the same genus is true, not in the sense that they are both species of the same genus, but in the sense that they are the principles of the same species. So, if the intellectual substance and the body existed apart from one another, they would be species of diverse genera; but by being united, they are of one and the same genus as principles of it.

[4] Nor is the *third argument* valid. For from the fact that the intellectual substance is in matter it does not follow that it is a material form, because that soul is not present in matter in the sense of being embedded in it or wholly enveloped by it, but in another way, as we have pointed out.

1. See above, ch. 68.
2. See above, ch. 56, ¶14–18.

[5]   As to the *fourth argument*, the fact that an intellectual substance is united to the body as its form does not prevent the intellect from being, as the philosophers say, separate from the body. For in the soul two things must be taken into consideration: its essence, and its power. Through its essence the soul gives being to such and such a body; by its power it performs its proper operations. Accordingly, if a psychic operation is carried out by means of a bodily organ, then the power of the soul which is the principle of that operation must be the act of that part of the body whereby such an operation is performed; thus, sight is the act of the eye. But, if the soul's operation is not effected by means of a bodily organ, then its power will not be the act of a body. And this is what is meant by saying that the intellect is *separate*; nor does separateness in this sense prevent the substance of the soul of which the intellect is a power (namely, the intellective soul) from being the act of the body, as the form which gives being to such a body.

[6]   Concerning the *fifth argument*, let it be said that because the soul is in its substance the form of the body, it does not follow that every operation of the soul must be performed by means of the body, so that every power of the soul will be the act of a bodily thing. For we have already proved that the human soul is not a form wholly embedded in matter, but among all other forms occupies a most exalted place above matter. That is why it can produce an operation without the body, as being operationally independent of the body; since neither is it existentially dependent on the body.

[7]   As for the arguments whereby Averroes endeavors to establish his theory,[3] they clearly fail to prove that an intellectual substance is not united to the body as its form.

[8]   For the terms which Aristotle applies to the possible intellect, namely, that it is *impassible, unmixed,* and *separate,* do not compel us to admit that an intellective substance is not united to the body as a form giving being. For these expressions are also true if we say that the intellective power,

3. See above, ch. 59.

which Aristotle calls the *power of insight*,[4] is not the act of an organ, as though it exercises its operation by it. This point, too, is made clear in his own demonstration, since he proves that this power is pure of all admixture, or is separate, because of the intellectual character of its operation, whereby it understands all things, and because a power is the source of a thing's operation.

[9] Clearly, that is why Aristotle's demonstration does not result in the proposition that the intellective substance is not united to the body as its form. For, if we maintain that the soul's substance is thus united in being to the body, and that the intellect is not the act of any organ, it will not follow that the intellect has a *particular nature*—I refer to the natures of sensible things—since the soul is not held to be a *harmony*,[5] nor the *form of an organ*. (As Aristotle in *De anima* II says[6] of the sense-power, it is a *certain form of an organ*.) None of these things is true of man's soul, because the intellect has no operation in common with the body.

[10] Now, by saying that the intellect is *free from all admixture*, or is *separate*, Aristotle does not mean to exclude its being a part or power of the soul which is the form of the whole body. This is clear from what he says toward the end of *De anima* I in opposing those who maintained that the soul has diverse parts of itself in diverse parts of the body: "If the whole soul holds together the whole body, it is fitting that each part of the soul should hold together a part of the body. But this seems an impossibility. For it is difficult to imagine what bodily part the intellect will hold together, or how it will do this."[7]

[11] Moreover, from the fact that the intellect is not the act of any part of the body, it clearly does not follow that its receptiveness is that of prime matter, for intellectual receptiveness and operation are altogether without a corporeal organ.

4. See above, ch. 61.
5. See above, ch. 64.
6. Aristotle, *De anima*, II, 12 (424a 29, 32).
7. Aristotle, *De anima*, I, 5 (411b 15).

[12]   Nor, again, does union with the body rob the intellect of its infinite power, since that power is not placed in a magnitude, but is rooted in the intellectual substance, as was said.

Chapter 70.

THAT ACCORDING TO THE WORDS OF ARISTOTLE THE INTELLECT MUST BE SAID TO BE UNITED TO THE BODY AS ITS FORM

[1]   Now, since Averroes seeks to conform his doctrine especially by appealing to the words and proof of Aristotle,[1] it remains for us to show that in the Philosopher's judgment we must say that the intellect, as to its substance, is united to the body as its form.

[2]   For Aristotle proves in the *Physics*[2] that in movers and things moved it is impossible to proceed to infinity. Hence, he concludes to the necessity of a first moved thing, which either is moved by an immobile mover or moves itself. And of these two he takes the second, namely, that the first movable being moves itself; for *what is through itself is always prior to that which is through another*. Then he shows that a self-mover necessarily is divided into two parts, part moving and part moved; whence it follows that the first self-mover must consist of two parts, the one moving, the other moved. Now, every thing of this kind is animate.[3] The first movable being, namely, the heaven, is therefore animate in Aristotle's opinion. So it is expressly stated in *De caelo* II[4] that the heaven is animate, and on this account we must attribute to it differences of position not only in relation to us, but also in relation to itself. Let us, then, ask with what kind of soul Aristotle thinks the heaven to be animated.

[3]   In *Metaphysics* XI[5] Aristotle proves that in the heaven's

1. See above, ch. 59, ¶2–6.
2. Aristotle, *Physics*, VIII, 5 (256a 17ff.).
3. Aristotle, *De caelo et mundo*, II, 2 (284b 33).
4. Aristotle, *De caelo et mundo*, II, 2 (285a 30).
5. Aristotle, *Metaphysics*, XI, 7 (1072a 20ff.).

movement two factors are to be considered: something that moves and is wholly unmoved, and something that moves and is also moved. Now, that which moves without being moved moves as an object of desire; nor is there any doubt that it moves as a thing desirable by that which is moved. And he shows that it moves not as an object of concupiscent desire, which is a sense desire, but of intellectual desire; and he therefore says that the first unmoved mover is an *object of desire and understanding*. Accordingly, that which is moved by this mover, namely, the heaven, desires and understands in a nobler fashion than we, as he subsequently proves. In Aristotle's view, then, the heaven is composed of an intellectual soul and a body. He indicates this when he says in *De anima* II that "in certain things there is intellect and the power of understanding, for example, in men, and in other things like man or superior to him,"[6] namely, the heaven.

[4] Now the heaven certainly does not possess a sensitive soul, according to the opinion of Aristotle; otherwise, it would have diverse organs, and this is inconsistent with the heaven's simplicity. By way of indicating this fact, Aristotle goes on to say that "among corruptible things, those that possess intellect have all the other powers,"[7] thus giving us to understand that some incorruptible things, namely, the heavenly bodies, have intellect without the other powers of the soul.

[5] It will therefore be impossible to say that the intellect makes contact with the heavenly bodies by the instrumentality of phantasms. On the contrary, it will have to be said that the intellect, by its substance, is united to the heavenly body as its form.

[6] Now, the human body is the noblest of all lower bodies, and by its equable temperament most closely resembles the heaven, which is completely devoid of contrariety; so that in Aristotle's judgment the intellectual substance is united to the human body not by any phantasms, but as its form.

[7] As for the heaven being animate, we have spoken of this

6. Aristotle, *De anima*, II, 3 (414b 19).
7. Aristotle, *De anima*, II, 3 (415a 9).

not as though asserting its accordance with the teaching of the faith, to which the whole question is entirely irrelevant. Hence, Augustine says in the *Enchiridion*: "Nor is it certain, to my mind, whether the sun, moon, and all the stars belong to the same community, namely, that of the angels; although to some they appear to be luminous bodies devoid of sense or intelligence."[8]

Chapter 71.

THAT THE SOUL IS UNITED TO THE BODY
WITHOUT INTERMEDIATION

[1]   It can be inferred from the foregoing that the soul is united to the body immediately, no medium being required to unite the soul to the body, whether it be the phantasms, as Averroes holds,[1] or the body's powers, as some say, or the corporeal spirit, as others have asserted.

[2]   For we have shown[2] that the soul is united to the body as its form. Now, a form is united to matter without any medium at all, since to be the act of such and such a body belongs to a form by its very essence, and not by anything else. That is why, as Aristotle proves in *Metaphysics* VIII,[3] there is nothing that makes a unitary thing out of matter and form except the agent which reduces the potentiality to act, for matter and form are related as potentiality and act.

[3]   Even so, it can be said that there is a medium between the soul and the body, not, however, from the point of view of being, but of movement and the order of generation. Respecting movement, we find such a medium, since the movement of the body by the soul entails a certain order among movables and movers. For the soul performs all its operations through its powers; thus, it moves the body by means of its

8. St. Augustine, *Enchiridion*, I, 58 (*PL*, 40, col. 260).
1. See above, ch. 59, ¶8.
2. See above, ch. 68 and 70.
3. Aristotle, *Metaphysics*, VIII, 6 (1045b 21).

power, and, and, again, the members by means of the [vital] spirit, and, lastly, one organ by means of another. And in the line of generation, a certain medium is found in the fact that dispositions to a form precede the form's reception in matter, but are posterior to it in being. That is why the body's dispositions, which make it the proper perfectible subject of such and such a form, may thus be called intermediaries between the soul and the body.

Chapter 72.

THAT THE WHOLE SOUL IS IN THE WHOLE BODY AND IN EACH OF ITS PARTS

[1] In the light of the same considerations it can be shown that the whole soul is present in the whole body and in its several parts.

[2] For the proper act must reside in its proper perfectible subject. Now, the soul is the act of an organic body,[1] not of one organ only. It is, therefore, in the whole body, and not merely in one part, according to its essence whereby it is the body's form.

[3] Moreover, the soul is the form of the whole body in such fashion as to be also the form of each part. For, were it the form of the whole and not of the parts, it would not be the substantial form of that body; thus, the form of a house, which is the form of the whole and not of each part, is an accidental form. That the soul is the substantial form both of the whole and of the parts, is clear from the fact that not only the whole but also the parts owe their species to it. This explains why it is that, when the soul departs, neither the whole body nor its parts remain of the same species as before; the eye or flesh of a dead thing are so called only in an equivocal sense.[2] Consequently, if the soul is the act of each part, and an act is in the thing whose act it is, it follows that the soul is by its essence in each part of the body.

1. Aristotle, *De anima*, II, 1 (412b 1).
2. Aristotle, *De partibus animalium*, I, 3 (641a 18).

[4]   And this is manifestly true of the whole soul. For since a whole is spoken of in relation to parts, the word *whole* must be taken in various senses, according to the meaning of *parts*. Now, the term *part* has a double signification; it may refer to the quantitative division of a thing (thus, two cubits is a part of three cubits), or to a division of its essence (form and matter are in this sense said to be parts of a composite). Accordingly, *whole* is used in reference both to quantity and to the perfection of the essence. Now, whole and part quantitatively so called appertain to forms only accidentally, namely, so far as the forms are divided when the quantitative subject in which they reside is divided. But whole and part as applied to the perfection of the essence are found in forms essentially. Respecting this kind of totality, which belongs to forms essentially, it is therefore clear that the whole of every form is in the whole subject and the whole of it in each part; just as *whiteness*, by its total essence, is in a whole body, so is it in each part. The case is different with a totality that is ascribed to forms accidentally, for in this sense we cannot say that the whole whiteness is in each part. If, then, there exists a form which is not divided as a result of its subject being divided—and souls of perfect animals are such forms— there will be no need for a distinction, since only one totality befits things of that kind; and it must be said unqualifiedly that the whole of this form is in each part of the body. Nor is this difficult to grasp by one who understands that the soul is not indivisible in the same way as a point, and that an incorporeal being is not united to a corporeal one in the same way as bodies are united to one another, as we explained above.[3]

[5]   Nor is it incongruous that the soul, since it is a simple form, should be the act of parts so diverse in character. For in every case the matter is adapted to the form according to the latter's requirements. Now, the higher and simpler a form is, the greater is its power; and that is why the soul, which is the highest of the lower forms, though simple in substance, has a multiplicity of powers and many operations. The soul, then, needs various organs in order to perform its operations,

3. See above, ch. 56, ¶2–7.

and of these organs the soul's various powers are said to be the proper acts; sight of the eye, hearing of the ears, etc. For this reason perfect animals have the greatest diversity of organs; plants, the least.

[6] Reflection on the fact that the soul needs various organs for the performance of its multifarious activities was the occasion for some philosophers to say that the soul is in some particular part of the body. Thus, Aristotle himself says in the *De motu animalium*[4] that the soul is in the heart, because one of the soul's powers is ascribed to that part of the body. For the motive power, of which Aristotle was treating in that work, is principally in the heart, through which the soul communicates movement and other such operations to the whole body.

Chapter 73.

THAT THERE IS NOT ONE POSSIBLE INTELLECT IN ALL MEN

[1] On the basis of what has already been said it can be clearly demonstrated that there is not one possible intellect of all present, future and past men, as Averroes imagined.[1]

[2] For it has been proved that the substance of the intellect is united to the human body as its form.[2] But one form cannot possibly exist in more than one matter, because the proper act comes to be in the proper potentiality, since they are proportioned to one another. Therefore, there is not one intellect of all men.

[3] Moreover, every mover ought to have its proper instruments; the flute-player uses one kind of instrument, the builder another. Now, the intellect is related to the body as its mover, as Aristotle shows in *De anima* III.[3] So, just as it is

4. Aristotle, *De motu animalium*, X (703a 14).
1. Averroes, *Commentarium magnum in Aristotelis de Anima*, III, t.c. 5 (p. 406, lines 575–576; p. 407, lines 595–596).
2. See above, ch. 68.
3. Aristotle, *De anima*, III, 10 (433a 14).

impossible for the builder to use a flute-player's instruments, so is it impossible for the intellect of one man to be the intellect of another.

[4]   Again, Aristotle in De anima I takes the ancients to task for discussing the soul without saying anything about its proper recipient, "as if it were possible, as in the Pythagorean fables, that any soul might put on any body."[4] It is, then, impossible for the soul of a dog to enter the body of a wolf, or for a man's soul to enter any body other than a man's. But the proportion between man's soul and man's body is the same as between this man's soul and this man's body. Therefore, the soul of this man cannot possibly enter a body other than his own. But it is this man's soul by which this man understands: man understands by his soul, as Aristotle puts it in De anima I.[5] Hence, this man and that man have not the same intellect.

[5]   Then, too, a thing owes its being and its unity to the same principle, for unity and being are consequent upon one another. But every thing has being through its form. Therefore, a thing's unity follows upon the unity of its form. Hence, there cannot possibly be one form of diverse individual things. But the form of this particular man is his intellective soul. Therefore, it is impossible that there should be one intellect for all men.

[6]   Now, if it be said that this man's sensitive soul is distinct from that man's, and that to this extent there is not one man although there is one intellect—such an argument cannot stand. For each thing's proper operation is a consequence and a manifestation of its species. Now, just as the proper operation of an animal is sensation, so the operation proper to man is understanding, as Aristotle says in Ethics I.[6] It is therefore necessary that just as this individual is an animal because it possesses the power of sensation, as Aristotle remarks in De anima II,[7] so is he a man in virtue of that by which he under-

4. Aristotle, De anima, I, 3 (407b 22).
5. Aristotle, De anima, I, 4 (408b 14).
6. Aristotle, Nicomachean Ethics, I, 7 (1098a 2, 8).
7. Aristotle, De anima, II, 2 (413b. 3).

stands. But "that whereby the soul, or man through the soul, understands," is the possible intellect, as the same philosopher says in *De anima* III.[8] This individual, then, is a man through the possible intellect. Now, suppose that this man has a distinct sensitive soul from that man's, and yet not a distinct possible intellect but one and the same possible intellect. The consequence is obviously impossible, namely, that this man and that man will be two animals, but not two men. Therefore, there is not one possible intellect of all men.

[7] Now, the Commentator Averroes replies to these arguments[9] by saying that the possible intellect comes into contact with us through its form, that is, by the intelligible species, whose single subject is the phantasm existing in us and which is distinct in distinct subjects. Thus, the possible intellect is particularized in diverse subjects, not by reason of its substance but of its form.

[8] It is clear from what has been said above[10] that this reply is worthless. For, if the possible intellect makes contact with us only in that way, man's understanding is rendered impossible, as we have shown.[11]

[9] But, even if we supposed that the contact in question sufficed to account for man's knowing, Averroes' reply still fails to solve the arguments we adduced. For in the Averroistic theory under consideration nothing pertaining to the intellect save only the phantasm will be particularized[12] in accordance with the number of men. Nor will this phantasm itself be particularized so far as it is actually understood, because in this state it exists in the possible intellect, being abstracted from material conditions by the agent intellect. But the phantasm, as understood potentially, is not above the level of being of the sensitive soul; so that this man will still remain indistinguishable from that man, except as concerns the sensitive

8. Aristotle, *De anima*, III, 4 (429a 22).
9. See above, ch. 59, ¶8.
10. *Ibid.*
11. *Ibid.*
12. Literally, numbered. See Averroes, *op. cit.*, III, t.c. 5 (p. 405, lines 513–520).

soul; and there will follow the incongruity previously noted, namely, that this and that man are not several men.

[10]   Moreover, a thing derives its species, not from that which is in potentiality, but from that which is in act. Yet the phantasm, as particularized, has only a potentially intelligible being. Therefore, it is not to the phantasm as particularized that this individual owes the specific character of intellective animal, which is the nature of man. And so we have the same result as before, namely, that the thing from which man's specific nature is derived is not particularized in diverse subjects.

[11]   Again, the source of a living thing's species is its first and not its second perfection, as is clear from what Aristotle says in *De anima* II.[13] But the phantasm is not the first but a second perfection, for the imagination is "a movement resulting from the exercise of a sense-power,"[14] as we read in the same work. Therefore, it is not to the particularized phantasm that man owes his specific nature.

[12]   Phantasms that are potentially understood are distinct. But the source of a thing's specific nature must be one, since of one thing there is one specific nature. Therefore, man does not derive his specific nature through phantasms as particularized in diverse subjects and hence as potentially understood.

[13]   The source of man's specific nature must always remain the same in the same individual as long as the individual continues to be; otherwise, the individual would not always be of one and the same species, but sometimes of this one and sometimes of that one. But phantasms do not always remain the same in one man; rather, some new ones appear, while some old ones pass away. Therefore, the human individual neither acquires his specific nature through the phantasm nor by its means is he brought into contact with the principle of his specific essence, namely, the possible intellect.

[14]   Now, if it be argued that this man does not derive his specific nature from the phantasms themselves but from the powers in which the phantasms reside, namely, imagination,

13. See above, ch. 61, ¶2.
14. Aristotle, *De anima*, III, 3 (429a 2).

memory, and cogitation—the latter, which Aristotle in *De anima* III calls the *passive intellect*,[15] being proper to man—even so the same impossibilities ensue. For, since the cogitative power is operationally limited to particular things, makes its judgments on the basis of particular intentions, and acts by means of a bodily organ, it is not above the generic level of the sensitive soul. Now, man is not a man in virtue of his sensitive soul, but an animal. Therefore, it still remains that the only thing particularized in us is that which belongs to man as an animal.

[15] Moreover, the cogitative power, since it operates by means of an organ, is not that whereby we understand, for understanding is not the operation of an organ. Now, that whereby we understand is that by which man is man, since understanding is man's proper operation, flowing from his specific nature. Consequently, it is not by the cogitative power that this individual is a man, nor is it by this power that man differs substantially from the brutes, as the Commentator imagines.

[16] Nor, again, does the cogitative power bear any ordered relationship to the possible intellect whereby man understands, except through its act of preparing the phantasms for the operation of the agent intellect which makes them actually intelligible and perfective of the possible intellect. But this activity of the cogitative power does not always remain the same in us. By its means, therefore, man cannot possibly be brought into contact with the principle of the human species, nor can he receive his specific nature from it. Clearly, the counter-argument cited above is therefore to be completely rejected.

[17] Furthermore, that whereby a thing operates or acts is a principle not only of the being of the operation flowing from it, but also of the multiplicity or unity involved. Thus, there is from the same heat but one heating or active calefaction, though there may be many things heated, many passive calefactions according to the number of different things heated simultaneously by the same heat. Now, the possible intellect

15. See above, ch. 60, ¶1.

is that by which the soul understands, as Aristotle says in De anima III.[16] Hence, if the possible intellect of this and that man is numerically one and the same, then the act of understanding will of necessity be one and the same in both men; which is obviously impossible, since a single operation cannot belong to distinct individuals. Therefore, this and that man cannot have the one possible intellect.

[18]   Now, if it be argued that the very act of understanding is multiplied in accordance with the diversity of phantasms, the contention is baseless. For, as has been said, the one action of the one agent is multiplied only according to the diverse subjects into which that action passes. But understanding, willing, and the like, are not actions that pass into external matter; on the contrary, they remain in the agent as perfections of that very agent, as Aristotle makes clear in Metaphysics IX.[17] Therefore, one act of understanding of the possible intellect cannot be multiplied by means of a diversity of phantasms.

[19]   The phantasms, moreover, are in a certain manner related to the possible intellect as the active to the passive. In this connection Aristotle remarks in De anima III that to understand is in a certain way to be passive.[18] Now, the passivity of the patient is diversified according to the diverse forms or species of the agents, not according to their numerical diversity. For the one passive subject is heated and dried at the same time by two active causes, heating and drying; two heating agents do not produce two heatings in one heatable thing, but only one heating, unless, perchance, those agents be distinct species of heat. For, since two heats specifically the same cannot be present in one subject, and movement is numbered in relation to its terminal point, if the movement take place at one time and in the same subject, there cannot be a double heating in one subject. I mean that this is the case unless another spcies of heat is involved, as in the seed there is said to be the heat of fire, of heaven, and of the soul.[19]

16. Aristotle, De anima, III, 4 (429a 10).
17. Aristotle, Metaphysics IX, 8 (1050a 34.)
18. Aristotle, De anima, III, 4 (429a 12).
19. Cf. St. Thomas Aquinas, Summa Theologiae, I, 118, 1, ad 3.

Hence, the possible intellect's act of understanding is not multiplied in accordance with the diversity of phantasms, except
as concerns its understanding of diverse species (so we may
say that its act of understanding is different in the case of
understanding a man and understanding a horse); on the
contrary, one act of understanding these things befits all men
at the same time. Therefore, it will still follow that the act of
understanding is numerically the same in this and that man.

[20] Again, the possible intellect understands man, not as
this man, but simply as *man*, according to man's specific nature. Now, this nature of man's is one, regardless of the multiplication of phantasms, whether in one man or in several,
according to the diverse human individuals to which phantasms properly speaking belong. Consequently, the multiplication of phantasms cannot cause the multiplication of the
possible intellect's act of understanding with respect to a
single species. We are, then, left with the same result as before, namely, numerically one action of many different men.

[21] Also, the possible intellect is the proper subject of the
habit of science, because its act is scientific consideration.
But, if an accident is one, it is multiplied only in reference to
its subject; so that, if there is one possible intellect of all men,
then specifically the same habit of science—the habit of gram-
mar, for instance—will of necessity be numerically the same
in all men; which is inconceivable. Therefore, the possible intellect is not one in all.

[22] But to this they [the Averroists] reply that the subject
of the habit of science is not the possible intellect but the
passive intellect and the cogitative power.[20]

[23] This, however, is impossible. For, as Aristotle proves in
Ethics II, "from like acts, like habits are formed, which in turn
give rise to like acts."[21] Now, the habit of science is formed
in us by acts of the possible intellect, and we are capable of
performing those acts according to the habit of science.
Therefore, the habit of science is in the possible, and not the
passive, intellect.

20. See above, ch. 60, ¶1.
21. Aristotle, *Nichomachean Ethics*, II (1103b 8ff.).

[24]   It is with respect to the conclusions of demonstrations, moreover, that there is science. For a demonstration is "a syllogism productive of scientific knowledge," as Aristotle says in *Posterior Analytics* I.[22] Now, the conclusions of demonstrations are universals, and so, too, are their principles. Therefore, science will reside in that power which is cognizant of universals. But the passive intellect has no knowledge of universals, but only of particular intentions. Hence, it is not the subject of the habit of science.

[25]   Then, too, against this [Averroistic theory about the passive intellect] are a number of arguments adduced above, when we were treating of the possible intellect's union with man.[23]

[26]   Seemingly, the fallacy of locating the habit of science in the passive intellect resulted from the observation that men are more or less apt for scientific studies according to the various dispositions of the cogitative and imaginative powers.

[27]   This aptitude, however, depends on these powers as on remote dispositions, as it likewise depends on a fine sense of touch and on bodily temperament. In this connection, Aristotle remarks in *De anima* II[24] that men possessed of a highly developed sense of touch and of soft flesh are "mentally well endowed." Now, the habit of science gives rise to an aptitude for reflection, being the proximate principle of that action; for the habit of science must perfect the power whereby we understand, so that it acts easily at will, even as the other habits perfect the powers in which they inhere.

[28]   Moreover, the dispositions of the cogitative and imaginative powers are relative to the object, namely, the phantasm, which, because of the well-developed character of these powers, is prepared in such a way as to facilitate its being made actually intelligible by the agent intellect. Now, dispositions relative to objects are not habits, but dispositions relative to powers are habits. Thus, the habit of fortitude is not a disposition whereby frightening things become endurable, but a

22. Aristotle, *Posterior Analytics*, I, 2 (71b 17).
23. See above, ch. 60.
24. Aristotle, *De anima*, II, 9 (421a 23, 26).

disposition by which the irascible part of the soul is disposed to endure such things. It is therefore evident that the habit of science is not in the passive intellect, as the Commentator says, but rather in the possible intellect.

[29] And if there is one possible intellect for all men, it must be granted that if (as the Averroists assert) men have always existed, then the possible intellect has always existed, and much more the agent intellect, because "the agent is superior to the patient," as Aristotle says.[25] Now, if both the agent and the recipient are eternal, the things received must be eternal. It would then follow that the intelligible species existed from all eternity in the possible intellect; so, in that case, the latter receives no intelligible species anew. But it is only as the subjects from which intelligible species may be derived that sense and imagination have any necessary role to play in the understanding of things. Therefore, neither sense nor imagination will be necessary for understanding. And thus we shall come back to Plato's theory that we do not acquire knowledge through the senses, but are awakened by them to the remembrance of things we knew before.[26]

[30] To this Averroes replies[27] that the intelligible species have a twofold subject: the possible intellect, wherein they have eternal being; the phantasm, as ground of their newness. So too, the subject of the visible species is twofold: the thing outside the soul, and the power of sight.

[31] But this reply cannot stand, because the action and perfection of an eternal thing could not possibly depend on something temporal. And phantasms are temporal, new ones springing up in us every day from the senses. It follows that the intelligible species whereby the possible intellect is actualized and operates cannot depend on the phantasms, as the visible species depends on things outside the soul.

[32] Nothing receives what it already has, since, as Aristotle remarks,[28] the recipient must be devoid of the thing received.

25. Aristotle, *De anima*, III, 5 (430a 18).
26. Plato, *Meno*, passim.
27. See above, ch. 59 and beginning of this chapter.
28. Aristotle, *De anima*, III, 4 (429a 22).

Now, prior to my sensation or yours, intelligible species were present in the possible intellect, for our predecessors would have had no understanding of anything unless the possible intellect had been actualized by the intelligible species. Nor can it be said that these species already received into the possible intellect have ceased to exist, for the possible intellect not only receives but also preserves what it receives; that is why in *De anima* III[29] it is called *the place of species*. Hence, species are not received from our phantasms into the possible intellect. Therefore, it would be useless for our phantasms to be made actually intelligible by the agent intellect.

[33]   Likewise, "The presence in the recipient of the thing received accords with the recipient's manner of being.[30] But the intellect, in itself, transcends movement. Therefore, what is received into it is received in a fixed and immovable manner.

[34]   Since the intellect is a higher power than the sense, its unity must be greater. This explains the observed fact of one intellect exercising judgment upon diverse kinds of sensible things belonging to diverse sensitive powers. And from this we can gather that the operations belonging to the various sensitive powers are united in the one intellect. Now, some of the sensitive powers only receive—the senses, for instance; while some retain, as imagination and memory, which therefore are called *store-houses*.[31] The possible intellect, then, must both receive and retain what it has received.

[35]   It is idle, moreover, to say that in the realm of natural things what is acquired as the result of movement has no abiding reality but immediately ceases to be. The opinion of those who say that all things are always in motion is rejected in the light of the fact that motion necessarily terminates in repose. Much less, therefore, can it be said that what is received into the possible intellect is not preserved.

[36]   Again, if from the phantasms in us the possible intellect comes into possession of no intelligible species because it has already received from the phantasms of our predecessors,

29. Aristotle, *De anima*, III, 4 (429a 27).
30. Cf. *Liber de causis*, XII (p. 171).
31. See below, ch. 74, ¶2.

then for the same reason it receives from none of the phantasms of those whom others preceded. But, if the world is eternal, as the Averroists say, there has never existed a person without predecessors. It follows that the possible intellect never receives any species from phantasms. There was then no point in Aristotle's having posited the agent intellect in order to make the phantasms actually intelligible.[32]

[37] The apparent consequence of all this, furthermore, is that the possible intellect has no need of phantasms in order to understand. Now, it is the possible intellect by which we understand. It will, therefore, follow that we need not have senses and phantasms in order to understand. And this is manifestly false, as well as being contrary to the judgment of Aristotle.[33]

[38] Now, it may be said that for the same reason we would not need a phantasm in order to consider the things whose species are retained in the possible intellect, even if there are many possible intellects in many different persons. Not only is this objection contrary to Aristotle, who says that "the soul in no wise understands without a phantasm,"[34] it is also clearly irrelevant. For the possible intellect, like every substance, operates in a manner consonant with its nature. Now, it is by its nature the form of the body. Hence, it does indeed understand immaterial things, but it sees them in something material. An indication of this is that in teaching universal notions particular examples are employed, so that the universals may be viewed in them. Hence, the possible intellect, before possessing the intelligible species, is related in one way to the phantasms which it needs, and in another way after receiving that species; before, it needs that phantasm in order to receive from it the intelligible species, and thus the phantasm stands in relation to the possible intellect as the object moving the latter; but, after the species has been received into the possible intellect, the latter needs the phantasm as the instrument or foundation of its species, so that the possible intellect is then related to the phantasm as efficient cause.

32. See below, ch. 78, ¶2, 7.
33. Aristotle, *De anima*, III, 8 (432a 6).
34. Aristotle, *De anima*, III, 7 (431a 17).

For by the intellect's command there is formed in the imagination a phantasm corresponding to such and such an intelligible
species, the latter being mirrored in this phantasm as an ex-
emplar in the thing exemplified or in the image. Consequently,
were the possible intellect always in possession of the species,
it would never stand in relationship to the phantasms as recipient to object moving it.

[39]   Then, too, the possible intellect, according to Aristotle,
is that "whereby the soul and man understand."[35] But, if the
possible intellect is one in all men and is eternal, then all the
intelligible species of the things that are or have been known
by any men whatever must already be received in it. Therefore, each of us, since we understand by the possible intellect,
and, in fact, our act of understanding is itself the possible intellect's act of understanding, will understand all that is or
has been understood by anyone whatever; which is plainly
false.

[40]   Now, to this the Commentator replies[36] that we do not
understand by the possible intellect except so far as it is in contact with us through our phantasms. And since phantasms
are not the same in all, nor disposed in the same manner,
neither is whatever one person understands understood by another. And this reply seems to be consistent with things previously said. For, even if the possible intellect is not one, we
do not understand the things whose species are in the possible
intellect without the presence of phantasms disposed for this
purpose.

[41]   But, that this reply cannot wholly avoid the difficulty
is made clear as follows. When the possible intellect has been
actualized by the reception of the intelligible species, *it can
act of itself*, as Aristotle says in *De anima* III.[37] This accounts
for the experienced fact that when we have once acquired
knowledge of a thing, it is in our power to consider it again
at will. And since we are able to form phantasms adapted to
the thinking that we wish to do, they are no hindrance to us

35. Aristotle, *De anima*, III, 4 (429a 11).
36. Averroes, *op. cit.*, III, t.c. 5 (p. 404, lines 501–520).
37. Aristotle, *De anima*, III, 4 (429b 7).

[in our reconsideration of things], unless, perhaps, there be an obstacle on the part of the organ to which the phantasm belongs, as in madmen and those afflicted with lethargy, who cannot freely exercise their imagination and memory. For this reason Aristotle says in *Physics* VIII[38] that one already possessed of the habit of science, though he be considering potentially, needs no mover to bring him from potentiality to act, except a remover of obstacles, but is himself able to exercise his knowledge at will. If, however, the intelligible species of all sciences are present in the possible intellect— which the hypothesis of its unicity and eternity necessarily implies—then that intellect will require phantasms, just as one already in possession of a science needs them in order to think in terms of that science; this the intellect cannot do without phantasms. Therefore, since every man understands by the possible intellect as a result of its being actualized by the intelligible species, every man will be able to apply his mind at will to the things known in every science. This is manifestly false, since in that case no one would need a teacher in order to acquire a science. Therefore, the possible intellect is not one and eternal.

Chapter 74.

CONCERNING THE THEORY OF AVICENNA, WHO SAID THAT INTELLIGIBLE FORMS ARE NOT PRESERVED IN THE POSSIBLE INTELLECT

[1] What Avicenna has to say, however, seems to conflict with the arguments given above, for he asserts in his *De anima*[1] that the intelligible species do not remain in the possible intellect except when they are being actually understood.

[2] Avicenna endeavors to prove this by arguing that, as long as the apprehended forms remain in the apprehending power, they are actually apprehended, since [as Aristotle says] "sense

38. Aristotle, *Physics*, VIII, 4 (255b 2).
1. Avicenna, *De anima*, V, 6 (foll. 26rb-26va).

is actualized by being identified with the thing actually sensed" and, similarly, "the intellect in act is one with the thing actually understood."[2] So, it seems that whenever sense or intellect becomes one with the thing sensed or understood, as the result of possessing its form, there is actual apprehension through sense or intellect. And Avicenna says that the powers wherein are preserved the forms not actually apprehended are not powers of apprehension, but store-houses thereof; for example, the imagination, which is the store-house of sense-apprehended forms, and the memory, which, he says, is the store-house of intentions apprehended without the senses—the sheep's apprehension of the wolf as its enemy, for instance. Now, it happens that these powers preserve forms not actually apprehended, so far as they possess bodily organs wherein forms are received in a manner closely resembling apprehension. Accordingly, the apprehensive power, by turning to these store-houses, apprehends actually. Now, the possible intellect certainly is an apprehensive power, and certainly it has no corporeal organ. Hence, Avicenna concludes that it is impossible for the intelligible species to be preserved in the possible intellect, except while it understands actually. There are, then, the following alternatives: either the intelligible species themselves must be preserved in some bodily organ or in some power having such an organ; or the intelligible forms are of necessity self-existent, our possible intellect being to them as a mirror to the things seen in it; or the intelligible species have to be infused anew into the possible intellect whenever it understands actually. Now, the first of these three is impossible, because forms existing in powers which employ bodily organs are only potentially intelligible; and the second is the opinion of Plato, which Aristotle refutes in the Metaphysics.[3] So, Avicenna takes the third, namely, that whenever we understand actually, the agent intellect, which he says is a separate substance, infuses intelligible species into our possible intellect.

[3]   Now, if anyone attacks Avicenna by arguing that on his theory there is no difference between a man when he first

2. Aristotle, De anima, III, 2 (425b 27); III, 4 (430a 3).
3. Aristotle, Metaphysics, I, 9 (990b 1ff.).

learns and when afterwards he wishes to consider actually what he had learned before, Avicenna replies that learning simply consists "in acquiring the perfect aptitude for uniting oneself with the agent intellect so as to receive the intelligible form from it"; so that before learning there exists in man the bare potentiality for such reception, and learning is, as it were, the *potentiality adapted*.

[4] In apparent harmony with this position is Aristotle's proof, given in the *De memoria*[4] that the memory is in the sensitive and not the intellective part of the soul; whence it seems to follow that the retention of the intelligible species is not the function of the intellective part.

[5] But, if this position is examined carefully, it will be seen that in principle it differs little or not at all from that of Plato. For Plato maintained that intelligible forms are separate substances, from which knowledge poured into our souls, while Avicenna asserts that knowledge flows into our souls from one separate substance, the agent intellect. Now, so far as the manner of acquiring knowledge is concerned, it makes no difference whether it be caused by one or several separate substances; in either case, it follows that our knowledge is not caused by sensible things—a consequence clearly contradicted by the fact that a person who lacks one sense lacks, also, the knowledge of those sensible things which are known through that sense.

[6] And a mere innovation is the statement[5] that by casting its gaze upon the singulars present in the imagination the possible intellect is illuminated by the light of the agent intellect so as to know the universal, and that the actions of the lower powers—imaginative, memorative, cogitative—make the soul a fit subject for receiving the influx of the agent intellect. For it is a matter of observation that our soul is the more disposed to receive from separate substances, the further removed it is from corporeal and sensible things; by withdrawing from the lower we approach the higher. The notion that the soul is disposed to receive the influx of a separate intelligence

4. Aristotle, *De memoria et reminiscentia*, I (450a 12).
5. Avicenna, *De anima*, V, 5 (fol. 25rb).

by reflecting upon corporeal phantasms is, therefore, without verisimilitude.

[7]   Now, Plato followed the root-principle of his position more consistently, because he held that sensible things do not dispose the soul to receive the influx of separate forms, but merely awaken the intellect to consider the things the knowledge of which it had received from an external cause. For he asserted that knowledge of all things knowable was caused in our souls from the beginning by separate forms. Learning he therefore declared to be a kind of remembering. And this is a necessary consequence of his position, for, since separate substances are immobile and ever the same, the knowledge of things always shines forth from them into our soul, which is the fit subject of that knowledge.

[8]   Moreover, the presence in the recipient of the thing received accords with the recipient's manner of being. Now, the possible intellect exists in a more stable manner than corporeal matter. Therefore, since forms flowing into corporeal matter from the agent intellect are according to Avicenna preserved in that matter, much more are they preserved in the possible intellect.

[9]   Again, intellective cognition is more perfect than sensitive; so that, if there is something to preserve things apprehended by the senses, this will be all the more true of things apprehended by the intellect.

[10]   Likewise, we see that distinct things, which in a lower order of powers belong to distinct powers, in a higher order belong to one. Thus, the common sense apprehends the things sensed by all the proper senses. It follows that apprehension and preservation, which in the sensitive part of the soul are functions of distinct powers, must be united in the highest power, namely, the intellect.

[11]   Then, too, according to Avicenna,[6] the agent intellect causes all sciences by way of influx. Hence, if to learn is simply to be made apt for union with that intellect, then he who learns one science does not learn that one more than another; which is obviously false.

6. Avicenna, De anima, V, 6 (fol. 26ra).

[12] This doctrine of Avicenna's is also clearly contrary to Aristotle, who says in *De anima* III[7] that the possible intellect is the *place of species*, a phrase having the same meaning as Avicenna's *store-house of intelligible species*.

[13] Moreover, Aristotle goes on to say[8] that when the possible intellect acquires knowledge, it is *capable of acting on its own initiative*, although it is not actually understanding. Therefore, it has no need of the influx of any higher agent.

[14] He also says in *Physics* VIII[9] that, before learning, a man is in a state of essential potentiality with respect to knowledge and therefore needs a mover to bring him to a state of actual knowledge, but, when he has already learned, he needs no mover essentially so called. Therefore, the influx of the agent intellect is unnecessary for him.

[15] And in *De anima* III Aristotle says that "phantasms are to the possible intellect what sensibles are to the senses."[10] So, it is clear that intelligible species in the possible intellect are derived from the phantasms, not from a separate substance.

[16] The arguments seemingly contrary to this conclusion are not difficult to solve. For the possible intellect is completely actualized with respect to the intelligible species when actually exercising its power; when it is not so doing, it is not in their regard completely actualized, but is in a state between potentiality and act. And Aristotle remarks that, when this part, namely, the possible intellect, "has become each of its objects, it is said to be actually possessed of knowledge; and this happens when it is capable of acting on its own initiative, yet, even so, its condition is one of potentiality, in a certain sense, but not in the same sense as before learning or discovering."[11]

[17] Now, the memory is located in the sensitive part of the soul, because its scope is limited to things subject to deter-

7. Aristotle, *De anima*, III, 4 (429a 27).
8. Aristotle, *De anima*, III, 4 (429b 8).
9. Aristotle, *Physics*, VIII, 4 (255a 33ff.).
10. Aristotle, *De anima*, III, 7, 8 (431a 14; 432 a 8).
11. Aristotle, *De anima*, III, 4 (429b 5).

minate times; there is memory only of what is past. Therefore, since memory does not abstract from singular conditions, it does not belong to the intellective part of the soul, which is cognizant of universals. This, however, does not stand in the way of the possible intellect's retentiveness of intelligibles, which abstract from all particular conditions.

Chapter 75.

SOLUTION OF THE SEEMINGLY DEMONSTRA-
TIVE ARGUMENTS FOR THE UNITY OF THE
POSSIBLE INTELLECT·

[1]   We must now show the inefficacy of the arguments put forward with the object of proving the unity of the possible intellect.[1]

[2]   For it seems that every form which is one specifically and many in number is individuated by matter; because things one in species and many in number agree in form and differ in matter. Therefore, if the possible intellect is multiplied numerically in different men, while being specifically one, then it must be individuated in this and that man by matter. But this individuation is not brought about by matter which is a part of the intellect itself, since in that case the intellect's receptivity would be of the same genus as that of prime matter, and it would receive individual forms; which is contrary to the nature of intellect. It remains that the intellect is individuated by that matter which is the human body and of which the intellect is held to be the form. But every form individuated by matter of which that form is the act is a material form. For the being of a thing must stem from that to which it owes its individuation; since just as common principles belong to the essence of the species, so individuating principles belong to the essence of this individual thing. It therefore follows that the possible intellect is a material form, and, consequently, that it neither receives anything nor oper-

1. See below, ¶2-4. Cf. Averroes, *Commentarium magnum in Aristotelis de Anima*, III, t.c. 5 (e.g., pp. 401–405, lines 424–527).

ates without a bodily organ. And this, too, is contrary to the nature of the possible intellect. Therefore, the possible intellect is not multiplied in different men, but is one for them all.

[3]   Also, if the possible intellect in this and that man were distinct, then the species understood would be numerically distinct in this and that man, though one in species. For the possible intellect is the proper subject of species actually understood, so that, with a multiplication of possible intellects, the intelligible species must be multiplied numerically in those diverse intellects. Now, species or forms which are specifically the same and numerically diverse are individual forms. And these cannot be intelligible forms, because intelligibles are universal, not particular. Therefore, the possible intellect cannot be multiplied in diverse human individuals; it must be one in all.

[4]   And again, the master imparts the knowledge that he possesses to his disciple. Hence, either he conveys numerically the same knowledge or a knowledge numerically, but not specifically, diverse. The latter seems impossible, because in that case the master would cause his own knowledge to exist in his disciple, even as he causes his own form to exist in something else by begetting one specifically like to himself; and this seems to apply to material agents. It follows that the master causes numerically the same knowledge to exist in the disciple. But, unless there were one possible intellect for both persons, this would be impossible. So, the existence of one possible intellect for all men seems to be a necessary conclusion.

[5]   Nevertheless, just as this doctrine is devoid of truth, as we have shown,[2] so the arguments put forward to confirm it are easy of solution.

[6]   As to the *first argument* adduced above, we admit that the possible intellect is specifically one in different men and yet is numerically many; though this is *not* to be taken so as to emphasize the fact that man's parts are not ascribed to his generic or specific essence as such, but only as principles of the whole man. Nor does it follow that the possible intellect is a material form dependent on the body for its being.

2. See above, ch. 73.

For just as it belongs to the human soul by its specific nature to be united to a particular species of body, so this particular soul differs only numerically from that one as the result of having a relationship to a numerically different body. In this way are human souls individuated in relation to bodies, and not as though their individuation were caused by bodies; and so the possible intellect, which is a power of the soul, is individuated likewise.

[7] *Averroes' second argument* fails because it does not distinguish between that by which one understands and that which is understood. The species received into the possible intellect is not that which is understood; for, since all arts and sciences have to do with things understood, it would follow that all sciences are about species existing in the possible intellect. And this is patently false, because no science, except logic and metaphysics, is concerned with such things. And yet, in all the sciences, whatever is known is known through those species. Consequently, in the act of understanding, the intelligible species received into the possible intellect functions as the thing by which one understands, and not as that which is understood, even as the species of color in the eye is not that which is seen, but that by which we see. And that which is understood is the very intelligible essence of things existing outside the soul, just as things outside the soul are seen by corporeal sight. For arts and sciences were discovered for the purpose of knowing things as existing in their own natures.

[8] Nor need we follow Plato in holding that, because science is about universals, universals are self-subsisting entities outside the soul. For, although the truth of knowledge requires the correspondence of cognition to thing, this does not mean that these two must have the same mode of being. For things united in reality are sometimes known separately; in a thing that is at once white and sweet, sight knows only the whiteness, taste only the sweetness. So, too, the intellect understands, apart from sensible matter, a line existing in sensible matter, although it can also understand it with sensible matter. Now, this diversity comes about as a result of the diversity of intelligible species received into the intellect, the

species being sometimes a likeness of quantity alone, and sometimes a likeness of a quantitative sensible substance. Similarly, although the generic nature and the specific nature never exist except in individual things, the intellect nevertheless understands those natures without understanding the individuating principles; and to do this is to understand universals. Thus, there is no incompatibility between the fact that universals do not subsist outside the soul, and that in understanding universals the intellect understands things that do exist outside the soul. The intellect's understanding of the generic or specific nature apart from the individuating principles is due to the condition of the intelligible species received into it, for the species is immaterialized by the agent intellect through being abstracted from matter and material conditions whereby a particular thing is individuated. Consequently, the sensitive powers are unable to know universals; they cannot receive an immaterial form, since whatever is received by them is always received in a corporeal organ.

[9] Hence, it does not follow that the intelligible species are numerically one in this or that knower; otherwise, this and that person's act of understanding would be numerically one, since operation follows upon the form which is the principle of the species. But in order that there be one thing understood, there must be a likeness of one and the same thing; and this is possible if the intelligible species are numerically distinct. For there is no reason why there should not be several different images of one thing; it is thus that one man is seen by several. Hence, the existence of several intelligible species in several persons is not incompatible with the intellect's knowledge of the universal.

[10] Nor does it then follow, if intelligible species are several in number and specifically the same, that they are not actually intelligible but only potentially intelligible, like other individual things. For to be individual is not incompatible with being actually intelligible, since, on the supposition that the possible and agent intellects are separate substances not united to the body but self-subsistent, it must be said that they are themselves individual things; and yet they are intel-

ligible. No; it is materiality that is incompatible with intelligibility, a sign of this being the fact that for the forms of material things to be made actually intelligible they must be abstracted from matter. Hence, things whose individuation is effected by particular signate matter are not actually intelligible, but nothing prevents things whose individuation is not due to matter from being actually intelligible. Now, intelligible species, in common with all other forms, are individuated by their subject, which in this case is the possible intellect. That is why the possible intellect, being immaterial, does not deprive of actual intelligibility the species which it individuates.

[11]   Moreover, just as individuals in the realm of sensible things are not actually intelligible if there be many of them in one species—for example, horses or men—so neither are sensible individuals which are unique in their species, as this particular sun and this particular moon. But species are individuated in the same way by the possible intellect, whether there be several such intellects or only one; yet they are not multiplied in the same way in the one species. Hence, so far as the actual intelligibility of the species received into the possible intellect is concerned, it makes no difference whether there be one or several possible intellects in all men.

[12]   Then, too, the possible intellect, according to Averroes, is the last in the order of intelligible substances, which in his view are several. Nor can it be denied that some of the higher substances are cognizant of things which the possible intellect knows; for in the movers of the spheres are present the forms of the things caused by the movement of a sphere, as he himself says. Hence, even if there is but one possible intellect, it will still follow that the intelligible forms are multiplied in different intellects.

[13]   Now, while we have said that the intelligible species received into the possible intellect is not that which is understood but that whereby one understands, this does not prevent the intellect, by a certain reflexion, from understanding itself, and its act of understanding, and the species whereby it understands. Indeed, it understands its own act of under-

standing in two ways: particularly, for it understands that it presently understands; universally, so far as it reasons about the nature of its act. So, likewise, the intellect understands both itself and the intelligible species in two ways: by perceiving its own being and its possession of an intelligible species—and this is a kind of particular knowing; by considering its own nature and that of the intelligible species, which is a universal knowing. It is in this latter mode that the intellect and the intelligible are treated in the sciences.

[14] As to the *third argument*, its solution emerges from what has already been said. For Averroes' statement that knowledge in the disciple and in the master is numerically one is partly true and partly false. It is numerically one as concerns the thing known; it is not numerically one either in respect of the intelligible species whereby the thing is known, or of the habit of knowledge itself. Nor does this entail the consequence that the master causes knowledge in the disciple in the same way as fire generates fire. For things are not in the same fashion generated by nature as by art; fire generates fire naturally, by making actual the form of fire potentially present in the matter, whereas the master causes knowledge in his disciple by way of art, since this is the aim of the art of demonstration, which Aristotle teaches in the *Posterior Analytics*; for demonstration is "a syllogism productive of scientific knowledge," as he says in that work.[3]

[15] It must be borne in mind, however, that according to Aristotle's teaching in *Metaphysics* VII[4] there are some arts wherein the matter is not an active principle productive of the art's effect. The art of building is a case in point, since in wood and stone there is no active force tending to the construction of a house, but only a passive aptitude. On the other hand, there exists an art whose matter is an active principle tending to produce the effect of that art. Such is the art of medicine, for in the sick body there is an active principle conducive to health. Thus, the effect of an art of the first kind is never produced by nature, but is always the result of

3. Aristotle, *Posterior Analytics*, I, 2 (71b 17).
4. Aristotle, *Metaphysics*, VII, 9 (1034a 13).

the art; every house is an artifact. But the effect of an art of the second kind is the result both of art and of nature without art, for many are healed by the action of nature without the art of medicine. Now, in those things that can be done both by art and by nature, *art imitates nature*;[5] if the cause of a person's illness is something cold, nature cures him by heating; and that is why the physician, if his services are needed in order to cure the patient, does so by applying heat. Now, the art of teaching resembles this art. For in the person taught there is an active principle conducive to knowledge, namely, the intellect, and there are also those things that are naturally understood, namely, first principles. Knowledge, then, is acquired in two ways: by discovery without teaching, and by teaching. So, the teacher begins to teach in the same way as the discoverer begins to discover, that is, by offering to the disciple's consideration principles known by him, since *all learning results from pre-existent knowledge*;[6] by drawing conclusions from those principles; and by proposing sensible examples, from which the phantasms necessary for the disciple's understanding are formed in the soul. And since the outward action of the teacher would have no effect without the inward principle of knowledge, whose presence in us we owe to God, the theologians remark that *man teaches by outward ministration, but God by inward operation*. So, too, is the physician said to minister to nature in the practice of his art of healing. Thus, knowledge is caused in the disciple by his master, not by way of natural action, but of art, as was said.

[16]   Furthermore, since the Commentator locates the habits of science in the passive intellect as their subject,[7] the unicity of the possible intellect does nothing whatever to effect a numerical unity of knowledge in disciple and master. For the passive intellect certainly is not the same in different individuals, since it is a material power. That is why this argument is wide of the mark even in terms of Averroes' own position.

5. Aristotle, *Physics*, II, 2 (194a 23).
6. Aristotle, *Posterior Analytics*, I, 1 (71a 1).
7. See above, ch. 60, ¶1.

Chapter 76.

THAT THE AGENT INTELLECT IS NOT A
SEPARATE SUBSTANCE, BUT PART
OF THE SOUL

[1] From the foregoing it can be inferred that neither is there one agent intellect in all,[1] as maintained by Alexander[2] and by Avicenna,[3] who do not hold there is one possible intellect for all.

[2] For, since agent and recipient are proportionate to one another, to every passive principle there must correspond a proper active one. Now, the possible intellect is compared to the agent intellect as its proper patient or recipient, because the agent intellect is related to it as *art to its matter;*[4] so that if the possible intellect is part of the human soul and is multiplied according to the number of individuals, as was shown,[5] then the agent intellect also will be part of the soul and multiplied in like manner, and not one for all.

[3] Again, the purpose for which the agent intellect renders the species actually intelligible is not that they may serve as means of understanding on its part, especially as a separate substance, because the agent intellect is not in a state of potentiality; this purpose, on the contrary, is that the possible intellect may understand by those species which the agent intellect has made actually intelligible. Thus, the function of the agent intellect in regard to the intelligible species is simply to render them fit vehicles for the possible intellect's understanding. Now, the agent intellect makes them to be

1. Cf. Averroes, *Commentarium magnum in Aristotelis de Anima,* III, t.c. 20, *passim.*
2. Alexander of Aphrodisias, *De intellectu et intellecto* (pp. 76–77, 82).
3. Avicenna, *De anima,* V, 5, 6 (foll. 25rb–26rb); *Metaphysics,* IX, 3 (foll. 104rb).
4. Aristotle, *De anima,* III, 5 (430a 13).
5. See above, ch. 73, ¶2–6.

such as it is itself; for *every agent produces its like*.[6] Therefore, the agent intellect is proportionate to the possible intellect; and since the possible intellect is a part of the soul, the agent intellect will not be a separate substance.

[4] Just as prime matter is perfected by natural forms, which are outside the soul, so the possible intellect is perfected by forms actually understood. Natural forms, however, are received into prime matter, not by the action of some separate substance alone, but by the action of a form of the same kind, namely, a form existing in matter; thus, this particular flesh is begotten through a form in this flesh and these bones, as Aristotle proves in *Metaphysics* vii.[7] If the possible intellect is a part of the soul and not a separate substance, as we have shown,[8] then the agent intellect, by whose action the intelligible species are made present in the possible intellect, will not be a separate substance but an active power of the soul.

[5] Also, Plato held that the cause of our knowledge is Ideas, which he said were separate substances: a theory disproved by Aristotle in *Metaphysics* i.[9] Now, it is certain that our knowledge depends on the agent intellect as its first principle. So, if the agent intellect were a separate substance, there would be little or no difference between this opinion and the Platonic theory referred to, which the Philosopher has refuted.

[6] Then, too, if the agent intellect is a separate substance, its action must be continuous and not interrupted; or at least it is not continued or interrupted at our will—this in any case must be said. Now, the function of the agent intellect is to make phantasms actually intelligible. Therefore, either it will do this always or not always. If not always, this, however, will not be by our choosing. Yet we understand actually when the phantasms are made actually intelligible. Hence it follows that either we always understand or that it is not in our power to understand actually.

6. Aristotle, *De generatione et corruptione*, I, 7 (324a 11).
7. Aristotle, *Metaphysics*, VII, 8 (1033b 5ff.).
8. See above, ch. 59.
9 Aristotle, *Metaphysics*, I, 9 (990b 1ff.).

[7] A separate substance, furthermore, has one and the same relationship to all the phantasms present in any men whatever, just as the sun stands in the same relation to all colors. Persons possessed of knowledge perceive sensible things, but so also do the ignorant. Hence, the same phantasms are in both, and these phantasms will in like manner be made actually intelligible by the agent intellect. Therefore, both will understand in similar fashion.

[8] Even so, it can be said that the agent intellect is, in itself, always acting, but that the phantasms are not always made actually intelligible, but only when they are disposed to this end. Now, they are so disposed by the act of the cogitative power, the use of which is in our power. Hence, to understand actually is in our power. And this is the reason why not all men understand the things whose phantasms they have, since not all are possessed of the requisite act of the cogitative power, but only those who are instructed and habituated.

[9] This reply, however, seems not entirely adequate. For the disposition to understand which the cogitative power causes must either be a disposition of the possible intellect to receive intelligible forms flowing from the agent intellect, as Avicenna says, or a disposition of the phantasms to be made actually intelligible, as Averroes and Alexander declare. But the former seems incongruous, because the possible intellect by its very nature is in potentiality with respect to species actually intelligible, so that it bears the same relationship to them as a transparent medium to light or to color-species. Now, a thing equipped by nature to receive a certain form needs no further disposition to that form, unless there happen to be contrary dispositions in it, as the matter of water is disposed to the form of air by the removal of cold and density. But there is nothing contrary in the possible intellect that could prevent it from receiving any intelligible species whatever; for the intelligible species even of contraries are not contrary in the intellect, as Aristotle proves in *Metaphysics* VII,[10] since one is the reason of the knowledge of the other. And any falsity occurring in the intellect's affirmative or negative judgments is due, not to the presence in the possible intel-

10. Aristotle, *Metaphysics*, VII, 7 (1032b 2).

lect of certain things understood, but to its lack of certain things. In and of itself, therefore, the possible intellect needs no preparation in order to receive the intelligible species issuing from the agent intellect.

[10]   Moreover, colors made actually visible by light unfailingly impress their likeness upon the transparent body and, consequently, upon the power of sight. Therefore, if the very phantasms which the agent intellect has illumined did not impress their likeness on the possible intellect, but only disposed it to receive them, the phantasms would not bear the same relationship to the possible intellect as colors to the faculty of sight, as Aristotle maintains.[11]

[11]   According to this [Avicennian theory], the phantasms would not be essentially necessary for our understanding, nor, then, would the senses; but necessary only accidentally, as things so to speak inciting and preparing the possible intellect to accomplish its receptive function. This is part of the Platonic doctrine, and is contrary to the order in which art and science come to birth in the mind, as Aristotle explains it in *Metaphysics* I,[12] and in the *Posterior Analytics*, where he says that "memory results from sensation; one experience from many memories; from many experiences the universal apprehension which is the beginning of science and art."[13] This position of Avicenna's, however, is in accord with what its author says about the generation of natural things.[14] For he asserts that the actions of all lower agents have merely the effect of preparing matter to receive the forms which flow into their matters from the separate agent intellect. So, too, for the same reason, he holds that the phantasms prepare the possible intellect, and that the intelligible forms emanate from a separate substance.

[12]   Similarly, on the hypothesis that the agent intellect is a separate substance it would seem incongruous that the phantasms should be prepared by the cogitative power so as to be

11. Aristotle, *De anima*, III, 5 (430a 15).
12. Aristotle, *Metaphysics*, I, 1 (980b ff.).
13. Aristotle, *Posterior Analytics*, II, 15 (100a 3).
14. Avicenna, *Metaphysics*, IX, 5 (foll. 105rb–vb).

actually intelligible and move the possible intellect. For, seemingly, this agrees with the position of those who say that the lower agents are merely dispositive causes with respect to the ultimate perfection [of a thing], the source of which is a separate agent: a position contrary to the judgment expressed by Aristotle in *Metaphysics* VII.[15] For the human soul would seem to be not less perfectly fitted for understanding than the lower things of nature for their proper operations.

[13] Then, too, among these lower things the more noble effects are produced not only by higher agents but also require agents of their own genus; for *the sun and man generate a man.*[16] Likewise, we observe that among other perfect animals, some less noble are generated entirely by the sun's action, without an active principle of their own genus; so it is with animals engendered by putrefaction. Now, understanding is the noblest effect found in this world of lower things. Therefore, it is not enough to ascribe this effect to a remote agent, unless a proximate one is also assigned. This argument, however, does not militate against Avicenna, because he holds that any animal can be generated without seed.[17]

[14] Again, the effect intended reveals the agent. Hence, animals engendered by putrefaction are not intended by a lower nature, but only by a higher one, because they are produced by a higher agent alone; for this reason Aristotle says in *Metaphysics* VII[18] that their production is fortuitous. On the other hand, animals generated from seed are intended both by the higher and the lower nature. Now, this effect which consists in abstracting universal forms from phantasms is intended by us, and not merely by a remote agent. Hence, there must exist in us a proximate principle of such an effect; and this is the agent intellect, which, therefore, is not a separate substance but a power of our soul.

[15] And again, present in the nature of every mover is a principle sufficient for its natural operation. If this operation

15. Aristotle, *Metaphysics*, VII, 8 (1033b 26).
16. Aristotle, *Physics*, II, 2 (194b 13).
17. Avicenna, *De natura animalium*, XV, 1 (foll. 59rb–60ra).
18. Aristotle, *Metaphysics*, VII, 7 (1032a 29).

consists in an action, then the nature contains an active principle; for instance, the powers of the nutritive soul of plants. But, if this operation is a passion, the nature contains a passive principle, as appears in the sensitive powers of animals. Now, man is the most perfect of all lower movers, and his proper and natural operation is understanding, which is not accomplished without a certain passivity, in that the intellect is passive to the intelligible; nor again, without action, in that the intellect makes things that are potentially intelligible to be actually so. Therefore, the proper principles of both these operations must be in man's nature, nor must either of them have being in separation from his soul. And these principles are the agent and the possible intellects.

[16]   Also, if the agent intellect is a separate substance, it is manifest that it is above man's nature. Now, an operation which man performs solely by the power of a supernatural substance is a supernatural operation; for instance, the working of miracles, prophesying, and other like things which men do by God's favor. Since man cannot understand except by the power of the agent intellect, understanding will not be for man a natural operation if the agent intellect is a separate substance. Nor in that case can man be defined as being *intellectual* or *rational*.

[17]   Furthermore, no thing operates except by virtue of a power formally in it. Hence, Aristotle in *De anima* II[19] shows that the thing whereby we live and sense is a form and an act. Now, both actions—of the agent intellect and of the possible intellect as well—are proper to man, since man abstracts from phantasms, and receives in his mind things actually intelligible. For, indeed, we should not have become aware of these actions had we not experienced them in ourselves. It follows that the principles to which we ascribe these actions, namely, the possible and agent intellects, must be powers formally existing in us.

[18]   And if it be argued that these actions are attributed to man so far as those intellects are in contact with us, as Aver-

19. Aristotle, *De anima*, II, 2 (414a 13).

roes claims,[20] we refer to our previous proof[21] that the possible intellect's conjunction with us does not suffice as a means of understanding on our part, if, as Averroes maintains, it is a separate substance. And, clearly, the same thing is true of the agent intellect. For the agent intellect stands in the same relation to the intelligible species received into the possible intellect as art to the artificial forms which it produces in matter, as the example used by Aristotle in *De anima* III makes clear.[22] But art-forms are artistically inoperative, attaining only to a formal likeness, and that is why the subject of these forms cannot through them exercise the action of a maker. Therefore, neither can man exercise the operation of the agent intellect through the presence in him of intelligible species made actual by the agent intellect.

[19] Again, a thing that cannot initiate its proper operation without being moved by an external principle is moved to operate rather than moves itself. Thus, irrational animals are moved to operate rather than move themselves, because every one of their operations depends on an extrinsic principle which moves them. For the sense, moved by an external sensible object, places an impress upon the imagination, thus giving rise to an orderly process in all the powers, down to the motive ones. Now, man's proper operation is understanding, and of this the primary principle is the agent intellect, which makes species intelligible, to which species the possible intellect in a certain manner is passive; and the possible intellect, having been actualized, moves the will. Therefore, if the agent intellect is a substance outside man, all man's operation depends on an extrinsic principle. Man, then, will not act autonomously, but will be activated by another. So, he will not be master of his own operations, nor will he merit either praise or blame. All moral science and social intercourse thus will perish; which is unfitting. Therefore, the agent intellect is not a substance separate from man.

20. See above, ch. 59, ¶8.
21. See above, ch. 59, ¶9–13.
22. Aristotle, *De anima*, III, 5 (430a 17).

Chapter 77.

THAT IT IS NOT IMPOSSIBLE FOR THE POSSIBLE AND AGENT INTELLECT TO EXIST TOGETHER IN THE ONE SUBSTANCE OF THE SOUL

[1] Perhaps someone will think it impossible for one and the same substance, namely, that of our soul, to be in potentiality to all intelligibles, as becomes the possible intellect, and to actualize them, as becomes the agent intellect. For nothing acts so far as it is in potentiality, but so far as it is in act. That is why it will seem impossible for the agent and possible intellect to exist concurrently in the one substance of the soul.

[2] Upon close examination, however, it is seen that this concurrence entails nothing incongruous or difficult. For nothing prevents one thing from being in one respect potential in relation to some other thing, and actual in another respect, as we observe in things of nature; air is actually damp and potentially dry, and the reverse is true of earth. Now, this same interrelationship obtains between the intellective soul and the phantasms. For the intellective soul has something actual to which the phantasm is potential, and is potential to something present actually in the phantasm; since the substance of the human soul is possessed of immateriality, and, as is clear from what has been said,[1] it therefore has an intellectual nature— every immaterial substance being of this kind. But this does not mean that the soul is now likened to this or that determinate thing, as it must be in order to know this or that thing determinately; for all knowledge is brought about by the likeness of the thing known being present in the knower. Thus, the intellectual soul itself remains potential with respect to the determinate likenesses of things that can be known by us, namely, the natures of sensible things. It is the phantasms which present these determinate sensible natures to us. But

1. See above, ch. 68.

these phantasms have not yet acquired intelligible actuality, since they are likenesses of sensible things even as to material conditions, which are the individual properties, and, moreover, the phantasms exist in material organs. Consequently, they are not actually intelligible. They are, however, potentially intelligible, since in the individual man whose likeness the phantasms reflect it is possible to receive the universal nature stripped of all individuating conditions. And so, the phantasms have intelligibility potentially, while being actually determinate as likenesses of things. In the intellective soul the opposite was the case. Hence, there is in that soul an active power vis-à-vis the phantasms, making them actually intelligible; and this power is called the *agent intellect;* while there is also in the soul a power that is in potentiality to the determinate likenesses of sensible things; and this power is the *possible intellect.*

[3] That which exists in the soul, however, differs from what is found in natural agents. For in the latter, one thing is in potentiality to something according to the same manner of being as that of its actual presence in something else; the matter of air is in potentiality to the form of water in the same way as it is in water. That is why natural bodies, which have matter in common, are mutually active and passive in the same order. On the other hand, the intellective soul is not in potentiality to the likenesses of things in the phantasms, according to the mode of their presence therein, but according as they are raised to a higher level by abstraction from material individuating conditions, thus being made actually intelligible. The action of the agent intellect on the phantasm, therefore, precedes the reception by the possible intellect, so that operational primacy here is ascribed not to the phantasms, but to the agent intellect. And for this reason Aristotle says[2] that the agent intellect is related to the possible intellect *as art to its matter.*

[4] A quite similar case would be that of the eye, if, being transparent and receptive of colors, it were endowed with sufficient light to make colors actually visible; even as certain

2. Aristotle, *De anima*, III, 5 (430a 13).

animals are said to illuminate objects for themselves by the light of their own eyes, and so they see more at night and less by day, for their eyes are weak, being activated by a dim light and confused by a strong one. There is something comparable to this in our intellect, which, "as regards things which are most evident of all, is as the eyes of the owl to the blaze of day;[3] so that the little intelligible light which is connatural to us suffices for our act of understanding.

[5] It is clear that the intelligible light connatural to our soul suffices to cause the action of the agent intellect, if one considers the necessity of affirming the existence of the agent intellect. For the soul was found to be in potentiality to intelligible things, as the senses are to sensible things; since, just as we do not always sense, so neither do we always understand. Now, these intelligibles which the human intellective soul understands were asserted by Plato to be intelligible of themselves, namely, Ideas, so that in his doctrine there was no necessity of an agent intellect: an intellect having an active role with respect to intelligibles. But, if this doctrine were true, it would follow necessarily that the more intelligible in their own nature things are, the greater would be our understanding of them; which is manifestly false. For the nearer things are to our senses, the more intelligible they are to us, though in themselves they are less intelligible. That is why Aristotle was impelled to maintain that those things which are intelligible to us are not existing entities intelligible in themselves, but are made intelligible from sensibles. Aristotle, therefore, saw the necessity of admitting a power capable of doing this, namely, the agent intellect. So, the function of that intellect is to make intelligibles proportionate to our minds. Now, the mode of intellectual light connatural to us is not unequal to the performance of this function. Nothing, therefore, stands in the way of our ascribing the action of the agent intellect to the light of our soul, and especially since Aristotle compares the agent intellect to a light.[4]

3. Aristotle, *Metaphysics*, Iα, 1 (993b 10).
4. Aristotle, *De anima*, III, 5 (430a 13).

Chapter 78.

THAT ARISTOTLE HELD NOT THAT THE AGENT INTELLECT IS A SEPARATE SUBSTANCE, BUT THAT IT IS A PART OF THE SOUL

[1] Now, since a number of persons agree with the Avicennian theory dealt with above,[1] in the belief that it is the position of Aristotle, we must show from his own words that in his judgment the agent intellect is not a separate substance.

[2] For Aristotle says[2] that in "every nature we find two factors, the one material, which, like the matter in every genus, is in potentiality to all the things contained under it, the other causal, which, like the efficient cause, produces all the things of a given genus, the latter factor standing to the former as art to its matter"; and therefore, Aristotle concludes, "these two factors must likewise be found within the soul." The quasi-material principle in the soul is "the (possible) *intellect wherein all things become intelligible*"; the other principle, having the role of efficient cause in the soul, "is the intellect by which all things are made" (namely, actually intelligible), and this is the agent intellect, "which is like a habit," and not a power. Aristotle explains what he means by calling the agent intellect a *habit*, when he goes on to speak of it as a *kind of light*, for "in a certain way light makes potential colors to be colors actually," that is to say, so far as it makes them actually visible. And this function in regard to intelligibles is attributed to the agent intellect.

[3] These considerations clearly imply that the agent intellect is not a separate substance, but, rather, a part of the soul; for Aristotle says explicitly that the possible and agent intellects are *differences of the soul*, and that they are *in the soul*. Therefore, neither of them is a separate substance.

[4] Aristotle's reasoning also proves the same point. For in every nature containing potentiality and act we find something

1. See above, ch. 76.
2. Aristotle, *De anima*, III, 5 (430a 10).

which, having the character of matter, is in potentiality to the things of that genus, and something in the role of an efficient cause which actualizes the potentiality; similarly, in the products of art there is art and matter. But the intellective soul is a nature in which we find potentiality and act, since sometimes it is actually understanding, and sometimes potentially. Consequently, in the nature of the intellective soul there is something having the character of matter, which is in potentiality to all intelligibles—and this is called the *possible intellect;* and there also is something which, in the capacity of an efficient cause, makes all in act—and this is called the *agent intellect.* Therefore, both intellects, on Aristotle's showing, are within the nature of the soul, and have no being separate from the body of which the soul is the act.

[5]   Aristotle says, moreover, that the agent intellect is *a sort of habit like light.* Now, by a habit we mean, not something existing by itself, but something belonging to one who has it. Therefore, the agent intellect is not a substance existing separately by itself, but is part of the human soul.

[6]   Yet, what this Aristotelian phrase means is not that the effect produced by the agent intellect may be called a habit, as though the sense were that the agent intellect makes man to understand all things, and this effect is like a habit. "For the essence of habit," as the Commentator, Averroes, says on this very text,[3] "consists in this, that its possessor understands by means of that which is proper to him—understands by himself and whenever he wills, with no need of anything extrinsic"; since Averroes explicitly likens to a habit, not the effect itself, but "the intellect by which we make all things."

[7]   Nevertheless, the agent intellect is not to be thought of as a habit such as we find in the second species of quality and in reference to which some have said that the agent intellect is the *habit of principles.* For this habit of principles is derived from sensible things, as Aristotle proves in *Posterior Analytics* II;[4] and thus it must be the effect of the agent intellect, whose function is to make actually understood the phantasms,

3. Averroes, *Commentarium magnum in Aristotelis de Anima,* III, t.c. 18 (p. 438, lines 26–29).
4. Aristotle, *Posterior Analytics,* II, 19 (99b 20ff.).

which are potentially understood. Now, the meaning of habit is grasped in terms of its distinction from *privation* and *potentiality*; thus, every *form* and *act* can be called a *habit*. This is clearly what Aristotle has in mind, because he says that the agent intellect is a habit in the same way as "light is a habit."

[8] Now, Aristotle goes on to say[5] that *this intellect*, namely, the agent intellect *is separate, unmixed, impassible, and an actually existing substance.* And of these four perfections attributed to that intellect, Aristotle had previously ascribed[6] two to the possible intellect, namely, *freedom from admixture and separate existence.* The third—*impassibility*—he had applied to it in showing the distinction between the impassibility of the senses and that of the possible intellect, pointing out that if *passivity* be taken broadly, the possible intellect is passive so far as it is in potentiality to intelligibles. The fourth perfection—*substantial actuality*—Aristotle simply denies of the possible intellect, saying that it was "in potentiality to intelligibles, and none of these things was actual before the act of understanding."[7] Thus, the possible intellect shares the first two perfections with the agent intellect; in the third it agrees partly, and partly differs; but in the fourth the agent intellect differs altogether from the possible intellect. Aristotle goes on to prove in a single argument[8] that these four perfections belong to the agent intellect: "*For always the agent is superior to the patient, and the* (active) *principle to the matter.*" For he had already said that the agent intellect is like an efficient cause, and the possible intellect like matter. Now, through this proposition, as a demonstrative mean, the first two perfections are inferred as follows: "The agent is superior to the patient and to matter. But the possible intellect, which is as patient and matter, is separate and unmixed, as was proved before. Much more, therefore, is the agent possessed of these perfections." The other perfections are inferred through this middle proposition, as follows: "The agent is superior to the patient and to matter by being compared to the latter as

5. Aristotle, *De anima*, III, 5 (430a 18).
6. Aristotle, *De anima*, III, 4 (429a 11, 20).
7. Aristotle, *De anima*, III, 4 (429b 5).
8. Aristotle, *De anima*, III, 5 (430a 18).

an agent and an actual being to a patient and a potential being. But the possible intellect is, in a certain way, a patient and a potential being. Therefore, the agent intellect is a non-passive agent and an actual being." Now, from those words of Aristotle, it evidently cannot be inferred that the agent intellect is a separate substance; rather, that it is *separate* in the same sense of the term as he had previously applied to the possible intellect, namely, *as not having an organ*. Aristotle's statement that the agent intellect is an *actual substantial being* is not incompatible with the fact that the substance of the soul is in potentiality, as was shown above.[9]

[9]   The Philosopher goes on to say[10] that *actual knowledge is identical with its object*. On this text the Commentator remarks[11] that the agent intellect differs from the possible, because that which understands and that which is understood are the same in the agent intellect, but not in the possible intellect. But this clearly is contrary to Aristotle's meaning. For Aristotle had used the same words before in speaking of the possible intellect, namely, that "it is intelligible in precisely the same way as its objects are; since in things devoid of matter, the intellect and that which is understood are the same; for speculative knowledge and its object are identical."[12] For he plainly wishes to show that the possible intellect is understood as are other intelligible objects, from the fact that the possible intellect, so far as it is actually understanding, is identical with that which is understood. Moreover, Aristotle had remarked a little before that the possible intellect "is in a sense potentially whatever is intelligible, though actually it is nothing until it has exercized its power of understanding";[13] and here he explicitly gives us to understand that, by actually knowing, the possible intellect becomes its objects. Nor is it surprising that he should say this of the possible intellect, since he had already said[14] the same thing about sense and the

9. See above, ch. 77, ¶2–4.
10. Aristotle, De anima, III, 5 (430a 20).
11. Averroes, op. cit., III, t.c. 19 (p. 443, lines 86–90).
12. Aristotle, De anima, III, 5 (430a 3).
13. Aristotle, De anima, III, 4 (429b 31).
14. Aristotle, De anima, III, 2 (425b 27).

sensible object in act. For the sense is actualized by the species actually sensed and, similarly, the possible intellect is actualized through the intelligible species in act; and for this reason the intellect in act is said to be the very intelligible object itself in act. We must therefore say that Aristotle, having definitively treated of the possible and agent intellects, here begins his treatment of the intellect in act, when he says that *actual knowledge is identical with the thing actually known.*

[10] Continuing, Aristotle states: "Although in the individual, potential knowledge is in time prior to actual knowledge, it is not altogether prior even in time."[15] Indeed, in several places he employs this distinction between potentiality and act, namely, that act is in its nature prior to potentiality, but that, in time, potentiality precedes act in one and the same thing that is changed from potentiality to act; and yet, absolutely speaking, potentiality is not even temporally prior to act, since it is only by an act that a potentiality is reduced to act. That is why Aristotle says that the *intellect which is in potency*, namely, the possible intellect so far as it is in potency, is *temporally prior* to the intellect in act—and this, I say, *in one and the same subject.* Aristotle, however, adds: *but not altogether*, that is to say, not universally; because the possible intellect is reduced to act by the agent intellect, which again is in act, as he said, through some possible intellect brought into act; thus, Aristotle remarked in *Physics* III[16] that, before learning, a person needs a teacher, that he may be brought from potency to act. In these words, then, Aristotle explains the relationship which the possible intellect, as potential, bears to the intellect in act.

[11] Aristotle then declares: *But it is not at one time understanding and at another not,*[17] thus indicating the difference between the intellect in act and the possible intellect. For he had said earlier[18] that the possible intellect is not perpetually understanding, but sometimes is not actually understanding, namely, when it is in potentiality to intelligibles, and some-

15. Aristotle, *De anima*, III, 5 (430a 21).
16. Aristotle, *Physics*, III, 3 (202b 18).
17. Aristotle, *De anima*, III, 5 (430a 23).
18. Aristotle, *De anima*, III, 4 (430a 5).

times is actually understanding, namely, when it is actually identified with them. Now, the intellect becomes in act by the fact that it is the intelligibles themselves, as he had already said. Hence, it does not pertain to the intellect to understand sometimes and sometimes not to understand.

[12]   The Philosopher thereupon adds: *That alone is separate which truly is.* This remark cannot apply to the agent intellect, since it alone is not separate, for he had already spoken of the possible intellect as being separate. Nor can that statement be understood to refer to the possible intellect, since Aristotle had already said the same thing concerning the agent intellect. It remains that the above remark applies to that which includes both intellects, namely, to the intellect in act, of which he was speaking; because that alone in our soul which belongs to the intellect in act is separate and uses no organ; I mean that part of the soul whereby we understand actually and which includes the possible and agent intellect. And that is why Aristotle goes on to say that *this part of the soul alone is immortal and everlasting,* as being independent of the body in virtue of its separateness.

Chapter 79.

THAT THE HUMAN SOUL DOES NOT PERISH
WHEN THE BODY IS CORRUPTED

[1]   From what has been said, therefore, it can be clearly shown that the human soul is not corrupted when the body is corrupted.

[2]   For it was proved above[1] that every intellectual substance is incorruptible. But man's soul is an intellectual substance, as was shown.[2] It therefore follows that the human soul is incorruptible.

[3]   Again, no thing is corrupted with respect to that wherein its perfection consists, for mutations in regard to perfection

1. See above, ch. 55.
2. See above, ch. 56–68.

and corruption are contrary to one another. The perfection of the human soul, however, consists in a certain abstraction from the body. For the soul is perfected by knowledge and virtue, and it is perfected in knowledge the more it considers immaterial things, the perfection of virtue consisting in man's not submitting to the passions of the body, but moderating and controlling them in accordance with reason. Consequently, the soul is not corrupted by being separated from the body.

[4] Now, it may be said that the soul's perfection lies in its operational separation from the body, and its corruption in its existential separation therefrom. Such an argument misses the mark, for a thing's operation manifests its substance and its being, since a thing operates according as it is a being, and its proper operation follows upon its proper nature. The operation of a thing, therefore, can be perfected only so far as its substance is perfected. Thus, if the soul, in leaving the body, is perfected operationally, its incorporeal substance will not fail in its being through separation from the body.

[5] Likewise, that which properly perfects the soul of man is something incorruptible; for the proper operation of man, as man, is understanding, since it is in this that he differs from brutes, plants, and inanimate things. Now, it properly pertains to this act to apprehend objects universal and incorruptible as such. But perfections must be proportionate to things perfectible. Therefore, the human soul is incorruptible.

[6] Moreover, it is impossible that natural appetite should be in vain. But man naturally desires to exist forever. This is evidenced by the fact that being is that which all desire; and man by his intellect apprehends being not merely in the present, as brute animals do, but unqualifiedly. Therefore, man attains perpetual existence as regards his soul, whereby he apprehends being unqualifiedly and in respect of every time.

[7] Also, the reception of one thing in another accords with the recipient's manner of being. But the forms of things are received in the possible intellect according as they are actually intelligible; and they are actually intelligible according as they are immaterial, universal, and consequently incorruptible. Therefore, the possible intellect is incorruptible. The pos-

sible intellect, however, is part of the human soul, as we proved above.[3] Hence, the human soul is incorruptible.

[8]   Then, too, intelligible being is more permanent than sensible being. But in sensible things that which has the role of first recipient, namely, prime matter, is incorruptible in its substance; much more so, therefore, is the possible intellect, which is receptive of intelligible forms. Therefore, the human soul, of which the possible intellect is a part, is also incorruptible.

[9]   Moreover, *the maker is superior to the thing made,* as Aristotle says.[4] But the agent intellect actualizes intelligibles, as was shown above.[5] Therefore, since intelligibles in act, as such, are incorruptible, much more will the agent intellect be incorruptible. So, too, then, is the human soul, whose light is the agent intellect, as we have previously made clear.[6]

[10]   Again, a form is corrupted by three things only: the action of its contrary, the corruption of its subject, the failure of its cause; by the action of a contrary, as when heat is destroyed by the action of cold; by the corruption of its subject, as when the power of sight is destroyed through the destruction of the eye; by the failure of its cause, as when the air's illumination fails through the failure of its cause, the sun, to be present. But the human soul cannot be corrupted by the action of a contrary, for nothing is contrary to it; since, through the possible intellect, it is cognizant and receptive of all contraries. Nor can the human soul be destroyed through the corruption of its subject, for we have already shown[7] that it is a form independent of the body in its being. Nor, again, can the soul be destroyed through the failure of its cause, since it can have no cause except an eternal one, as we shall prove later on.[8] Therefore, in no way can the human soul be corrupted.

3. See above, ch. 59, ¶9–17; cf. ch. 73 and 76.
4. Aristotle, *De anima,* III, 5 (430a 18).
5. See above, ch. 76, ¶3ff.
6. See above, ch. 78, ¶2, 5.
7. See above, ch. 68, ¶6–12.
8. See below, ch. 87.

[11] Furthermore, if the soul perishes as the result of the body's corruption, then its being must be weakened through the debility of the body. But if a power of the soul is weakened for that reason, this occurs only by accident, namely, in so far as that power has need of a bodily organ. Thus, the power of sight is debilitated through the weakening of its organ—accidentally, however. The following considerations will make this point clear. If some weakness were attached to the power through itself, it would never be restored as the result of the organ's being restored; yet it is a fact of observation that, however much the power of sight may seem to be weakened, if the organ is restored, then the power is restored. That is why Aristotle says, in *De anima* I, "that if an old man were to recover the eye of a youth, he would see just as well as the youth does."[9] Since, then, the intellect is a power of the soul that needs no organ—as we proved above[10]—it is not weakened, either through itself or accidentally, by old age or any other bodily weakness. Now, if in the operation of the intellect fatigue occurs, or some impediment because of a bodily infirmity, this is due not to any weakness on the part of the intellect itself, but to the weakness of the powers which the intellect needs, namely, of the imagination, the memory, and the cognitive power. Clearly, therefore, the intellect is incorruptible. And since it is an intellective substance, the human soul likewise is incorruptible.

[12] This conclusion also comes to light through the authority of Aristotle. For he says in *De anima* I that *the intellect is evidently a substance and is incapable of being destroyed.*[11] And it can be inferred from what has been said already[12] that this remark of Aristotle's cannot apply to a separate substance that is either the possible or the agent intellect.

[13] The same conclusion also follows from what Aristotle says in *Metaphysics* XI, speaking against Plato, namely, "that moving causes exist prior to their effects, whereas formal causes are simultaneous with their effects; thus when a man is healed,

9. Aristotle, *De anima*, I, 4 (408b 22).
10. See above, ch. 68, ¶12.
11. Aristotle, *De anima*, I, 4 (408b 18).
12. See above, ch. 61 and 78.

then health exists,"[13] and not before—Plato's position, that
the forms of things exist prior to the things themselves, to the
contrary notwithstanding. Having said this, Aristotle adds:
But we must examine whether anything also survives afterwards. "For in some cases there is nothing to prevent this—
the soul, for example, may be of this sort, not every soul, but
the intellect."[14] Since Aristotle is speaking of forms, he clearly
means that the intellect, which is the form of man, remains
after the matter, which is the body.

[14] It is also clear from these texts of Aristotle that, while
he maintains that the soul is a form, he does not say it is non-
subsistent and therefore corruptible—an interpretation which
Gregory of Nyssa attributes to him.[15] For Aristotle excludes
the intellective soul from the generality of other forms, in saying that *it remains after the body, and is a certain substance.*

[15] The doctrine of the Catholic faith is in agreement on
these matters. For in the work *On the Teachings of the
Church* there is this statement: "We believe that man alone is
possessed of a subsistent soul, which continues to live even
after divesting itself of the body, and is the animating principle of the senses and powers; nor does the soul die with the
body, as the Arabian asserts, nor after a short period of time,
as Zeno would have it, because it is a living substance."[16]

[16] This eliminates the error of the ungodly, in whose person Solomon says: "We are born of nothing, and after this
we shall be as if we had not been" (Wis. 2:2); and in whose
person again Solomon says: "The death of man and of beasts
is one, and the condition of them both is equal: as man dieth,
so they also die: all things breathe alike, and man hath nothing
more than beast" (Eccle. 3:19). For Solomon clearly is not
speaking in his own person but in that of the godless, since
at the end of the book he adds in a decisive manner: "Before

13. Aristotle, Metaph ics, XI, 3 (1070a 21).
14. Aristotle, Metaphysics, XI, 3 (1070a 24).
15. St. Gregory of Nyssa, De anima, serm. 1 (PG, 45, col. 200; cf.
    40, col. 560).
16. Gennadius, De ecclesiasticis dogmatibus, XVI, (PL, 42, col.
    1216).

the dust return into its earth, from whence it was, and the spirit return to Him Who gave it" (Eccle. 12:6–7).

[17] Furthermore, there are myriad passages of sacred Scripture which proclaim the immortality of the soul.

Chapters 80 and 81.

ARGUMENTS TO PROVE THAT THE CORRUPTION
OF THE BODY ENTAILS THAT OF THE SOUL
[AND THEIR SOLUTION]

[1] There are certain arguments which would seem to prove the impossibility of human souls remaining after the body.

[2] For, if human souls are multiplied in accordance with the multiplication of bodies, as was shown above,[1] then the souls cannot remain in their multiple being when the bodies are destroyed. One of two alternatives, therefore, follows ineluctably: either the human soul perishes utterly, or only one soul remains. And, seemingly, this state of affairs would accord with the theory of those who maintain that what is one in all men is alone incorruptible, whether this be the agent intellect only, as Alexander declares, or, in the Averroistic doctrine, the possible along with the agent intellect.[2]

[3] Moreover, the formal principle [*ratio*] is the cause of specific diversity. But, if many souls remain after the corruption of bodies, they must be mutually diverse; for just as there is identity where there is unity of substance, so those things are diverse which are substantially many. Now, in souls that survive the death of the bodies which they inform, the only possible diversity is of a formal character, since such souls are not composed of matter and form—a point proved above[3] with respect to every intellectual substance. It therefore follows that those souls are specifically diverse. Nevertheless, souls are not changed to another species as a result of the

1. See above, ch. 75, ¶6ff.
2. See above, ch. 73 and 76.
3. See above, ch. 50 and 51.

body's corruption, because whatever is changed from species to species is corrupted. Consequently, even before souls were separated from their bodies, they were specifically diverse. Now, composite things owe their specific nature to their form. It follows that individual men will be specifically diverse— an awkward consequence. It is, therefore, seemingly impossible that a multiplicity of human souls should survive their bodies.

[4]   Then, too, for those who espouse the doctrine of the eternity of the world it would seem utterly impossible to maintain that a multiplicity of human souls remain after the death of the body. For, if the world exists from eternity, then movement did, too, so that generation likewise is eternal. But in that case an infinite number of men have died before us. If, then, the souls of the dead remain in their multiple being after death, it must be said that there actually exist now an infinite number of souls of men already dead. This, however, is impossible, because the actually infinite cannot exist in nature.[4] Hence it follows, on the hypothesis of the world's eternity, that souls do not remain many after death.

[5]   Also, "That which comes to a thing and departs from it, without the latter being corrupted, accrues to it accidentally";[5] for this is the definition of an accident. Thus, if the soul is not corrupted as the result of its severance from the body, it would follow that the soul is united to the body accidentally, and, further, that man is an accidental being, composed of body and soul. In that case, too, we should be faced with the consequence that there is no human species, for one species does not result from things joined together by accident; white man, for example, is not a species.

[6]   A completely inoperative substance, moreover, cannot possibly exist. All psychic operation, however, is corporeally determined, as we see by induction. For the soul's nutritive powers function through the bodily qualities, and by a bodily

4. Cf. St. Thomas Aquinas, *Summa Theologiae*, I, 7, 4.
5. Cf. Porphyry, *Isagoge* (4a 25), in *Commentaria in Aristotelem Graeca*, IV, pt. 1. (Also in *PL*, 64, col. 132.)

instrument acting upon the body, which is perfected by the soul, which is nourished and increased, and from which the seed is separated for generative purposes. Secondly, all the operations of the powers belonging to the sensitive soul are executed through bodily organs, some of them entailing a certain bodily transmutation, as in those which are called passions of the soul, for instance, love, joy, and the like. And again, while understanding is not an operation carried out through any bodily organ, nevertheless its objects are the phantasms, which stand in relation to it as colors to the power of sight; so that, just as sight cannot function in the absence of colors, so the intellective soul is incapable of understanding without phantasms. Moreover, to enable it to understand, the soul needs the powers which prepare the phantasms so as to render them actually intelligible, namely, the cogitative power and the memory—powers which, being acts of certain bodily organs and functioning through them, surely cannot remain after the body perishes. And that is why Aristotle says that *the soul never understands without a phantasm*,[6] and that *it understands nothing without the passive intellect*,[7] which he terms the cogitative power, and which is destructible. This explains why he says in *De anima* I[8] that *man's understanding is corrupted through the decay of some inward part*, namely, the phantasm, or the passive intellect. Aristotle also remarks in *De anima* III[9] that after death we do not remember what we know in life. Evidently, then, no operation of the soul can remain after death. Therefore, neither does its substance continue to be, since no substance can exist without operation.

[7] [Chapter 81] Now, because these arguments arrive at a false conclusion, as was shown above,[10] we must endeavor to solve them. And first of all, it must be understood that whatever things have to be adapted and proportioned to one another simultaneously derive their multiplicity or unity, each from its own cause. Therefore, if the being of one thing depends on

6. Aristotle, *De anima*, III, 7 (431a 17).
7. Aristotle, *De anima*, III, 5 (430a 25).
8. Aristotle, *De anima*, I, 4 (408b 24).
9. Aristotle, *De anima*, III, 5 (430a 23).   10. See above, ch. 79.

another, its unity or multiplicity likewise depends thereon; otherwise, its unity or multiplicity depends on some other extrinsic cause. Thus, form and matter must always be mutually proportioned and, as it were, naturally adapted, because the proper act is produced in its proper matter. That is why matter and form must always agree with one another in respect to multiplicity and unity. Consequently, if the being of the form depends on matter, its multiplication, as well as its unity, depends on matter. But if this is not the case, then the form will have to be multiplied in accordance with the multiplication of the matter, that is to say, together with the matter and in proportion to it; yet not in such a manner that the unity or multiplicity of the form itself depends upon the matter. It has been shown,[11] however, that the human soul is a form not depending in its being on matter. It therefore follows that souls are multiplied in accordance with the multiplication of bodies, yet the latter will not be the cause of the multiplication of souls. And for this reason it does not follow that, with the destruction of bodies, the plurality of souls ceases, as the *first argument* concluded.

[8]   From this the reply to the *second argument* also clearly emerges. For not every diversity of form causes diversity in species, but that diversity alone which concerns formal principles, or otherness in respect of the intelligible essence of the form; for obviously, the form of this and that fire is essentially distinct, yet neither the fire nor its form is specifically diverse. Thus, a multiplicity of souls separated from their bodies is due to the substantial diversity of the forms, since the substance of this soul is other than the substance of that soul. This diversity, nevertheless, does not result from a diversity in the essential principles of the soul itself, nor from otherness in respect of the intelligible essence of the soul, but from diversity in the commensuration of souls to bodies, since this soul is adapted to this and not to that body, and that soul to another body, and so in all other instances. And such adaptabilities remain in souls even after the bodies have perished, even as their substances remain, as not depending in their being on bodies. For souls are in their substances the forms of bodies;

11. See above, ch. 68.

otherwise, they would be united to their bodies accidentally, so that from the union of soul and body there would result a thing not essentially, but only accidentally, one. Now, it is as forms that souls have to be adapted to bodies. Clearly, that is why these diverse adaptabilities remain in separated souls, and consequently explains their enduring plurality.

[9]   For some advocates of the eternity of the world the *third argument* cited above has been the occasion of their lapsing into various bizarre opinions. For some admitted the conclusion unqualifiedly, declaring that human souls perish utterly with their bodies. Others said that of all souls there remains a single separate entity common to them all, namely, the agent intellect, according to some, or, in addition, the possible intellect, according to others. Still others maintained that souls continue to exist in their multiplicity after the death of the bodies; yet, on pain of having to admit an infinite number of souls, these persons averred that the same souls are united to different bodies after a certain period of time has elapsed. This was the Platonists' theory, of which we shall treat further on.[12] Avoiding all these inferences, another group of thinkers held that it is not impossible for separate souls to be actually infinite in number. For in the case of things devoid of mutual order, to be actually infinite is to be infinite accidentally, and those thinkers saw no incongruity in admitting this. Such is the position of Avicenna and Algazel. Aristotle does not tell us explicitly which of these opinions he himself shared, but he does expressly affirm the eternity of the world. Nevertheless, of all the opinions cited above, the last one is not inconsistent with the principle laid down by him. For in *Physics* III[13] and in *De caelo* I[14] he proves that there is no actual infinity in natural bodies, but he does not prove that there is no actual infinity in immaterial substances.[15] In any case it is certain that this question presents no difficulty to those who profess the Catholic faith, and do not posit the eternity of the world.

12. See below, ch. 83.
13. Aristotle, *Physics*, III, 5 (205a 10 – 205b 38).
14. Aristotle, *De caelo et mundo*, I, 5.
15. Aristotle appears not to have dealt explicitly with this latter question. Cf. James F. Anderson, *The Cause of Being* (St. Louis, 1952), pp. 92f.

[10]   Moreover, if the soul remains in existence after the death of the body, it does not follow that it must have been accidentally united to it, as the *fourth argument* concluded. For an accident is described as *that which can be present or absent without the corruption of the subject composed of matter and form*. However, if this statement is applied to the principles of the composite subject, it is found to be false; because it is clear, as Aristotle shows in *Physics* I,[16] that prime matter is ungenerated and incorruptible. That is why prime matter remains in its essence when the form departs. Nevertheless, the form was united to it not accidentally but essentially, since it was joined to it according to one act of being. The soul likewise is united to the body as regards one act of being, as was shown above.[17] Therefore, although the soul continues to exist after the body has passed away, it is nevertheless united to the body substantially and not accidentally. Now, prime matter does not remain in act after the form's departure, except in relation to the act of another form, whereas the human soul remains in the same act; and the reason for this is that the human soul is a form and an act, while prime matter is a being only potentially.

[11]   The proposition advanced in the *fifth* argument, namely, that no operation can remain in the soul when separated from the body, we declare to be false, in view of the fact that those operations do remain which are not exercised through organs. Such are the operations of understanding and willing. Those operations, however, do not endure which are carried out by means of bodily organs, and of such a kind are the operations of the nutritive and sensitive powers.

[12]   Nevertheless it must be borne in mind that the soul understands in a different manner when separated from the body and when united to it, even as it exists diversely in those cases; for a thing acts according as it is. Indeed, although the soul, while united to the body, enjoys an absolute being not depending on the body, nevertheless the body is the soul's housing, so to speak, and the subject that receives it. This explains why the soul's proper operation, understanding, has

16. Aristotle, *Physics*, I, 9 (192a 28).
17. See above, ch. 68, ¶3–5.

its object, namely, the phantasm, in the body, despite the fact that this operation does not depend on the body as though it were effected through the instrumentality of a bodily organ. It follows that, so long as the soul is in the body, it cannot perform that act without a phantasm; neither can it remember except through the powers of cogitation and memory, by which the phantasms are prepared, as stated above.[18] Accordingly, understanding, so far as this mode of it is concerned, as well as remembering, perishes with the death of the body. The separated soul, however, exists by itself, apart from the body. Consequently, its operation, which is understanding, will not be fulfilled in relation to those objects existing in bodily organs which the phantasms are; on the contrary, it will understand through itself, in the manner of substances which in their being are totally separate from bodies, and of which we shall treat subsequently.[19] And from those substances, as from things above it, the separated soul will be able to receive a more abundant influx, productive of a more perfect understanding on its own part. There is an indication of this even in the young. For the more the soul is freed from preoccupation with its body, the more fit does it become for understanding higher things. Hence, the virtue of temperance, which withdraws the soul from bodily pleasures, is especially fruitful in making men apt in understanding. Then, too, sleeping persons, their bodily senses being dormant, with no disturbance of the humours or vapors to impede their mental processes, are, under the influence of higher beings, enabled to perceive some things pertaining to the future which transcend the scope of human reason. And this is all the more true of those in a fainting condition or in ecstasy, since such states involve an even greater withdrawal from the bodily senses. Nor does this come to pass undeservedly. For, since the human soul, as we have shown already,[20] is situated on the boundary line between corporeal and incorporeal substances, *as though it existed on the horizon of eternity and time,* it approaches to the highest by withdrawing from the lowest. Consequently, when the soul shall be completely separated from the body,

18. See above, ch. 80, ¶6.
19. See below, ch. 96–101.
20. See above, ch. 68, ¶6.

it will be perfectly likened to separate substances in its mode of understanding, and will receive their influx abundantly.

[13] Therefore, although the mode of understanding vouchsafed to us in the present life ceases upon the death of the body, nevertheless another and higher mode of understanding will take its place.

[14] Now, recollection, being an act performed through a bodily organ, as Aristotle shows in the *De memoria*,[21] cannot remain in the soul after the body, unless *recollection* be taken equivocally for the understanding of things which one knew before. For there must be present in the separate soul even the things that it knew in this life, since the intelligible species are received into the possible intellect inexpugnably, as we have already shown.[22]

[15] As for the other operations of the soul, such as loving, rejoicing, and the like, one must beware of equivocation. For sometimes such operations are taken inasmuch as they are passions of the soul, and in this sense they are acts of the sensible appetite appertaining to the concupiscible and irascible powers, entailing some bodily change. And thus they cannot remain in the soul after death, as Aristotle proves in the *De anima*.[23] Sometimes, however, such operations are taken for a simple act of the will, in the absence of all passion. That is why Aristotle says in Book VII of the *Ethics* that God rejoices in a single and simple operation;[24] and in Book X that in the contemplation of wisdom there is *marvelous delight*;[25] and in Book VIII he distinguishes the *love of friendship* from the *love* that is a passion.[26] Now, since the will is a power employing no organ, as neither does the intellect, it is plain that these things of which we are speaking remain in the separated soul, so far as they are acts of the will.

[16] From the preceding arguments, therefore, it cannot be concluded that the soul of man is mortal.

21. Aristotle, *De memoria et reminiscentia*, I (451a 20).
22. See above, ch. 74, ¶8ff.
23. Aristotle, *De anima*, I, 4 (408b 26).
24. Aristotle, *Nicomachean Ethics*, VII, 14 (1154b 26).
25. Aristotle, *Nicomachean Ethics*, X, 7 (1177a 26).
26. Aristotle, *Nicomachean Ethics*, VIII, 5 (1157b 28).

Chapter 82.

THAT THE SOULS OF BRUTE ANIMALS ARE NOT IMMORTAL

[1]   This truth can be clearly inferred from what has been already said.

[2]   For we demonstrated above[1] that no operation of the sensitive part of the soul can be performed without the body. In the souls of brute animals, however, there is no operation superior to those of the sensitive part, since they neither understand nor reason. This is evident from the fact that all animals of the same species operate in the same way, as though moved by nature and not as operating by art; every swallow builds its nest and every spider spins its web, in the same manner. The souls of brutes, then, are incapable of any operation that does not involve the body. Now, since every substance is possessed of some operation, the soul of a brute animal will be unable to exist apart from its body; so that it perishes along with the body.

[3]   Likewise, every form separate from matter is understood in act, for the agent intellect renders species intelligible in act by way of abstraction, as we see from what was said above.[2] But, if the soul of the brute animal continues to exist after its body has passed away, then that soul will be a form separate from matter, and therefore a form understood in act. And yet, as Aristotle says in De anima III,[3] *with things separate from matter, that which understands is identical with that which is understood.* It follows that the soul of a brute animal, if it survives the body, will be intellectual; and this is impossible.

[4]   Then, too, in every thing capable of attaining a certain perfection, we find a natural desire for that perfection, since

1. See above, ch. 66 and 67.
2. See above, ch. 77.
3. Aristotle, De anima, III, 4 (430a 3).

good is what all things desire,[4] yet in such fashion that each thing desires the good proper to itself.[5] In brutes, however, we find no desire for perpetual existence, but only a desire for the perpetuation of their several species, since we do observe in them the desire to reproduce and thereby perpetuate the species—a desire common also to plants and to inanimate things, though not as regards desire proper to an animal as such, because animal appetite is consequent upon apprehension. For, since the apprehending power of the sensitive soul is limited to the here and now, that soul cannot possibly be cognizant of perpetual existence. Nor, then, does it desire such existence with animal appetite. Therefore, the soul of a brute animal is incapable of perpetual existence.

[5]   Moreover, as Aristotle remarks in Ethics x,[6] pleasures perfect operations. Hence, a thing's activity is directed to that object wherein it takes pleasure, as to its end. But all the pleasures of brute animals have reference to the preservation of their body; thus, they delight in sounds, odors, and sights only to the extent that they signify for them food or sex, the sole objects of all their pleasures. All the activities of such animals, then, have but a single end: the preservation of their bodily existence. Thus, there is in them no being whatever which is independent of the body.

[6]   The teaching of the Catholic faith is in harmony with this doctrine. For in the Old Testament we read, concerning the soul of the brute animal, that "the life of all flesh is in the blood" (Lev. 17:14; cf. Gen. 9:4-5), which seemingly means that the existence of such souls depends on the permanence of the blood. And it is said in the work On the Teachings of the Church:[7] "We declare that man alone has a subsistent soul," that is, a soul having life of itself; and that "the souls of brute animals perish along with their bodies."

[7]   Aristotle likewise states, in De anima II, that "the intel-

4. Aristotle, Nicomachean Ethics, I, 1 (1094a 2).
5. Aristotle, Nicomachean Ethics, VIII, 2 (1155b 23).
6. Aristotle, Nicomachean Ethics, X, 4 (1174b 23).
7. Gennadius, De ecclesiasticis dogmatibus, XVI–XVII (PL, 42, col. 1216).

lective part of the soul differs from the other parts as the incorruptible from the corruptible."[8]

[8] This eliminates Plato's theory that the souls even of brute animals are immortal.[9]

[9] Nevertheless, it would seem possible to show that the souls of such animals are immortal. For, if a thing possesses an operation through itself, distinctly its own, then it is subsisting through itself. But the sensitive soul in brutes enjoys an operation through itself, wherein the body has no part, namely, motion; for a mover is compounded of two parts, the one being mover and the other moved. Since the body is a thing moved, it remains that the soul is exclusively a mover, and, consequently, is subsisting through itself. Hence, the soul cannot be corrupted by accident, when the body is corrupted, for only those things are corrupted by accident which do not have being through themselves. Nor can the soul be corrupted through itself, since it neither has a contrary nor is composed of contraries. The result of the argument, therefore, is that the soul is altogether incorruptible.

[10] And, seemingly, Plato's argument that every soul is immortal[10] comes to the same thing, namely, that *the soul is a self-mover*; and everything of this sort must be immortal. For the body dies only when its mover departs from it, and a thing cannot abandon itself. That is why Plato inferred that a thing which moves itself cannot die. And thus he came to the conclusion that every soul possessed of the power of motion, even that of brute animals, is immortal. Now, we have remarked that this argument is reductively the same as the preceding one, since, given Plato's position that nothing moves without being moved, a thing that moves itself is a mover through itself and therefore has an operation through itself.

[11] Now, Plato also maintained that the sensitive soul enjoys an operation of its own, not only in respect to movement, but also as regards sensation.[11] For he said that sensation is a

8. Aristotle, *De anima*, II, 2 (413b 26).
9. Cf. Plato, *Phaedo*, 105E, 106B.
10. Cf. Plato, *Phaedrus*, 245C–246A.
11. Cf. Plato, *Theaetetus*, 160C.

movement of the sensing soul itself, and that the soul, thus moved, moved the body to sensation;[12] wherefore Plato said, in defining sense, that it is *the motion of the soul through the body.*[13]

[12]   Now, these Platonic dicta are patently false. For the act of sensation is not an act of movement; rather, to sense is to be moved; since, through the sensible objects' altering the condition of the senses in acting upon them, the animal is made actually sentient from being only potentially so. However, it cannot be maintained that the passivity of the sense in respect of the sensible is the same as that of the intellect in relation to the intelligible, so that sensation could then be an operation of the soul without a bodily instrument, just as understanding is. This is impossible, because the intellect grasps things in abstraction from matter and material conditions, which are individuating principles, whereas the sense does not, being manifestly limited to the perception of particulars, while the intellect attains to universals. Clearly, then, the senses are passive to things as existing in matter, but not the intellect, which is passive to things according as they are abstracted. Thus, in the intellect there is passivity in utter independence of corporeal matter, but not in the senses.

[13]   Moreover, diverse senses are receptive of diverse sensible objects—sight of colors, hearing of sounds, and so on. And it is quite clear that this diversity stems from the diverse dispositions of the organs. The organ of sight, for instance, is, necessarily, in potentiality to all colors, and the organ of hearing to all sounds. But, if this sense-receptivity occurred without a corporeal organ, then the same power would be receptive of all sensible objects; for an immaterial power is of itself related indifferently to all such qualities; and that is why the intellect, which employs no bodily organ, is cognizant of all sensible things. Without a bodily organ, then, no sensation takes place.

[14]   There is also the fact that sense is overwhelmed by an exceedingly high degree of intensity on the part of its objects; but the intellect is not, because *he who understands the higher intelligibles is more and not less able to understand*

12. Cf. Plato, *Philebus*, 34A.
13. Cf. Plato, *Timaeus*, 43C.

other things.[14] Hence, the state of passivity brought about in the sense by the sensible differs in kind from that which the intelligible causes in the intellect; the latter occurs without a bodily organ, the former with a bodily organ, the harmonious structure of whose parts is shattered by the pre-eminent power of some sensible objects.

[15] Now, Plato's statement, that *the soul is self-moving*, appears true in the light of our observations of bodily things. For no body seems to move without being moved, and Plato accordingly asserted that every mover is moved. Moreover, since it is impossible to proceed to infinity, every thing moved being moved by something else, he laid it down that the first mover, in each and every order of things, moves itself. It therefore followed that the soul, being the first mover in the order of animal movements, is a self-moving reality.

[16] This conclusion, however, is seen to be false, for two reasons. *First*, because it has been proved in Book I of this work[15] that whatever is moved through itself is a body; since, then, the soul is not a body, it cannot possibly be moved except by accident.

[17] The *second reason* is this. A mover, precisely as such, is in act; the thing moved, as such, is in potentiality; and nothing can be in act and in potentiality in the same respect. The same thing, therefore, cannot possibly be mover and moved in the same respect, so that, if a thing is said to move itself, one part of it must be mover and the other part moved. And this is what is meant by saying that an animal moves itself, for the animal's soul is the mover and its body the moved. Now, Plato did not hold that the soul is a body, although he did use the word *movement* in this connection, and in the proper sense of the term, movement belongs to bodies. But it was not this meaning that Plato had in mind; rather, he was taking *movement* in a more universal, extended sense, as applying to any operation, even as Aristotle does in *De anima* III: "Sensation and understanding are certain movements."[16]

14. Cf. Aristotle, *De anima*, III, 4 (429b 35).
15. *SCG*, I, ch. 13, ¶5, 10.
16. Aristotle, *De anima*, III, 7 (431a 6).

But in this case movement is the act, not of that which exists potentially, but of that which is perfect. So, in saying that the soul moves itself, Plato meant that it acts without the help of the body, whereas just the reverse is true of other forms, incapable as they are of exercising any action whatever apart from matter. (It is not any separately existing heat that produces heat, but only something hot.) Plato wishes to conclude from this that every soul capable of causing movement is immortal, for that which by its essence is endowed with operation can likewise enjoy an essential mode of existence.

[18]   But we have shown already that the brute animal's operation of sensing is impossible without the body. And this impossibility is all the more apparent in the case of the operation of appetite. For all things pertaining to sense appetite manifestly involve some bodily change; that is why they are called passions of the soul.

[19]   From these points it follows that movement is itself no organless operation of the sensitive soul. For it is only through sense and appetite that the soul of the brute animal moves; since the power designated as the executor of movement makes the animal's members obedient to the appetite's command. Thus, the powers of which we speak are of the sort that perfect the body as regards its being moved, rather than powers of actively moving.

[20]   It is, then, clearly impossible for any operation of the brute animal's soul to be independent of its body. And from this it can be inferred with necessity that the soul of the brute perishes with the body.

Chapter 83.

THAT THE HUMAN SOUL BEGINS TO EXIST
WHEN THE BODY DOES

[1]   Now, since the same things are found both to begin to be and to end, someone might suppose that, because the

human soul will not cease to exist, neither will it have begun to exist, but, on the contrary, has always been. And it would seem possible to prove this by the following arguments.

[2] That which will never cease to be has the power to exist forever. But no such thing can ever be truly said *not to be*; for the extent of a thing's existential duration is exactly commensurate with its power of existing. But of every thing which has begun to exist, it is at some time true to say that *it is not*. Therefore, that which will never cease to exist, at no time begins to be.

[3] Moreover, just as the truth of intelligible things is imperishable, so is that truth, of itself, eternal; because it is necessary, and whatever is necessary is eternal, for what is necessary to be cannot possibly not be. Now, the imperishable being of the soul is demonstrated from the imperishability of intelligible truth.[1] Hence, by the same reasoning, the soul's eternity can be proved from the eternal being of intelligible truth.

[4] Also, a thing that lacks several of its principal parts is not perfect. But, clearly, the principal parts of the universe are intellectual substances, in the genus of which human souls belong, as we have shown above.[2] If every day as many human souls begin to exist as men are born, then, obviously, many of the principal parts of the universe are added to it daily, so that it lacks a multiplicity of things. Consequently, the universe is imperfect. But this is impossible.

[5] Then, too, some draw their arguments from the authority of Sacred Scripture. For in Genesis (2:2) it is said that "on the seventh day God ended His work which He had made: and He rested from all His work which He had done." But, if God made new souls every day, this would not be true. Therefore, no new human souls ever begin to exist, but they have existed from the beginning of the world.

[6] Hence, for these and similar reasons, proponents of the doctrine of the world's eternity have said that, just as the

1. See above, ch. 79, ¶5ff.
2. See above, ch. 68.

human soul is incorruptible, so has it existed from all eternity. That is why the upholders of the theory of the immortality of human souls in their multiple existence—I refer to the Platonists—asserted that they have existed from eternity, and are united to bodies at one time and separated from them at another, these vicissitudes following a fixed cyclical pattern throughout set periods of years.[3] Advocates of the theory that human souls are immortal in respect of some single reality, pertaining to all men, which remains after death, declared, however, that this one entity has endured from all eternity; whether it be the agent intellect alone, as Alexander held, or, together with this, the possible intellect, as Averroes maintained.[4] Aristotle, also, seems to be making the same point when, speaking of the intellect, he says that it is not only incorruptible, but also *everlasting*.[5]

[7]   On the other hand, some who profess the Catholic faith, yet are imbued with the teachings of the Platonists, have taken a middle position. For, since the Catholic faith teaches that nothing is eternal except God, these persons maintain, not that human souls are eternal, but that they were created with, or rather before, the visible world, yet are fettered to bodies anew. Among these Christians, Origen was the first exponent of this theory,[6] and a number of his disciples followed suit. The theory, indeed, survives to this day among heretics, the Manicheans, for example, siding with Plato in proclaiming the eternity and transmutation of souls.

[8]   Now, all these opinions can be easily shown to have no foundation in truth. For it has already been proved that there does not exist only one possible agent intellect for all men.[7] Hence, it remains for us to proceed against those theories which, while envisaging the existence of many human souls, maintain that they existed before bodies, either from eternity, or from the foundation of the world. The incongruity of such a notion is exposed by the following arguments.

3. Cf. Plato, *Timaeus*, 42BC; *Phaedrus*, 246A, 248C–249B.
4. See above, ch. 80, ¶2.
5. Aristotle, *De anima*, III, 5 (430a 18, 23).
6. Origen, *Peri Archon*, II, 9 (PG, 11, col. 226).
7. See above, ch. 59 and 76.

[9] For, it has already been established[8] that the soul is united to the body as its form and act. Now, although act is prior in its nature to potentiality, nevertheless in one and the same thing it is temporally posterior to it; for a thing is moved from potentiality to act. Thus, seed, which is potentially living,[9] preceded the soul, which is the act of life.

[10] Moreover, it is natural to every form to be united to its proper matter; otherwise, that which is made of form and matter would be something preternatural. But that which befits a thing naturally is attributed to it before that which befits it preternaturally, because the latter is in it by accident, the former, through itself. Now, that which is by accident is always posterior to that which is through itself. It is, therefore, becoming to the soul to be united to the body before being separated from it. The soul, then, was not created before the body to which it is united.

[11] Again, every part existing in separation from its whole is imperfect. Now, the soul, being a form, as has been proved,[10] is a part of the specific nature of man. Hence, as long as it exists through itself apart from the body, it is imperfect. But in the order of natural things, the perfect is prior to the imperfect. It would, therefore, be inconsistent with the order of nature were the soul created apart from the body before being united to it.

[12] And again, if souls are created without bodies, it must be asked how they are united to bodies. This union could be effected in but two ways: by violence or by nature. Now, everything violent is against nature, so that if the union of soul and body is brought about by violence it is not natural. Hence, man, who is composed of both, is something unnatural; which is obviously false. There is also the consideration that intellectual substances are of a higher order than the heavenly bodies. But in the latter there is nothing violent or contrary. Much less, therefore, does any such thing exist in intellectual substances.

8. See above, ch. 68.
9. Cf. Aristotle, *De generatione animalium,* II, 3 (737a 17).
10. See above, ch. 68.

[13]   Now, if the union of souls to bodies is natural, then, in their creation, souls had a natural desire to be united to bodies. Now, natural appetite immediately issues in act if no obstacle stands in the way, as we see in the movement of heavy and light bodies; for nature always works in the same way. So, unless something existed to prevent it, souls would have been united to bodies from the very beginning of their creation. But whatever obstructs the realisation of natural appetite does violence to it. That at some time souls existed in separation from bodies was therefore the result of violence. And this is incongruous, not only because in such substances there can be nothing violent, as was shown, but also because the violent and the unnatural, being accidental, cannot be prior to that which is in keeping with nature, nor can they be consequent upon the total species.

[14]   Furthermore, since everything naturally desires its own perfection, it pertains to matter to desire form, and not conversely. But the soul is compared to the body as form to matter, as was shown above.[11] Therefore, the union of the soul to the body is not brought about in response to the desire of the soul, but, rather, of the body.

[15]   Now, the argument may be raised that union with the body is natural to the soul, as well as separation from it, according to various periods of time. But such a notion seems impossible. For changes that take place naturally in a subject are accidental, such as youth and old age; so that, if its union with, and separation from the body are for the soul natural changes, then union with the body will be an accident of the soul. The human being constituted by this union therefore will not be an essential but an accidental being.

[16]   Then, too, whatever is subject to alternate phases of existence according to various periods of time is subject to the movement of the heaven, which the whole course of time follows. But intellectual and incorporeal substances, including separately existing souls, transcend the entire realm of bodily things. Hence, they cannot be subject to the movements of the heavenly bodies. Therefore, it is impossible that they

11. See above, ch. 68 ¶2–5.

should be naturally united during one period of time and separated during another, or that they should naturally desire this at one time, and that at another.

[17] On the other hand, the hypothesis that souls are united to bodies neither by violence nor by nature, but by free choice, is likewise impossible. For no one voluntarily enters into a state worse than the previous one, unless he be deceived. But the separate soul enjoys a higher state of existence than when united to the body; especially according to the Platonists, who say that through its union with the body, the soul forgets what it knew before, its power to contemplate truth in a pure manner thus being checked.[12] Hence, the soul is not willingly united to the body unless it be the victim of deception. But there can be nothing in the soul that could cause deception, since, for the Platonists, the soul is possessed of all knowledge. Nor can it be said that the soul's judgment, proceeding from universal scientific knowledge and applied to a particular matter of choice, is overwhelmed by the passions, as in the incontinent; for no passions of this sort occur without bodily change, and, consequently, they cannot exist in the separate soul. We are, then, left with the conclusion that, if the soul had existed before the body, it would not be united to the body of its own will.

[18] Moreover, every effect issuing from the concurrent operation of two mutually unrelated wills is fortuitous, as in the case of a person who goes out to shop and meets his creditor in the market place without any prior arrangement between the two. Now, the will of the generative agent, whereon the body's production depends, is independent of the will of the separate soul which wills to be united. It follows that the union of the soul and body is fortuitous, since it cannot be effected without the concurrence of both wills. Thus, the begetting of a man results not from nature, but from chance, which is patently false, since it occurs in the majority of cases.

[19] Now, again, the theory may be advanced that the soul is united to the body by divine decree, and not by nature, nor of its own will. But such a supposition also seems inadmissible

12. Cf. Plato, *Timaeus, Meno, passim.*

on the hypothesis that souls were created before bodies. For God established each thing in being in a mode congruent with its nature. Hence, in the Book of Genesis (1: 10, 31) it is said of each creature: "God saw that it was good," and of all creatures collectively: "God saw all the things that He had made, and they were very good." If, then, God created souls separate from bodies, it must be said that this manner of being is more suitable to their nature. But it is not becoming to the ordering of things by the divine goodness to relegate them to a lower state, but, rather, to raise them to a higher. Hence, it could not have been by God's ordinance that the soul was united to the body.

[20]   Moreover, it is inconsistent with the order of divine wisdom to raise up lower things to the detriment of higher things. But generable and corruptible bodies have the lowest rank in the order of things. Hence, it would not have been consistent with the order of divine wisdom to ennoble human bodies by uniting pre-existing souls to them, since this would be impossible without detriment to the latter, as we have already seen.

[21]   Having this point in mind—for he asserted that human souls had been created from the beginning—Origen said that they were united to bodies by divine decree, but as a punishment. For Origen thought that souls had sinned before bodies existed, and that according to the gravity of their sin, souls were shut up in bodies of higher or lower character, as in so many prisons.

[22]   This doctrine, however, is untenable, for, being contrary to a good of nature, punishment is said to be an evil. If, then, the union of soul and body is something penal in character, it is not a good of nature. But this is impossible, for that union is intended by nature, since natural generation terminates in it. And again, on Origen's theory, it would follow that man's being would not be a good according to nature, yet it is said, after man's creation: "God saw all the things that He had made, and they were very good."

[23]   Furthermore, good does not issue from evil save by accident. Therefore, if the soul's union with the body were due to

sin on the part of the separate soul, it would follow that this union is accidental, since it is a kind of good. In that case the production of man was a matter of chance. But such a thing is derogatory to God's wisdom, of which it is written that "It ordered all things in number, weight, and measure" (Wisd. 11:21).

[24] That notion also clearly clashes with apostolic doctrine. For St. Paul says of Jacob and Esau, that "when they were not yet born, nor had done any good or evil, it was said that the elder shall serve the younger" (Rom. 9:11–12). Hence, before this was said, their souls had not sinned at all, yet the Apostle's statement postdates the time of their conception, as Genesis (25:23) makes clear.

[25] Earlier,[13] in treating of the distinction of things, we leveled against Origen's position a number of arguments which may also be used here. Omitting them, therefore, we pass on to others.

[26] It must be said that the human soul either needs the senses or does not need them. Now, experience seems to show clearly that the former is true. For a person who lacks a certain sense has no knowledge of the sensible objects which are perceived through that sense; a man born blind has neither knowledge nor any understanding of colors. Furthermore, if the human soul does not require the senses in order to understand, then sensitive and intellective cognition in man would have no ordered relationship to one another. But experience demonstrates the contrary; for our senses give rise to memories, and from these we obtain experiential knowledge of things, which in turn is the means through which we come to an understanding of the universal principles of sciences and arts.[14] Now, nature is wanting in nothing that is necessary for the fulfillment of its proper operation; thus, to animals whose soul is endowed with powers of sense and movement nature gives the appropriate organs of sense and movement. Hence, if the human soul needs the senses in order to understand, then that soul would never have been made to be in the first place with-

13. See above, ch. 44.
14. Cf. Aristotle, *Posterior Analytics*, II, 19 (100a 3).

out the indispensable assistants which the senses are. But the senses do not function without corporeal organs, as we have seen.[15] The soul, therefore, was not made without such organs.

[27] The argument that the human soul does not need the senses in order to understand, and thus is said to have been created apart from the body, necessarily implies that, before being united to the body, the soul was by itself cognizant of all scientific truths. The Platonists indeed admitted this[16] in saying that Ideas, which according to Plato are the separate intelligible forms of things, are the cause of knowledge; and thus, the separate soul, having no obstacle confronting it, received full knowledge of all sciences. Therefore, since the soul is found to be ignorant when united to the body, it must be said that it forgets the knowledge which it previously possessed. The Platonists acknowledge this inference, also, adducing the following observation as indicative of its truth: If a man, however ignorant he may be, is questioned systematically about matters taught in the sciences, he will answer the truth; so, if a man has forgotten some of the things that he knew before, and a person proposes to him one by one the things he has forgotten, he recalls them to his memory. And from this they inferred that *learning was nothing else than remembering*. This theory then necessarily led to the conclusion that union with the body places an obstacle in the way of the soul's understanding. In no case, however, does nature unite a thing to that which impedes its operation; on the contrary, nature unites the thing to that which facilitates its operation. Thus, the union of body and soul will not be natural, so that man will not be a natural thing, nor will his engendering be natural; which, of course, is false.

[28] The ultimate end of every thing, moreover, is that which it strives to attain by its operations. But man, by all his proper operations fittingly ordered and rightly directed, strives to attain the contemplation of truth; for the operations of the active powers are certain preparations and dispositions to the contemplative powers. The end of man, therefore, is to arrive at the contemplation of truth. It is for this purpose, then,

15. See above, ch. 57, ¶8, 9.
16. Cf. Plato, *Timaeus, Meno*, passim.

that the soul is united to the body, and in this union does man's being consist. Therefore, it is not union with the body that causes the soul to lose knowledge which it had possessed; on the contrary, the soul is united to the body so that it may acquire knowledge.

[29] Then, too, if a person ignorant of the sciences is questioned about matters pertaining to the sciences, his answers will not be true, except with regard to the universal principles of which no one is ignorant, but which are known by all in the same way and naturally. But, if that ignorant person is questioned systematically later on, he will answer truly concerning matters closely related to the principles, by referring them to the latter; and he will go on answering truly as long as he is able to apply the power of first principles to the subjects about which he is questioned. This makes it quite clear, therefore, that through the primary principles new knowledge is caused in the person questioned. This new knowledge, then, is not caused by recalling to memory things previously known.

[30] Furthermore, if the knowledge of conclusions were as natural to the soul as knowledge of principles, then everyone's judgment concerning conclusions, as well as principles, would be the same, since things natural are the same for all. But not all persons share the same judgment in respect to conclusions, but only to principles. Clearly, then, the knowledge of principles is natural to us, but not the knowledge of conclusions. The non-natural, however, is acquired by us through the natural; thus it is through our hands that we produce, in the world of things outside us, all our artifacts. Therefore, we have no knowledge of conclusions except that which we acquire from principles.

[31] Again, since nature is always directed to one thing, of one power there must naturally be one object, as color of sight, and sound of hearing. Hence, the intellect, being one power, has one natural object, of which it has knowledge essentially and naturally. And this object must be one under which are included all things known by the intellect; just as under color are included all colors essentially visible. Now, this is none other than *being* [*ens*]. Our intellect, therefore,

knows being naturally, and whatever essentially belongs to a being as such; and upon this knowledge is founded the knowledge of first principles, such as the *impossibility of simultaneously affirming and denying*, and the like. Thus, only these principles are known naturally by our intellect, while conclusions are known through them; just as, through color, sight is cognizant of both common and accidental sensibles.

[32]   And again. That which we acquire through the senses did not exist in the soul before its union with the body. But our knowledge of principles themselves is derived from sensible things; if, for instance, we had not perceived some whole by our senses, we would be unable to understand the principle that *the whole is greater than its parts*; even as a man born blind is utterly insensible of colors. Therefore, neither did the soul prior to its union with the body have any knowledge of principles; much less, of other things. Hence, Plato's argument that the soul existed before its union with the body is without solidity.

[33]   There is also the argument that if all souls existed before the bodies to which they are united, it would then seemingly follow that the same soul is united to different bodies according to the vicissitudes of time—an obvious consequence of the doctrine of the eternity of the world. For from the hypothesis of the engendering of human beings from eternity it follows that an infinite number of human bodies have come into being and passed away throughout the whole course of time. Hence, two possibilities: either an actually infinite number of souls pre-existed, if each soul is united to a single body; or, if the number of souls is finite, then the same souls are united at one time to these particular bodies and at another time to those. And seemingly we would be faced with the same consequence if we held that souls existed before bodies but that they were not produced from eternity. For, even if it be supposed that the engendering of men has not always been in progress, nevertheless, in the very nature of the case, it indubitably can be of infinite duration; because every man is so constituted by nature that, unless he be impeded accidentally, he is able to beget another man, even as he himself was begotten of another. But this would be impossible if,

given the existence of a finite number of souls, one soul cannot be united to several bodies. That is why a number of proponents of the doctrine that souls exist before bodies espoused the theory of transmigration; which cannot possibly be true. Therefore, souls did not exist before bodies.

[34] Now, the impossibility of one soul's being united to diverse bodies is clearly seen in the light of the following considerations. Human souls do not differ specifically from one another, but only numerically; otherwise, men also would differ specifically, one from the other. Material principles, however, are the source of numerical distinction. It follows that the distinction among human souls must be attributed to something material in character—but not so as to imply that matter is a part of the soul, because the soul is an intellectual substance, and no such substance has matter, as we have proved above.[17] It therefore remains that in the manner explained above[18] the diversity and plurality of souls result from their relationship to the diverse matters to which they are united; so that, if there are different bodies, they must have different souls united to them. One soul, then, is not united to several bodies.

[35] Moreover, it was shown above[19] that the soul is united to the body as its form. But forms must be proportionate to their proper matters, since they are related to one another as act to potentiality, the proper act corresponding to the proper potentiality. Therefore, one soul is not united to a number of bodies.

[36] We argue further from the fact that the power of the mover must be proportionate to the thing movable by it, for not every power moves every movable. But, even if the soul were not the form of the body, it could not be said that the soul is not the body's mover, for we distinguish the animate from the inanimate by sense and movement. It therefore follows that the distinction among souls must correspond to the distinction among bodies.

17. See above, ch. 50 and 51.
18. See above, ch. 80 and 81.
19. See above, ch. 68, ¶2–5.

[37] Likewise, in the realm of things subject to generation and corruption it is impossible for one and the same thing to be reproduced by generation; for generation and corruption are movements in respect of substance, so that in things generated and corrupted the substance does not remain the same, as it does in things moved locally. But, if one soul is united successively to different generated bodies, the self-same man will come into being again through generation. This follows necessarily for Plato, who said that man is a "soul clothed with a body."[20] This consequence also holds for any others. For a thing's unity follows upon its form, even as its being does, so that those things are one in number whose form is one in number. It is, therefore, impossible for one soul to be united to different bodies. From this it follows, too, that souls were not in existence before bodies.

[38] With this truth the Catholic faith expressly agrees. For it is said in a Psalm (32:15): "He who hath made the hearts of every one of them"; namely, because God created a soul specially for each one, and neither created them all together, nor united one to different bodies. In this connection also we read in the work *On the Teachings of the Church*: "We declare that human souls were not created from the beginning together with other intellectual natures, nor all at the same time, as Origen imagines."[21]

Chapter 84.

SOLUTION OF THE PRECEDING ARGUMENTS

[1] The arguments in proof of the thesis that souls have existed from eternity, or that at least they existed before bodies,[1] are easily solved.

[2] As to the first argument, the statement that the soul

20. See above, ch. 57, ¶4, 5.
21. Gennadius, *De ecclesiasticis dogmatibus*, XIV (PL, 42, col. 1216).
1. See above, ch. 83, ¶2–7.

has the power to exist always, must be granted. But it must be borne in mind that the power and potentiality of a thing extend not to what was, but to what is or will be; hence, there is no possibility with respect to things past. Therefore, from the fact that the soul has the power to exist always it can be concluded, not that the soul always was, but that it always will be.

[3] Moreover, that to which a power is ordained does not follow from the power except on the supposition of the latter's existence. Therefore, though the soul have the power to exist always, it cannot be inferred that the soul does exist always, except after it has actually received this power; and if it is assumed that the soul has received this power from eternity, the point that has to be proved, namely, the soul's existence from eternity, will be begged.

[4] The *second argument*, concerning the eternity of the truth which the soul understands, calls for a distinction. In one way, this eternity can be taken to refer to the thing understood; in another, to that by which it is understood. In the first case, the thing understood would be eternal, but not the one who understands; in the second, eternity would be on the side of the soul which understands. Now, the understood truth is eternal, not in the latter but in the former reference; since, as we have already clearly shown,[2] the intelligible species, whereby our soul understands truth, come to us repeatedly from the phantasms through the operation of the agent intellect. It cannot, then, be inferred that the soul is eternal, but that the truths understood are based upon something eternal; for, indeed, their foundation is in the first truth, as in the universal cause embracing all truth. But the soul stands in relation to this eternal entity, not as subject to form, but as thing to proper end, since the true is the good of the intellect, and its end. Now, argument concerning a thing's duration can be drawn from its end, just as the question of its beginning is arguable through its efficient cause; for, indeed, a thing ordained to an eternal end must be capable of enduring forever. That is why the soul's immortality can be proved from the eternity of intelligible truth, but not its eternity. And what

2. See above, ch. 76, ¶14, 17.

we have already said on the question of the eternity of creatures[3] makes it quite clear that the eternity of the soul cannot
be demonstrated from the eternity of its efficient cause.

[5]   The third argument, in regard to the perfection of the
universe, is void of necessity. For the perfection of the universe envisages species, not individuals; since the universe is
constantly receiving the addition of myriad individuals of
pre-existing species. Human souls, however, do not differ in
specific nature but only in number, as was shown above.[4]
Hence, it is not incompatible with the perfection of the universe if new souls be created.

[6]   And from this we see the solution of the fourth argument. For in the Book of Genesis (2:2) it is said at the same
time that "God ended His work," and that "He rested from all
His work which He had done." Hence, just as the consumma-
tion or perfection of creatures is considered in terms of species,
not individuals, so God's resting must be understood to refer
to cessation from forming new species, but not new individuals, of which others specifically alike have existed before.
Thus, since all human souls are of one species, and likewise
all men, it is not inconsistent with God's rest if He creates
new souls every day.

[7]   Now, it should be known that in Aristotle we do not
find the statement that the human intellect is eternal; yet he
customarily says this of those things which he thinks have
existed always. But he does say that the human intellect is
everlasting;[5] and this can be said of those things that always
will be, even if they have not always been. Hence, when Aristotle, in Metaphysics XI, excepted the intellective soul from
the condition of other forms, he did not say that it was prior
to matter, but Plato said this of the Ideas; and so it would
seem that Aristotle might consistently have said something of
the sort here about the soul; but what he did say was that the
soul remains after the body.[6]

3. See above, ch. 31–38.
4. See above, ch. 81, ¶8.
5. See above, ch. 61, ¶4, and 78, ¶12.
6. Aristotle, Metaphysics, XI, 3 (1070a 25).

Chapter 85.

THAT THE SOUL IS NOT MADE OF GOD'S SUBSTANCE

[1] Things already said make it quite clear that the soul is not of God's substance.

[2] For it was shown in Book I of this work[1] that the divine substance is eternal, and that no perfection of it has any beginning. Human souls, however, did not exist before bodies, as we have just shown.[2] Therefore, the soul cannot be made of God's substance.

[3] It was likewise shown in Book I that God cannot be the form of anything.[3] But the human soul is, as proved above,[4] the form of the body. Therefore, it is not of the divine substance.

[4] Moreover, everything from which something is made is in potentiality to that which is made from it. But the divine substance is not in potentiality to anything, since it is pure act, as was shown in Book I[5] Therefore, neither the soul nor anything else can possibly be made from God's substance.

[5] Then, too, that from which something is made is in some way changed. But God is absolutely unchangeable, as was proved in Book I.[6] It is, therefore, impossible for anything to be made from Him.

[6] Furthermore, that the soul suffers variations in knowledge and virtue, and their opposites, is a fact of observation. But in God there is absolutely no variation, either through himself or by accident.[7]

[7] Also, it was shown in Book I that God is pure act, com-

1. SCG, I, ch. 15. 2. See above, ch. 83 and 84.
3. SCG, I, ch. 27. 4. See above, ch. 68.
5. SCG, I, ch. 16. 6. SCG, I, ch. 13, ¶3–33.
7. Ibid.

pletely devoid of potentiality.[8] But in the human soul we find both potentiality and act, since it contains the possible intellect, which is in potentiality to all intelligibles, as well as the agent intellect, as was shown above.[9] Therefore, it is not of God's nature that the human soul is made.

[8]   Again, since the divine substance is utterly indivisible,[10] the soul cannot be part of it, but only the whole substance. But the divine substance can be one only, as shown in Book I.[11] It therefore follows that of all men there is but one soul so far as intellect is concerned. And this was disproved above.[12] Therefore, the soul is not made of God's substance.

[9]   Now, the theory that the soul is part and parcel of God's own substance or nature seems to have had three sources: the doctrine that no substance is incorporeal; the doctrine that there is but one intellect for all men; the very likeness of our soul to God. As to the first source, some, having denied that any substance is incorporeal, asserted that God is the noblest body, whether it be air or fire or anything else putatively a principle, and that the soul was of the nature of this body. For, as Aristotle points out,[13] the partisans of this doctrine all attributed to the soul whatever to their mind had the character of a principle. So, from this position, it followed that the soul is of the substance of God. And from this root sprang the theory of Manes, who held that God is a luminous body extended through infinite space, and of this body, he said, the human soul is a fragment.[14]

[10]   This theory, however, was previously refuted by the demonstration that God is not a body,[15] as well as the proof that neither the human soul nor any intellectual substance is a body.[16]

[11]   As to the second source indicated above, some have

8. SCG, I, ch. 16.   9. See above, ch. 61 and 76.
10. SCG, I, ch. 18.   11. SCG, I, ch. 42.
12. See above, ch. 73–78.
13. Aristotle, De anima, I, 2 (404b 10).
14. Cf. St. Augustine, Confessions, IV, 16 (PL, 32, col. 706).
15. SCG, I, ch. 20.
16. See above, ch. 49 and 65.

held that of all men there is but a single intellect, whether an agent intellect alone, or an agent and a possible intellect together, as we explained above.[17] And since the ancients attributed divinity to every separate substance, it followed that our soul, the intellect by which we understand, is of the nature of the divine. And that is why in this age certain persons who profess the Christian faith and who posit a separately existing agent intellect explicitly identify the agent intellect with God.

[12]   Now, this whole doctrine of the unicity of man's intellect has already been refuted.[18]

[13]   In the very likeness of our soul to God may be found the *third source* of the theory that the soul is of the substance or nature of God Himself. For we find that understanding, which is thought to be proper to God above all, is possessed by no substance in this lower world except man—and this on account of his soul. It might, then, seem that the soul partakes of the nature of God; and this notion might appeal especially to persons firmly convinced of the immortality of the human soul.

[14]   This idea even seems to find support in the Book of Genesis (1:26), where, after the statement, "Let us make man to Our image and likeness," it is added: "God formed man of the slime of the earth; and breathed into his face the breath of life." From this text some wished to infer that the soul is of the very nature of God. For, since he who breathes into another's face puts forth into the latter numerically the same thing that was in himself, holy Scripture itself would here seem to imply that God put into man something divine in order to give him life.

[15]   But the likeness in question is no proof that man is a part of the divine substance, for man's understanding suffers from many defects—which cannot be said of God's. This likeness, then, is rather indicative of a certain imperfect image than of any consubstantiality. And, indeed, Scripture implies

17. See above, ch. 73–78.
18. *Ibid.*

this in saying that man was made "to the image" of God. And thus the "breathing" of which Genesis speaks signifies the pouring forth of life from God into man according to a certain likeness, and not according to unity of substance. So, too, "the spirit of life" is said to have been "breathed into his face," for, since the organs of several senses are located in this part of the body, life is more palpably manifested in the face. God, therefore, is said to have breathed the spirit into man's face, because He gave man the spirit of life, but not by detaching it from His own substance. For he who literally breathes into the face of someone—and this bodily breathing is evidently the source of the Scriptural metaphor—blows air into his face, but does not infuse part of his substance into him.

Chapter 86.

THAT THE HUMAN SOUL IS NOT TRANSMITTED WITH THE SEMEN

[1]   From points previously established it can be shown that the human soul is not transmitted with the semen, as though it were begotten by coition.

[2]   For any principles whatever whose operations cannot be without the body cannot without the body begin to be at all; a thing's way of being and its way of operating are in mutual accord, since everything operates inasmuch as it is a being. Contrariwise, those principles whose operations are performed without the body are not generated through the generation of the body. Now, the nutritive and sensitive soul cannot operate independently of the body, as we have seen before.[1] On the other hand, as we have likewise pointed out,[2] the intellective soul does not operate through any bodily organ. Therefore, the nutritive and sensitive souls are brought into being through the body's engendering; but not the intellective soul. The transmission of the semen, however, has as

1. See above, ch. 68, ¶10, 11.
2. See above, ch. 68, ¶12.

its aim the generation of the body. It is, therefore, through the transmission of the semen that the nutritive and sensitive souls begin to be; but this is not true of the intellective soul.

[3] Moreover, there are but two ways in which the human soul could conceivably originate through the transmission of the semen. First, it might be thought to exist in the semen actually, as though it were parted by accident from the soul of the generative agent, in the manner in which the semen is separated from the body. A case in point are annulose animals which live after being cut in two and which contain one soul actually and several potentially, since, when the body of such an animal is divided, the soul begins to exist actually in each living part. Second, the semen might be thought to possess a power productive of the intellective soul, and thus the latter would be held to exist virtually in the semen, but not actually.

[4] Now, the first of these is impossible for two reasons. One: since the intellective soul is the most perfect of souls and its power the highest, its proper perfectible subject is a body having many different organs through which its multifarious operations can be carried out; and that is why the soul cannot possibly be actually present in the semen separated from the body; for, indeed, not even the souls of perfect brute animals are multiplied by division, as with annulose animals. And the *second reason* is this. The intellect, which is the proper and principal power of the intellective soul, is not the act of any part of the body, and therefore it cannot be divided accidentally as a result of the body's being divided. Nor, then, can the intellective soul be so divided.

[5] The second[3] is also impossible. For it is by transmuting the body that the active power in the semen contributes to the generation of the animal; indeed, a power present in matter cannot act otherwise. But every form that is initiated through the transmutation of matter is dependent upon matter for its being, since by this means the form is made actual from being potential, and thus the material transmutation

---

3. Hypothetical way in which the human soul could originate through the transmission of the semen.

issues in the actual being of the matter through its union with the form. Hence, if in this way the form also begins to be simply, then the form will have no being at all except that which accrues to it through being united to a matter; that is to say, the form will be dependent on matter for its being. Hence, from the hypothesis that the human soul is brought into being through the active power in the semen it follows that its being depends upon matter, as with other material forms. But the contrary of this has already been proved.[4] The intellective soul, therefore, is in no way produced through the transmission of the semen.

[6] Moreover, every form brought into being through the transmutation of matter is educed from the potentiality of matter, for the transmutation of matter is its reduction from potentiality to act. Now, the intellective soul cannot be educed from the potentiality of matter, since it has already been shown[5] that the intellective soul altogether exceeds the power of matter, through having a materially independent operation, as was likewise proved above.[6] The intellective soul, therefore, is not brought into being through the transmutation of matter; nor, then, is it produced by the action of a power in the semen.

[7]   Then, too, the operation of no active power exceeds the genus to which that power belongs. But the intellective soul transcends the whole genus of bodies, since it enjoys an operation completely surpassing the range of bodily things, namely, the operation of understanding. Therefore, no corporeal power can produce the intellective soul. But every action of a power present in the semen is exercised through some bodily potency, since the formative power acts by means of a three-fold heat—the heat of fire, of the heaven, and of the soul. Therefore, the intellective soul cannot be produced by a power in the semen.

[8]   Furthermore, it is ridiculous to say that an intellective substance is either divided in consequence of the division of a body or produced by a power corporeal in nature. But, as was

4. See above, ch. 68 and 79.
5. See above, ch. 68, ¶12, and ch. 78.
6. Ibid.

previously shown,[7] the human soul is an intellectual substance. Therefore, it cannot be said that the soul is divided as
the result of the semen's being divided, or that it is brought
into being by an active power in the semen. In no way, then,
does the human soul begin to exist through the transmission
of the semen.

[9] Again, if the generation of a thing is the cause of a
thing's being, then its corruption will be the cause of its
ceasing to be. The corruption of the body, however, does not
cause the soul to cease to be, since the soul is immortal, as
was proved above.[8] Consequently, neither is the production of
the body the cause of the soul's entry into existence. But the
transmission of the semen is the proper cause of the engendering of the body. Hence, the transmission of the semen is not
the generating cause that brings the soul into being.

[10] Thus is excluded the error of Apollinaris and his followers, who said that "souls are generated by souls, just as
bodies are generated by bodies."[9]

Chapter 87.

THAT THE HUMAN SOUL IS BROUGHT INTO
BEING THROUGH THE CREATIVE ACTION
OF GOD

[1] On the basis of what has already been said, it can be
demonstrated that God alone brings the human soul into
being.

[2] There are but three possibilities: whatever is brought
into being is either generated through itself, or by accident, or
it is created. But the human soul is not generated through
itself, since it is not composed of matter and form, as was
shown above.[1] Nor is it generated by accident; for, since the

7. See above, ch. 68.
8. See above, ch. 79.
9. Cf. St. Gregory of Nyssa, *De anima*, (PG, 45, col. 206).
1. See above, ch. 50 and 65.

soul is the form of the body, it would be generated through the generation of the body, which results from the active power of the semen—a notion just now disproved. And, as was shown a while back,[2] the human soul begins to be, for it is not eternal, nor does it exist before the body. It therefore remains that it comes into being by way of creation. Now, it was shown above[3] that only God can create. Hence, He alone brings the human soul into being.

[3]   There is also the point, previously demonstrated,[4] that everything whose substance is not its being has an author of its being. But the human soul is not its being; this, as we proved in the same place, is the prerogative of God alone. The human soul, therefore, has an active cause of its being. Now, that which has being through itself is also actuated through itself; while that which does not have being through itself, but only together with another, is produced not through itself, but through this other thing being made; the form of fire emerges when the fire itself is produced. Now, it pertains to the human soul distinctively, in contrast to other forms, to be subsisting in its being, and to communicate to the body the being proper to itself.[5] The human soul therefore enjoys, through itself, a mode of production beyond that of other forms, which come to be by accident through the making of the composites. But, since the human soul does not have matter as part of itself, it cannot be made from something as from matter. It therefore remains that the soul is made from nothing. And thus, it is created. And in view of the previously demonstrated fact[6] that creation is the proper work of God, it follows that the soul is created immediately by God alone.

[4]   Moreover, as we have just proved,[7] things of the same genus come into being in the same way. But the soul belongs to the genus of intellectual substances, which cannot conceivably be brought into being except by way of creation.

2. See above, ch. 83.
3. See above, ch. 21.
4. See above, ch. 15.
5. See above, ch. 68.
6. See above, ch. 21.
7. See above, ch. 86, ¶2.

Therefore, it is through creation by God that the human soul comes into being.

[5] Furthermore, whatever is produced by an agent acquires therefrom either something that is the source of a thing's being in such and such a species, or it acquires being itself, purely and simply. Now, the soul cannot be brought into being in such a way as to acquire something having the character of a source of its being, as with things composed of matter and form, which are generated through acquiring an actual form; because the soul, being a simple substance, as we have already shown,[8] contains nothing that would be a source of its own being. Thus, the only way in which the soul is brought into being by an agent is by receiving from it being unqualifiedly speaking. Now, being itself is the proper effect of the first and universal agent. For secondary agents act by impressing the likenesses of their forms on the things they make, these likenesses being the forms of the thing made. Therefore, the soul cannot be brought into being save by the first and universal agent, namely, God.

[6] Then, too, the end of a thing corresponds to its source; for a thing achieves its perfection when it attains its proper source, whether by way of likeness to it, or in any manner whatsoever. Now, the end and ultimate perfection of the human soul lies in its transcending by knowledge and love the whole order of creatures, thus reaching up to the first principle, which is God. It is therefore He that is the proper principle of the soul's origin.

[7] This truth also seems to be implied in sacred Scripture, for in speaking of the formation of other animals, it ascribes their souls to other causes, as in the text: "Let the waters bring forth the creeping creatures with a living soul" (Gen. 1:20), and so it is with other things. But when man is spoken of later on, the creation of his soul by God is revealed: "God formed man of the slime of the earth, and breathed into his face the breath of life" (Gen. 2:7).

[8] And this does away with the error of those who maintained that souls were created by angels.

8. See above, ch. 50 and 65.

Chapter 88.

ARGUMENTS DESIGNED TO PROVE THAT THE HUMAN SOUL IS FORMED FROM THE SEMEN

[1] There are, however, certain arguments which seem to militate against what we have said above.[1]

[2] From the fact that man is an animal inasmuch as he has a sensitive soul, and the concept of *animal* applies univocally to man and other animals, it seems to follow that man's sensitive soul is of the same genus as the souls of other animals. Now, things of the same genus have the same manner of coming into being.[2] Hence, the sensitive soul of man, just as of other animals, comes into being through a power in the semen. But in man the intellective and sensitive soul are, as shown above,[3] the same in respect of substance. Seemingly, therefore, the intellective soul also is produced through a power in the semen.

[3] Moreover, as Aristotle teaches in the *De generation animalium*,[4] the fetus is an animal before becoming a man. But, during the time in which the fetus is an animal and not a man, it has a sensitive and not an intellective soul; and, just as in other animals, this sensitive soul in indubitably produced by the active power of the semen. And yet that same sensitive soul is potentially intellective, just as that animal is potentially a rational animal; and the notion that the supervening intellective soul is substantially distinct from the sensitive one has been refuted already.[5] It therefore seems that the substance of the intellective soul is derived from a power in the semen.

[4] Then, too, the soul, being the form of the body, is united

1. See above, ch. 86 and 87.
2. See above, ch. 86, ¶2, 7.
3. See above, ch. 58.
4. Aristotle, *De generatione animalium*, II, 3 (736b 3).
5. See above, ch. 58.

to the body according to the soul's own being. But things that are one in being are the term of one action and of one agent; for, if there were diverse agents, and, consequently, diverse actions, effects diverse in being would ensue. Hence, it is in the being of soul and body that the one action of one agent must terminate. But the body's production is clearly due to the action of a power in the semen. Hence, the soul, which is the body's form, is the effect of the same cause, and not of a separate agent.

[5] Furthermore, it is by a power present in the emitted semen that man generates things specifically like himself. But any univocal agent generates such things by causing the form of the effect generated, which owes its specific nature to that form. Consequently, the human soul, whence man derives his specific nature, is produced by a power in the semen.

[6] Then there is the argument of Apollinaris,[6] that whoever completes a work co-operates with the agent, so that, if souls are created by God, He is responsible for completing the generation of children who are sometimes born of adulterers; and thus God co-operates with adulterers—which seems incongruous.

[7] Also, in a book ascribed to Gregory of Nyssa,[7] there are arguments designed to prove the same thing. The author argues as follows. From the soul and the body there results one being, and this is one man. Hence, if the soul is made before the body, or the body before the soul, one and the same thing will be prior and posterior to itself; which does not seem possible. Body and soul, then, are produced simultaneously. But the formation of the body begins at the time when the semen is separated. Hence, the soul also is brought into being as a result of the separation of the semen.

[8] Seemingly imperfect, moreover, is the operation of an agent which does not produce a thing in its entirely, but only some part of it.[8] Suppose that God brought the soul into being and that the body was formed by a seminal power. Now, body

6. Cf. *loc. cit.*, ch. 86, ¶10.
7. St. Gregory of Nyssa, *De hominis opificio*, (PG, 44, col. 235).
8. *Ibid.*

and soul are parts of one being: man. So, on that hypothesis the operation of both God and the seminal power would seem to be imperfect; which obviously cannot be allowed. Therefore, man's soul and body are produced by one and the same cause. But man's body certainly is produced through a power residing in the semen. The same, therefore, is true of the soul.

[9] Again, in everything generated from seed, all the parts of the thing generated are together contained in the seed virtually, though they appear not to be present actually. "For example, in wheat or any other seed we observe that the plant itself, with stem, joints, fruit and tassel, are contained virtually in the original seed, and that afterwards the seed spreads forth and discloses itself, thus attaining perfection by a kind of natural resultance, without assuming anything extrinsic."[9] Now, the soul certainly is part of man. Therefore, the human soul is virtually contained in the human seed, and does not originate from any external cause.

[10] And again, things having the same development and the same term must have the same originative principle. But in the generation of a man we find the same development and term in the body as in the soul; for the manifestation of the soul's operations goes hand in hand with the development in shape and size of the members of the body, the operation of the nutritive soul appearing first, and afterwards, that of the sensitive soul, and lastly, when the bodily development is complete, the operation of the intellective soul.[10] Hence, both the body and the soul have the same source. But the body originates through the separation of the semen. The principle of the soul's origin is, therefore, the same.

[11] Furthermore, that which is conformed to a thing is made by the action of that to which it is conformed; the wax that is conformed to the seal receives this conformity from the seal's impress. Now, clearly, the body of a man or of any animal is conformed to its own soul, for its organs are disposed in a manner befitting the psychic operations which are to be exercised by those organs.[11] Hence, the body is formed by the

9. *Ibid.*
10. *Ibid.*
11. *Ibid*

action of the soul, and that is why Aristotle says in *De anima* 11[12] that *the soul is the efficient cause of the body.* But this would not be so if the soul was not present in the semen; for the body is formed by the semen's power. Therefore, the human soul is in the human seed, and thus owes its origin to the separation of that seed.

[12] Likewise, nothing lives except by a soul. But the semen is a living entity.[13] And this is evident for three reasons: because it is parted from a living being; because the semen exhibits vital heat and vital operation, which are the marks of a living thing; and because, if plant seeds were not possessed of life in themselves, they could not, when sown, obtain from the soil, which is inanimate, the heat indispensable to life. Therefore, the soul is in the semen, and thus originates with its separation.

[13] Moreover, if the soul did not, as we have shown,[14] exist before the body, nor begin to exist with the separation of the semen, it follows that the formation of the body came first, the newly created soul being infused into it afterwards. But this, if true, would imply that the soul is for the sake of the body, since what exists on another's account is posterior to it; the clothes are for the man. That notion, however, is not true, because the body is for the soul's sake; the end is always nobler. It must, therefore, be said that the soul originates simultaneously with the separation of the semen.

Chapter 89.

SOLUTION OF THE PRECEDING ARGUMENTS

[1] In order to facilitate the solution of these arguments, certain things must be premised in explanation of the order and process of the generation of man and of animals in general.

12. Aristotle, *De anima,* II, 4 (415b 10).
13. St. Gregory of Nyssa, *De hominis opificio* (PG, 44, col. 235).
14. See above, ch. 83.

[2]   To be taken into account first of all is the falsity of the opinion of those who say that the vital operations appearing in the embryo before its complete development do not proceed from a soul, or from a soul's power existing in the embryo, but from the soul of the mother. If this were true, the embryo would not even be an animal, since every animal consists of soul and body. Vital operations, moreover, do not issue from an extrinsic active principle, but from an internal power; and in this respect particularly are living things, to which self-movement properly belongs, seen to differ from the non-living. For the thing that is nourished assimilates the nourishment and thus must possess an active power of nutrition; what the agent effects is like to itself. And this fact is much more manifest in the operation of the senses; it is through a power existing in this person, and not in another, that he is enabled to see and to hear. Hence, nourishment and even sensation on the part of the embryo prior to its complete development cannot be attributed to the soul of the mother.

[3]   Nevertheless, it cannot be said that the soul in its complete essence is present in the semen from the very beginning, though its operations are not manifested because of the lack of organs. This is impossible in view of the fact that, since the soul is united to the body as its form, it is united only to a body of which it is properly the act. Now, a soul is the "act of an organic body."[1] Prior to the organization of the body, therefore, the soul is not in the semen actually, but only potentially or virtually. Thus, Aristotle says in De anima II that "seeds and fruits are endowed with life potentially so far as they are rid of," that is, lack, "a soul; whereas the thing of which the soul is the act has indeed the power of life, but is not without a soul."[2]

[4]   And the hypothesis of the soul's presence in the semen from the beginning would entail the further consequence that animal generation takes place solely by way of partition, as with annulose animals, where two are produced from one. For, if the semen were possessed of a soul at the moment of

1. Aristotle, De anima, II, 1 (412b 6).
2. Aristotle, De anima, II, 1 (412b 25).

its separation, it would then already be endowed with a substantial form. But in every case substantial generation precedes the substantial form; it never comes after it; and if any changes follow in the wake of the substantial form, they concern not the being but the well-being of the thing generated. Thus, the engendering of the animal would be completed with the mere alienation of the semen; and all subsequent changes would have no bearing upon the process of generation.

[5] But this theory would be even more ridiculous if applied to the rational soul. For, first, the soul cannot possibly be divided as the body is, so as to be present in the separated semen; and second, it would follow that in all extracopulative emissions of semen, without conception taking place, rational souls would nevertheless be multiplied.

[6] Another theory, likewise inadmissible, is stated as follows. From the moment of severance the soul is not present in the semen actually but virtually, because of the lack of organs; and yet this very power of the semen—itself a body potentially endowed with organs though actually without them—is, proportionately to the semen, a potential but not an actual soul. Moreover, since plant life requires fewer organs than animal life, from the moment that the organic development of the semen suffices for plant life, the aforesaid seminal power becomes a vegetative soul; and later, the organs having been perfected and multiplied still more, the same power is raised to the level of a sensitive soul; and finally, with the perfecting of the organs' form, the same soul becomes rational, not, indeed, by the action of that seminal power, but through the influx of an external agent. And for this reason the proponents of the theory suppose Aristotle to have said in the *De generatione animalium* that "the intellect is from without."[3] Now, this theory would involve the consequence that numerically one and the same power is at one time a purely vegetative soul, and afterwards a sensitive soul, the substantial form itself thus being perfected successively more and more. It would further follow both that the substantial form would be brought from potentiality to act, not all at once but in successive stages, and that generation is a continuous move-

3. Cf. Aristotle, *De generatione animalium*, II, 3 (736b 28).

ment, just as alteration is. Now, all these consequences are impossible in nature.

[7] But that theory would entail a consequence still more incongruous, namely, the mortality of the rational soul. For nothing formal in character that accrues to a corruptible thing makes it incorruptible by nature; in that case, the corruptible would be changed into the incorruptible, which is impossible, since *they differ in genus*, as Aristotle says in *Metaphysics* x.[4] In the process described above, however, the substance of the sensitive soul is held to be generated accidentally by the generated body, and hence that substance must necessarily be corruptible with the corruption of the body. Therefore, if the same soul becomes rational through the infusion into it of a kind of light, having the role of a form in its regard, for the sensitive is potentially intellective, then necessarily the rational soul perishes along with the body. But this is impossible, as we proved above,[5] and as the Catholic faith teaches.

[8] Therefore, the very same power which is separated, together with the semen, and is called the *formative* power, is not the soul, nor does it become the soul in the process of generation; but, being based, as on its proper subject, on the vital spirit which the semen contains as a kind of froth, this power is responsible for the formation of the body so far as it functions by virtue of the father's soul, to whom generation is attributed as the principal agent, and not by virtue of the soul of the subject conceived, even after the soul exists in that subject; for the latter does not generate itself, but is generated by the father. And the truth of this becomes quite clear if we survey the powers of the soul one by one. For, indeed, the body's formation cannot be attributed to the soul of the embryo by reason of the *generative power*; not only because that power does not function until the powers of nutrition and growth, which are its auxiliaries, have completed their work— for the generative function is the prerogative of that which already exists as a complete being—but also because the generative power has as its object, not the perfection of the in-

4. Aristotle, *Metaphysics*, X, 10 (1058b 28).
5. See above, ch. 79.

dividual itself, but the preservation of the species. Nor can the body's formation be attributed to the *nutritive power*, whose function is to assimilate nourishment to the subject nourished; and this is not the case here, since in the process of formation the nourishment is not assimilated to something already existing, but is brought to a form more perfect in character and one more closely resembling the father. So, neither can the formation of the body be ascribed to the *power of growth*, whose proper function is to produce change, not in the form, but only in quantity. And the *sensitive and intellective parts* clearly have no operation appropriate to such a formation. It therefore remains that the formation of the body, especially as concerns its primary and principal parts, is not due to the soul of the thing generated, nor to a formative power acting by virtue of the soul of the generated subject, but to a formative power acting by virtue of the generative soul of the father, the work of that soul being the production of that which is specifically like the generator.

[9] This formative power thus remains the same in the above-mentioned vital spirit from the beginning of the body's formation until the end. The species of the subject formed, however, does not remain the same; since at first it possesses the form of semen, afterwards of blood, and so on, until at last it arrives at that wherein it finds its fulfilment. For, although the generation of simple bodies does not proceed in serial order, since each of them possesses a form related immediately to prime matter, a progressive order must obtain in the generation of other bodies because of the many intermediate forms between the first elemental form and the ultimate form which is the object of the generative process; so that there are many generations and corruptions following one another.

[10] Nor is it inconsistent if the generation of an intermediate form takes place and then at once is interrupted, because the intermediate forms lack specific completeness, but are on the way toward that end. Thus, the reason why they are generated is not that they may remain in existence, but that the ultimate term of generation may be attained through them. And if the process of generation is not entirely continuous, and there are many intermediate generations, this is nothing to be won-

dered at; for such is the case, too, in alteration and growth, since neither of them is continuous throughout, local movement alone being truly continuous, as *Physics* VIII makes clear.[6]

[11] Therefore, the more noble a form is and the further removed it is from the elemental form, the more numerous must be the intermediate forms, through which the ultimate form is reached step by step, and, consequently, the intervening generative processes will be multiplied too. That is why, in the generation of an animal and a man, wherein the most perfect type of form exists, there are many intermediate forms and generations—and, hence, corruptions, because the generation of one thing is the corruption of another.[7] Thus, the vegetative soul, which is present first (when the embryo lives the life of a plant), perishes, and is succeeded by a more perfect soul, both nutritive and sensitive in character, and then the embryo lives an animal life; and when this passes away it is succeeded by the rational soul introduced from without,[8] while the preceding souls existed in virtue of the semen.

[12] With these considerations in mind, it is easy to answer the objections.[9]

To the *first objection,* that the sensitive soul must originate in the same way in man and in irrational animals because *animal* is predicated of them both univocally, we reply that this is not necessary. For, although the sensitive souls in man and brute are generically alike, they differ specifically, as do the things whose forms they are; since, just as the human animal differs specifically from the other animals by the fact that it is rational, so the sensitive soul of man differs specifically from the sensitive soul of the brute by the fact that it is also intellective. Therefore, in the soul of the brute there is nothing supra-sensitive, and, consequently, it transcends the body neither in being nor in operation; and that is why the brute soul must be generated together with the body and perish with the body. But in man the sensitive soul is possessed of intellective power over and above the sensitive nature and

6. Aristotle, *Physics,* VIII, 7 (261a 32).
7. Cf. Aristotle, *Physics,* III, 8 (203a 9).
8. See above, ch. 87.
9. See above, ch. 88.

is therefore raised above the body both in being and in operation; it is neither generated through the generation of the body, nor corrupted through the body's corruption. Thus, the diversity in mode of origin of the human and of the brute soul is not on the part of the sensitive faculty, from which the generic nature is derived, but on the part of the intellective faculty, whence the specific difference stems. Hence, it cannot be inferred that they are diverse generically, but only specifically.

[13] As to the *second objection*, to say that the thing conceived is an animal before a man does not prove that the rational soul is produced together with the semen. For the sensitive soul, by which it was an animal, does not remain, but is succeeded by a soul both sensitive and intellective in character, by which it is at once animal and man, as we have already made clear.

[14] In the *third objection*, the remark that the actions of diverse agents do not terminate in the production of one thing must be understood to refer to diverse agents that are not ordered to one another. For, if they are so ordered, they must have one effect; since the action of the primary efficient cause upon the effect of the secondary efficient cause is more powerful even than that which is exercised by the latter. This accounts for our observation of the fact that an effect produced by a principal agent through an instrument is more properly attributed to the principal agent than to the instrument. In some instances, however, the action of the principal agent attains to something in the effect produced, to which the action of the instrument does not attain. The vegetative power, for example, extends to the production of the form of flesh, which the instrument of that power, namely, the heat of fire, cannot produce, although it acts dispositively in regard to that effect by dissolving and consuming. Therefore, since every active power of nature is compared to God as an instrument to the primary and principal agent, nothing prevents the action of nature, in that self-same generated subject which is man, from terminating in a part of man, and not in the whole, the production of which is due to the action of God. The human body, therefore, is formed at the same time both

by the power of God, as principal and first agent, and by the power of the semen, as secondary agent; but it is God's action that produces the human soul, which the seminal power cannot produce, but to which it disposes.

[15] The answer to the *fourth objection* thus is clear; for a man begets that which is like himself in species, so far as his seminal power acts in a dispositive manner toward the ultimate form from which he derives his specific nature.

[16] Regarding the *fifth objection*, there is nothing incongruous in God's co-operating with adulterers in the action of nature; for it is not the nature of adulterers that is evil, but their will, and the action deriving from their seminal power is natural, not voluntary. Hence, it is not unfitting that God should co-operate in their action by bringing it to its final completion.

[17] Now, the inference drawn in the *sixth objection* clearly lacks necessity. For, even if it is granted that man's body is formed before the soul is created, or vice versa, it does not follow that one and the same man is prior to himself, because a man is not his body nor his soul. Rather, it follows that some part of him is prior to the other; and quite reasonably so, because matter is temporally prior to form—I mean, matter so far as it is in potentiality to form, and not as actually completed by a form, for in that state it is simultaneous with the form. It follows that the human body, so far as it is in potentiality to the soul, as not yet having one, precedes the soul in time; it is, then, not actually human, but only potentially human. However, when the body is actually human, as being perfected by the human soul, it neither precedes nor follows the soul, but is simultaneous with it.

[18] Nor does the argument follow that is put forward in the *seventh objection*, namely, that if the soul is not produced by the seminal power, but only the body, then the operation both of God and of nature is imperfect. The inference is false, because both the body and the soul are made by the power of God; although the formation of the body derives from Him by means of the natural power residing in the semen, whereas He produces the soul immediately. Nor does it follow that the

action of the seminal power is imperfect, since it fulfils its proper function.

[19] The *eighth argument* is likewise inconclusive. For, while it is true that the seed contains virtually whatever does not exceed the scope of a power corporeal in nature—such as the grass, the stalk, the joints, and so on—it cannot be concluded that the part of man which totally surpasses such a power is contained virtually in the seed.

[20] The *ninth argument*, to the effect that the operations of the soul seem to develop in the process of generation as the parts of the body develop, does not prove that the human soul and body have the same source; rather, it proves that the disposition of the body's parts is necessary for the soul's operation.

[21] The *tenth objection*, that the body is conformed to the soul and that, therefore, the soul forms a body like to itself, is partly true and partly false. This statement is true if referred to the soul of the begetter, but false if referred to the soul of the begotten; for, as regards its primary and principal parts, the body is not formed by the power of the latter's soul, but by that of the former, as we have just shown. So, too, is every matter configured to its form: a configuration which, however, is not brought about by the action of the thing generated, but by the action of the generating form.

[22] As to the *eleventh objection*, it is quite clear, from what has been said, that at the beginning of its separation the semen is only potentially animate; hence, it does not at that time have a soul actually, but virtually. In the process of generation the semen is, by its own power, endowed with a vegetative and a sensitive soul, which do not remain but pass away, being succeeded by a rational soul.

[23] Nor, again, is the reasoning in the *twelfth objection* conclusive. For, if the formation of the body precedes the human soul, it does not follow that the soul is for the sake of the body. Indeed, a thing is for the sake of another, in two ways. In one way, for the sake of the latter's operation, or preservation, or anything of the sort which follows upon being;

and such things are posterior to that on whose account they are; the clothes are for the man, and tools for the worker. In another way, for the sake of its being; and thus, a thing which is for the sake of another is prior to the latter in time, but posterior in nature. It is in this sense that the body is for the sake of the soul, just as in every case matter is for the sake of the form. But this would not be true if the joining of soul and body did not constitute a thing one in being, as those say who deny that the soul is the form of the body.

Chapter 90.

THAT AN INTELLECTUAL SUBSTANCE IS UNITED ONLY TO A HUMAN BODY AS ITS FORM

[1] Having shown[1] that a certain intellectual substance—the human soul—is united to a body as its form, we must now inquire whether any intellectual substance is united to any other body as its form. As to the heavenly bodies, we have, indeed, already presented[2] Aristotle's opinion on the question of their being animated by an intellectual soul, and have observed that Augustine leaves the matter in doubt. Bodies composed of elements, then, should be the focal point of the present inquiry.

[2] Now, it is quite clear that an intellectual substance is not united as form to such a body except a human one. For, were it united to a body other than the human, the latter would be either mixed or simple. But it cannot be united to a mixed body, because that body would have to be the most symmetrically structured one of its genus; and it is a fact of observation that mixed bodies have forms so much the more noble, the nearer they come to possessing an equable blending of their constituent parts. Thus, if the subject of a form of the noblest type, such as an intellectual substance, is a mixed body, it must possess that harmonious quality in the highest

1. See above, ch. 68.
2. See above, ch. 70, ¶2–4.

degree. And this explains why we find that flesh of fine texture[3] and a keen sense of touch, which reveal evenness of bodily temperament, are signs of mental acuteness.[4] Now, the most evenly tempered body is the human, so that, if an intellectual substance is united to a mixed body, the latter must be of the same nature as the human body; and its form, too, would be of the same nature as the human soul, if it were an intellectual substance. Hence, there would be no specific difference between the animal so constituted and man.

[3] It is likewise impossible for an intellectual substance to be united as form to a simple body, such as air, water, fire, or earth. For each of these bodies is of uniform character in the whole and in the parts; a part of air is of the same nature and species as the whole air, having, indeed, the same motion; and so it is with the other simple bodies. Like movers, however, must have like forms. Therefore, if any part of any one of those bodies—air, for example—is animated by an intellectual soul, then for that very reason the whole air and all its parts will be animated. But this manifestly is not so; for there is no evidence of vital operation in the parts of the air or of other simple bodies. Therefore, a substance of intellectual type is not united as form to any part of the air or of similar bodies.

[4] Moreover, if an intellectual substance is united as form to one of the simple bodies, it will either be endowed with an intellect only, or will have other powers such as those that belong to the sensitive or to the nutritive part, as in man. In the first case, there would be no point in its being united to a body. For every corporeal form has some operation proper to itself which is exercised through the body; whereas the intellect has no operation pertaining to the body, except by way of moving it; because understanding is not an operation that can be exercised through any bodily organ, and, for the same reason, neither is the act of the will. The movements of the elements, moreover, are derived from natural movers, namely, from generators; the elements do not move themselves. Hence, the mere possession of movement on their part does not imply that they are animated. But, if the intellectual

3. Literally, softness of flesh.
4. Cf. Aristotle, *De anima*, II, 9 (421a 21–26).

substance, hypothetically united to an element or a part of an element, is endowed with other psychic parts, then, since these parts are parts of certain organs, a diversity of organs will necessarily be found in the body of the element. But this is incompatible with its simplicity. An intellectual substance, therefore, cannot possibly be united as form to an element or to a part thereof.

[5] There is also the fact that the nearer a body is to prime matter, the less noble it is, being more in potentiality and less in complete act. The elements, however, are nearer than mixed bodies to prime matter, since they are the proximate matter of mixed bodies. Hence, the bodies of the elements are less noble in their specific nature than mixed bodies. Since, then, the nobler form belongs to the nobler body, it is impossible that the noblest form, namely, the intellective soul, should be united to bodies of the elements.

[6] Furthermore, if such bodies or any of their parts were animated by souls of the noblest type—the intellective— then the more closely bodies are annexed to the elements, the nearer they must be to life. Yet this evidently is not so, but rather the contrary; for plants have life in a lesser degree than animals, yet they are nearer to earth; and minerals, which are nearer still, have no life at all. Therefore, an intellectual substance is not united as form to an element or to a part thereof.

[7] Then, too, extreme contrariety is destructive of life in all corruptible agents; excessive heat or cold, wet or dryness, are fatal to animals and plants. Now, it is in the bodies of the elements especially that we find the extremes of these contraries. So, life cannot possibly exist in them. It is, therefore, impossible for an intellectual substance to be united to them as their form.

[8] Again, although the elements are incorruptible as a whole, each of their parts is corruptible as having contrariety. So, if some of their parts have cognitive substances united to them, it seems that the power of discerning things corruptive of them will be attributed to them in the highest degree. Now, this power is the sense of touch, which discriminates between hot and cold, and similar contraries; and for this reason, all

animals possess that sense, as something necessary for preservation from corruption. But the sense of touch cannot possibly be present in a simple body, since the organ of touch must not contain contraries actually but only potentially; and this is true of mixed and tempered bodies alone. It is, therefore, impossible that any parts of the elements should be animated by an intellective soul.

[9] And again, every living body has local motion of some kind through its soul; thus, the heavenly bodies—if in fact they are animated—have circular movement; perfect animals, a progressive movement; shell fish, a movement of expansion and contraction; plants, a movement of increase and decrease; and all these are in some way movements in respect of place. Yet in the elements there is no evidence of any motion deriving from a soul, but only of natural movements. Therefore, the elements are not living bodies.

[10] There is, however, another hypothesis, namely, that although an intellectual substance be not united to a body of an element, or to a part thereof, as its form, nevertheless it is united to it as its mover. Now, the former cannot be said of the air; for, since a part of air is not terminable through itself, no determinate part of it can have its own proper movement, by reason of which an intellectual substance may be united to it.

[11] Moreover, if an intellectual substance is naturally united to a body as a mover to its proper movable, then the motive power of that substance must be limited to the movable body to which it is united naturally; for in no case does the exercise of the power of a proper mover exceed its proper movable. But it seems ridiculous to say that the power of an intellectual substance does not, in discharging its function of moving, exceed a determinate part of an element, or some mixed body. Seemingly, then, it must not be said that an intellectual substance is in a natural fashion united to an elemental body as its mover, unless it is also united to it as its form.

[12] Furthermore, principles other than the intellectual substance can cause the movement of a body composed of elements. Therefore, intellectual substances would not need

to be naturally united to such bodies so as to account for this movement.

[13] This rules out the opinion of Apuleius and of certain Platonists, who said that "the demons are animals ethereal in body, endowed with reason, passive in soul, and of eternal duration"; as well as the theory of certain heathen thinkers, who, supposing the elements to be animated, instituted divine worship in their honor.[5] Likewise set aside is the opinion of those who say that angels and demons have bodies naturally united to them—bodies of the nature of the higher or lower elements.

Chapter 91.

THAT THERE ARE SOME INTELLECTUAL SUB-STANCES WHICH ARE NOT UNITED TO BODIES

[1] Now, the preceding considerations enable us to show that some intellectual substances exist in complete separation from bodies.

[2] For we have already shown[1] that when bodies perish the intellect retains its substantial character forever. And, indeed, if the substance of the intellect which remains be one in all, as some say,[2] it follows necessarily that it is separate in its being from the body; and thus our thesis is established, namely, that some intellectual substance subsists apart from a body. But, if a number of intellective souls remain after the bodies have perished, then it belongs to some intellectual substances to subsist apart from a body—especially in view of the demonstrated fact that souls do not pass from one body to another.[3] But to exist apart from bodies is an accidental competence on the part of souls, since they are naturally forms of bodies. Now, that which is through itself must be prior

5. See above, ch. 49, ¶11.
1. See above, ch. 79.
2. See above, ch. 80, ¶2, with ch. 73 and 76.
3. See above, ch. 83.

to that which is by accident. Therefore, there are some intellectual substances, prior in nature to souls, which, through themselves, enjoy subsistence without bodies.

[3] Furthermore, everything included in the essence of the genus must also be found in that of the species, whereas certain things belong to the latter which are not in the former; for instance, *rational* belongs to the essence of *man*, but not to the essence of *animal*. Now, whatever is of the essence of the species, but not of the genus, does not necessarily exist in all species of the genus; thus, there are many species of irrational animals. But it belongs to the intellectual substance, according to its genus, to be subsisting through itself, since it is, through itself, endowed with operation, as shown above.[4] Now, it is of the essence of a thing thus subsisting not to be united to another. Hence, it is not of the generic essence of an intellectual substance to be united to a body, although this is of the essence of that intellectual substance which is the soul. There are, then, some intellectual substances which are not united to bodies.

[4] Then, too, the higher nature in its lowest part touches the lower nature in its highest part. Now, the intellectual nature is higher than the corporeal, and it makes contact with it in one of its parts, namely, the intellective soul. Consequently, just as the body perfected by the intellective soul is the highest in the genus of bodies, so the intellective soul which is united to a body is the lowest in the genus of intellectual substances. Therefore, there are some intellectual substances not united to bodies which, in the order of nature, are superior to the soul.

[5] If in a genus, moreover, there exists something imperfect, then one finds a reality antecedent to it; a thing which, in the order of nature, is perfect in that genus, for the perfect is prior in nature to the imperfect. Now, forms existing in matters are imperfect acts, since they have not complete being. Hence, there are some forms that are complete acts, subsisting in themselves, and having a complete species. But every form that subsists through itself without matter is an intellectual

4. See above, ch. 51.

substance, since, as we have seen,[5] immunity from matter con-
fers intelligible being. Therefore, there are some intellectual
substances that are not united to bodies, for every body has
matter.

[6]   Then, too, it is possible for substance to be without
quantity, but not vice versa. "For substance is prior to the
other genera in time, in nature, and in knowledge."[6] But no
corporeal substance is without quantity. Hence, there can be
some things in the genus of substance that are completely
incorporeal. But all possible natures are found in the order
of things; otherwise, the universe would be imperfect. And
indeed, "in the case of eternal things, to be and to be possible
are one and the same."[7] Therefore, below the first substance,
God, who is not in a genus (as was shown in Book I of this
work[8]), and above the soul, which is united to a body, there
are some substances subsisting without bodies.

[7]   Furthermore, if in a thing composed of two entities the
less perfect one be found to exist through itself, then the one
which is more perfect and has less need of the other is also
found to exist in the same way. Now, as we have seen,[9] there
is in fact a substance composed of an intellectual substance
and a body. And a bodily thing existing through itself, is also
an observed fact—of which all inanimate bodies are evident
instances. All the more reason, then, for our finding intellectual substances that are not united to bodies.

[8]   Also, the substance of a thing must be proportionate to
its operation, because operation is the act and the good of the
operator's substance. Now, understanding is the proper operation of an intellectual substance. Hence, an intellectual substance must be the kind of substance to which such operation
belongs. But, since understanding is an operation that is not
exercised through a corporeal organ, it has no need of the body
except so far as intelligibles are taken from sensible things.
This is an imperfect way of understanding; the perfect way

5. See above, ch. 82.
6. Aristotle, *Metaphysics*, VI, 1 (1028a 32).
7. Aristotle, *Physics*, III, 4 (203b 28).
8. SCG, I, ch. 25.   9. See above, ch. 68.

consists in the understanding of things which in their very nature are intelligible; to understand only those things which are not intelligible in themselves but which are made intelligible by the intellect, is an imperfect way of understanding. Now, prior to every imperfect thing there must be something perfect in the same genus; so that above human souls, which understand by receiving from phantasms, there are some intellectual substances which understand things that are intelligible in themselves, without receiving knowledge from sensible things; and, therefore, such substances are by their nature entirely separate from bodies.

[9] Again, in *Metaphysics* XI[10] Aristotle reasons as follows. Movement that is continuous, regular, and in its own nature unfailing must be derived from a mover which is not moved, either through itself or by accident, as was proved in Book I of this work.[11] Moreover, a plurality of movements must proceed from a plurality of movers. The movement of the heaven, however, is continuous, regular, and in its nature unfailing; and besides the first movement, there are many such movements in the heaven, as the studies of the astronomers show. Hence, there must be several movers which are not moved, either through themselves or by accident. But, as we proved in that same Book,[12] no body moves unless it is itself moved; and an incorporeal mover united to a body is moved accidentally in keeping with the movement of the body, as we see in the case of the soul. Hence, there must be a number of movers which neither are bodies nor are united to bodies. Now, the heavenly movements proceed from an intellect, as we have also shown.[13] We therefore conclude to the existence of a plurality of intellectual substances that are not united to bodies.

[10] With this conclusion Dionysius is in agreement, when, speaking of the angels, he says that "they are understood to be immaterial and incorporeal."[14]

[11] Excluded hereby are the error of the Sadducees, who

10. Aristotle, *Metaphysics*, XI, 8 (1073a 25ff.).
11. *SCG*, I, ch. 20. 12. *Ibid.*, ¶23.
13. *Ibid.*; cf., above, ch. 70, ¶3.
14. Pseudo-Dionysius, *De divinis nominibus*, IV (PG, 3, col. 694).

said that "no spirit exists" (Acts 23:8); the doctrine of the natural philosophers of old, who maintained that every substance is corporeal;[15] as well as the position of Origen, who held that no substance, save the divine Trinity, can subsist apart from a body;[16] and, indeed, of all the other thinkers who hold that all the angels, both good and bad, have bodies naturally united to them.[17]

Chapter 92.

CONCERNING THE GREAT NUMBER OF
SEPARATE SUBSTANCES

[1]   In treating this problem, let it be noted that Aristotle attempts to prove that not only some intellectual substances exist apart from a body, but also that they are of the same number, neither more nor less, as the movements observed in the heaven.[1]

[2]   Now, Aristotle proves that no movements unobservable by us exist in the heaven, because every movement in the heaven exists by reason of the movement of some star—a thing perceptible to the senses; for the spheres are the conveyers of the stars, and the movement of the conveyer is for the sake of the movement of the conveyed. He proves also that there are no separate substances from which some movements do not arise in the heaven, for the heavenly movements are directed to the separate substances as their ends; so that, if there were any separate substances other than those which he enumerates, there would be some movements directed to them as their ends; otherwise, those movements would be imperfect. In view of all this, Aristotle concludes[2] that such substances are not more numerous than the movements that are and can be observed in the heaven; especially since there are not several

15. SCG, I, ch. 20, ¶34–37.
16. Origen, Peri Archon, I, 6 (PG, 11, col. 170).
17. See above, ch. 90, ¶13.
1. Aristotle, Metaphysics, XI, 8.
2. Aristotle, Metaphysics, XI, 8 (1073a 37).

heavenly bodies of the same species, so as to make possible the existence of several movements unknown to us.

[3] This proof, however, lacks necessity. For, as Aristotle himself teaches in *Physics* II,[3] with things directed to an end, necessity derives from the end, and not conversely. So if, as he says, the heavenly movements are ordained to separate substances as their ends, the number of such substances cannot be inferred with necessity from the number of the movements. For it can be said that there are some separate substances of a higher nature than those which are the proximate ends of the celestial movements; even so, the fact that craftsmen's tools are for those who work with them does not preclude the existence of other men who do not work with such tools themselves, but direct the workers. And, in point of fact, Aristotle himself adduces the preceding proof, not as necessary but as probable; for he says: "hence the number of the unchangeable substances and principles may probably be taken to be just so many; the assertion of necessity may be left to more powerful thinkers."[4]

[4] It therefore remains to be shown that the intellectual substances existing apart from bodies are much more numerous than the heavenly movements.

[5] Now, intellectual substances are in their genus transcendent with respect to all corporeal natures. Hence, the rank of such substances must be determined in accordance with their elevation above the corporeal nature. Now, some intellectual substances transcend the corporeal substance only in their generic nature, and yet, as we have seen,[5] are united to bodies as forms. And since intellectual substances enjoy a kind of being that is entirely independent of the body, as was shown above,[6] we find a higher grade of such substances, which, though not united to bodies as forms, are nevertheless the proper movers of certain determinate bodies. And the nature of an intellectual substance likewise does not depend on its producing movement, since the latter follows upon their principal operation,

3. Aristotle, *Physics*, II, 9 (199b 34ff.).
4. Aristotle, *Metaphysics*, XI, 8, (1074a 15).
5. See above, ch. 68.   6. See above, ch. 91.

which is understanding. Consequently, there will exist a still higher grade of intellectual substances, which are not the proper movers of certain bodies, but are superior to the movers.

[6] Moreover, just as an agent that acts by nature acts by its natural form, so an agent that acts by intellect acts by its intellectual form, as we see in those who act by art. Therefore, just as the former agent is proportionate to the patient by reason of its natural form, so the latter agent is proportionate to the patient and to the thing made, through the form in its intellect; that is to say, the intellective form is then such that it can be introduced by the agent's action into matter which receives it. Therefore, the proper movers of the spheres, which (if we wish to side with Aristotle here[7]) move by their intellect, must have such understandings as are explicable by the motions of the spheres and reproducible in natural things. But above intelligible conceptions of this sort there are some which are more universal. For the intellect apprehends the forms of things in a more universal mode than that in which they exist in things; and for this reason we observe that the form of the speculative intellect is more universal than that of the practical intellect, and among the practical arts, the conception of the commanding art is more universal than that of an executive art. Now, the grades of intellectual substances must be reckoned according to the grade of intellectual operation proper to them. Therefore, there are some intellectual substances above those which are the proper and proximate movers of certain determinate spheres.

[7] The order of the universe, furthermore, seems to require that whatever is nobler among things should exceed in quantity or number the less noble; since the latter seem to exist for the sake of the former. That is why the more noble things, as existing for their own sake, should be as numerous as possible. Thus we see that the incorruptible, or heavenly, bodies so far exceed the corruptible, or element-composed, bodies, that the latter are in number practically negligible by comparison. However, just as the heavenly bodies are nobler than those composed of elements—the incorruptible than the corruptible—so intellectual substances are superior

7. See above, ch. 70.

to all bodies, as the immovable and immaterial to the movable and material. The number of separate intellectual substances, therefore, surpasses that of the whole multitude of material things. Such substances, then, are not limited to the number of the heavenly movements.

[8] Then, too, it is not through the matter that the species of material things are multiplied, but through the form. Now, forms outside of matter enjoy a more complete and universal being than forms in matter, because forms are received into matter in keeping with the receptive capacity of matter. Hence, those forms which exist apart from matter, and which we call separate substances, are seemingly not less numerous than the species of material things.

[9] But we do not on this account say, with the Platonists,[8] that separate substances are the species of these sensible things. For, not being able to arrive at the knowledge of such substances except from sensible things, the Platonists supposed the former to be of the same species as the latter, or rather to be their species. In the same way, a person who had not seen the sun or the moon or the other stars, and had heard that they were incorruptible bodies, might call them by the names of these corruptible bodies, thinking them to be of the same species as the latter; which could not be so. And it is likewise impossible that immaterial substances should be of the same species as material ones, or that they should be the species of the latter. For the specific essence of these sensible things includes matter, though not this particular matter, which is the proper principle of the individual, just as the specific essence of man includes flesh and bones, but not this flesh and these bones which are principles of Socrates and Plato. Thus, we do not say that separate substances are the species of these sensible things, but that they are other species superior to them, inasmuch as the pure is nobler than the mixed. Those substances, then, must be more numerous than the species of these material things.

[10] Moreover, a thing is multipliable in respect of its intelligible being rather than its material being. For we grasp

8. Cf. Aristotle, *Metaphysics*, I, 6 (987b 7); 7 (988b 4).

with our intellect many things which cannot exist in matter. This accounts for the fact that any straight finite line can be added to mathematically, but not physically; and that rarefaction of bodies, the velocity of movements, and the diversity of shapes can be increased *ad infinitum* in thought, though not in nature. Now, separate substances are by their nature endowed with intelligible being. Therefore, greater multiplicity is possible in such substances than in material ones, considering the properties and the nature of both these kinds of being. But *in eternal things, to be and to be possible are one and the same.*[9] The multitude of separate substances is, therefore, greater than that of material bodies.

[11]   Now, to these things Holy Scripture bears witness. For it is said in the Book of Daniel (7:10): "Thousands of thousands ministered to Him, and ten thousand times a hundred thousand stood before Him." And Dionysius in his work, *The Celestial Hierarchy*,[10] writes that the number of those substances "exceeds all material multitude."

[12]   This excludes the error of those who say that the number of separate substances corresponds to the number of heavenly movements, or of the heavenly spheres, as well as the error of Rabbi Moses, who said[11] that the number of angels which Scripture affirms is not the number of separate substances, but of forces in this lower world; as if the concupiscible power were called the "spirit of concupiscence," and so on.

Chapter 93.

ON THE NON-EXISTENCE OF A PLURALITY OF
SEPARATE SUBSTANCES OF ONE SPECIES

[1]   From the preceding observations concerning these substances it can be shown that there are not several of them belonging to the same species.

9. Aristotle, *Physics*, III, 4 (203b 28).
10. Pseudo-Dionysius, *De caelesti hierarchia*, XIV (PG, 3, col. 322).
11. Moses Maimonides, *The Guide for the Perplexed*, pt. II, ch. 6, pp. 160–161.

[2] For it was shown above[1] that separate substances are certain subsisting quiddities. But the species of a thing is what is signified by the definition, which is the *sign of a thing's quiddity*.[2] Hence, subsisting quiddities are subsisting species. Therefore, several separate substances cannot exist unless they be several species.

[3] Moreover, things specifically the same, but numerically diverse, possess matter. For the difference that results from the form introduces specific diversity; from the matter, numerical diversity. But separate substances have no matter whatever, either as part of themselves or as that to which they are united as forms. It is therefore impossible that there be several such substances of one species.

[4] Then, too, the reason why there exist among corruptible things several individuals in one species is that the specific nature, which cannot be perpetuated in one individual, may be preserved in several.[3] Hence, even in incorruptible bodies there is but one individual in one species. The nature of the separate substance, however, can be preserved in one individual, because such substances are incorruptible, as was shown above.[4] Consequently, in those substances there is no need for several individuals of the same species.

[5] Furthermore, in each individual that which belongs to the species is superior to the individuating principle, which lies outside the essence of the species. Therefore, the universe is ennobled more by the multiplication of species than by the multiplication of individuals of one species. But it is in separate substances, above all, that the perfection of the universe consists. Therefore, it is more consonant with the perfection of the universe that they constitute a plurality, each diverse in species from the other, rather than a numerical multiplicity within one and the same species.

[6] Again, separate substances are more perfect than the heavenly bodies. But in the heavenly bodies, on account of their

1. See above, ch. 51 and 91.
2. Aristotle, *Topics*, I, 5 (101b 39).
3. Aristotle, *De anima*, II, 4 (415b 4).
4. See above, ch. 55.

very perfection, we find that one species contains only one individual; both because each of them exhausts the entire matter pertaining to its species, and because each heavenly body possesses perfectly the power of its species to fulfil in the universe that to which the species is ordered, as the sun and the moon exemplify conspicuously. For all the more reason, then, should we find in separate substances but one individual of the one species.

Chapter 94.

THAT THE SEPARATE SUBSTANCE AND THE SOUL ARE NOT OF THE SAME SPECIES

[1]   From the above we can proceed to prove that the soul is not of the same species as separate substances.

[2]   For the difference between the human soul and a separate substance is greater than that between one separate substance and another. But, as we have just shown,[1] all separate substances differ in species from one another. Much more, then, does a separate substance differ in species from the soul.

[3]   Moreover, the being proper to each thing accords with its specific nature; things diverse in the nature of their being are diverse in species. But the being of the human soul and of the separate substance is not of the same nature; for in the being of a separate substance the body cannot communicate, as, indeed, it can in the being of the human soul, which is united in being to the body as form to matter. The human soul, therefore, differs in species from separate substances.

[4]   Furthermore, that which of itself has species cannot be of the same species as that which of itself does not, but which is part of a species. Now, the separate substance is so endowed, but the soul, being part of the human species, is not. The soul, therefore, cannot possibly be of the same species as separate substances—unless, perchance, man be of the same species as they; which is clearly impossible.

1. See above, ch. 93.

[5] Then, too, the species of a thing is gathered from its proper operation; for the operation manifests the power, which reveals the essence. Now, understanding is the proper operation of the separate substance and of the intellective soul. But these two have an utterly different mode of understanding; the soul understands by receiving from phantasms; the separate substance does not, since it has no corporeal organs—which are the necessary loci of phantasms. It follows that the human soul and the separate substance are not of the same species.

Chapter 95.

HOW IN SEPARATE SUBSTANCES GENUS AND SPECIES ARE TO BE TAKEN

[1] We must now consider in what respect species is diversified in separate substances. For in materal things which are of diverse species and of one genus, the concept of the genus is taken from the material principle; the difference of species from the formal principle. Thus, the sensitive nature, whence the notion of animal is derived, is in man material with respect to the intellective nature, from which man's specific difference, rational, is obtained. Therefore, if separate substances are not composed of matter and form, as we have seen,[1] it is not clear how genus and specific difference can apply to them.

[2] It must, therefore, be known that the diverse species of things possess the nature of being [*ens*] in graded fashion. Thus, in the first division of being we at once find something perfect, namely, being through itself and being in act, and something imperfect, namely, being in another and being in potency. And passing thus from species to species, it becomes quite apparent that one species has an additional grade of perfection over another—animals over plants, and animals that can move about over those that cannot; while in colors one species is found to be more perfect than another the nearer it approaches to whiteness. Wherefore Aristotle says in *Metaphysics* VIII that "the definitions of things are like number, the

1. See above, ch. 50.

species of which is changed by the subtraction or addition of unity"[2]; just as in definitions the subtraction or addition of a difference gives us a new species. Hence, the essence of a determinate species consists in this, that the common nature is placed in a determinate grade of being. Now, in things composed of matter and form, the form has the character of a term, and that which is terminated by it is the matter or something material. The concept of the genus must, therefore, be taken from the material principle, and the specific difference from the formal principle. Accordingly, from genus and difference, as from matter and form, there results one thing. And just as it is one and the same nature that is constituted by the matter and the form, so the difference does not add to the genus a nature extraneous to it, but is a certain determination of the generic nature itself. For instance, suppose that the genus is *animal with feet*, and its difference, *animal with two feet*; this difference manifestly adds nothing extraneous to the genus.

[3]   Clearly, then, it is accidental to the genus and difference that the determination introduced by the difference be caused by a principle other than the nature of the genus; for the nature signified by the definition is composed of matter, as that which is determined, and form as that which determines. Therefore, if a simple nature exists, it will be terminated by itself, and will not need to have two parts, one terminating, the other terminated. Thus, the concept of the genus will be derived from the very intelligible essence of that simple nature; its specific difference, from its termination according as it is in such a grade of beings.

[4]   From this, also, we see that if there is a nature devoid of limits and infinite in itself, as was shown in Book I[3] to be true of the divine nature, neither genus nor species is applicable to it; and this agrees with the things we proved concerning God in that same Book.[4]

[5]   It is likewise clear from what has been said that no two

2. Aristotle, *Metaphysics*, VIII, 8 (1043b 37).
3. SCG, I, ch. 43.
4. SCG, I, ch. 25.

separate substances are equal in rank, but that one is naturally superior to another; because there are diverse species in separate substances according to the diverse grades allotted to them, and there are not here several individuals in one species.[5] And so it is that we read in the Book of Job (38:33): "Dost thou know the order of heaven?" While Dionysius says in *The Celestial Hierarchy*[6] that just as in the whole multitude of angels there is a highest, a middle, and a lowest hierarchy, so in each hierarchy there is a highest, a middle, and a lowest order, and in each order, highest, middle, and lowest angels.

[6] Now, this disposes of the theory of Origen, who said[7] that all spiritual substances, including souls, were created equal from the beginning; and that the diversity found among these substances—this one being united to a body and that one not, this one being higher and that one lower—results from a difference of merits. The theory is false, because we have just shown that this difference of grades is natural; that the soul is not of the same species as separate substances; that the latter are themselves not of the same species with one another; and that they are not equal in the order of nature.

Chapter 96.

THAT SEPARATE SUBSTANCES DO NOT RECEIVE THEIR KNOWLEDGE FROM SENSIBLE THINGS

[1] This point can be demonstrated from what has gone before.

[2] For sensibles by their very nature are the appropriate objects of sense-apprehension, as are intelligibles of intellectual apprehension. Thus, every cognitive substance that derives its knowledge from sensibles possesses sensitive knowledge, and, consequently, has a body united to it naturally, since such knowledge is impossible without a bodily organ. But it has

5. See above, ch. 93.
6. Pseudo-Dionysius, *De caelesti hierarchia*, X (PG, 3, col. 274).
7. Origen, *Peri Archon*, II, 9 (PG, 11, col. 230).

already been shown[1] that separate substances have no bodies
naturally united to them. Hence, they do not derive intellective
knowledge from sensible things.

[3] The object of a higher power, moreover, must itself be
higher. But the intellective power of a separate substance is
higher than that of the human soul, since, as we have also
shown,[2] the intellect with which the human soul is endowed
is the lowest in the order of intellects. And the object of that
intellect, we have seen,[3] is the phantasm, which, in the order
of objects, is higher than the sensible thing existing outside
the soul, as the order of cognitive powers clearly shows. Therefore, the object of a separate substance cannot be a thing
existing outside the soul, as that from which it derives its
knowledge immediately; nor can it be a phantasm. It therefore remains that the object of the separate substance's intellect is something higher than a phantasm. But in the order of
knowable objects, nothing is higher than a phantasm except
that which is intelligible in act. Separate substances, then,
do not derive intellectual knowledge from sensibles, but they
understand things which are intelligible even through themselves.

[4] Then, too, the order of intelligibles is in keeping with
the order of intellects. Now, in the order of intelligibles,
things that are intelligible in themselves rank above things
whose intelligibility is due solely to our own making. And all
intelligibles derived from sensibles must be of the latter sort,
because sensibles are not intelligible in themselves. But the
intelligibles which our intellect understands are derived from
sensibles. Therefore, the separate substance's intellect, being
superior to ours, has not as the object of its understanding
intelligibles received from sensibles, but those which are in
themselves intelligible in act.

[5] Furthermore, the mode of a thing's proper operation
corresponds proportionately to the mode of its substance and
nature. Now, a separate substance is an intellect existing by
itself and not in a body, so that the objects of its intellectual

1. See above, ch. 91.
2. *Ibid.*, ¶4.
3. See above, ch. 60, ¶17ff.

operation will be intelligibles having no bodily foundation. But all intelligibles derived from sensibles have some sort of basis in bodies; our intelligibles, for instance, are founded on the phantasms, which reside in bodily organs. Therefore, separate substances do not derive their knowledge from sensible things.

[6] Again, just as prime matter ranks lowest in the order of sensible things, and is, therefore, purely potential with respect to all sensible forms, so the possible intellect, being the lowest in the order of intelligible things, is in potentiality to all intelligibles, as we have already seen.[4] Now, in the order of sensibles the things above prime matter are in actual possession of their form, through which they are established in sensible being. Therefore, separate substances, which, in the order of intelligibles, are above the human possible intellect, are actually in intelligible being; for, an intellect receiving knowledge from sensibles, is in intelligible being, not actually, but potentially. The separate substance, therefore, does not receive knowledge from sensibles.

[7] And again, the perfection of a higher nature does not depend on a lower nature. Now, since the separate substance is intellectual, its perfection consists in understanding. Therefore, the act of understanding exercised by such substances does not depend on sensible things, in such fashion as to derive knowledge from them.

[8] And from this we see that in separate substances there is no agent and possible intellect, except, perhaps, in an equivocal sense. For a possible and an agent intellect are found in the intellective soul by reason of its receiving intellective knowledge from sensible things; since it is the agent intellect which makes intelligible in act the species received from such things, while the possible intellect is that which is in potentiality to the knowledge of all forms of sensibles. Since, then, separate substances do not receive knowledge from sensibles, no agent or possible intellect exists in them. And so it is that when Aristotle, in *De anima* III,[5] introduces the possible and agent intellects, he says that they must be located *in the soul.*

4. See above, ch. 78, ¶3.
5. Aristotle, *De anima*, III, 5 (430a 13).

[9]   It is likewise manifest that for such substances local distance cannot be a hindrance to knowledge. For local distance is through itself related to sense, but to intellect, only by accident, so far as it receives things from sense. The reason why local distance bears such a relationship to sense is that sensibles move the senses in respect of a determinate distance; whereas things intelligible in act, inasmuch as they move the intellect, are not in place, being separate from corporeal matter. Since separate substances do not derive intellective knowledge from sensible things, it follows that their knowledge is unaffected by local distance.

[10]   It is also quite clear that time does not enter into the intellectual operation of separate substances. For just as things intelligible in act are without place, so, too, are they outside of time; following upon local movement, time measures only such things as exist somehow in place. Thus, the understanding exercised by a separate substance is above time; whereas time touches our intellectual operation, through the fact that we obtain knowledge from phantasms, which have a determinate temporal reference. Hence, in composition and division our intellect always links up with time, past or future, but not in understanding *what a thing is*. For it understands *what a thing is* by abstracting intelligibles from sensible conditions; so that in this operation it grasps the intelligible apart from time and all conditions to which sensible things are subject. On the other hand, the intellect composes or divides by applying previously abstracted intelligibles to things; and in this application time is necessarily involved.

Chapter 97.

THAT THE INTELLECT OF A SEPARATE SUB-STANCE IS ALWAYS IN ACT OF UNDERSTANDING

[1]   The truth of this statement clearly emerges from what was said above.

[2] For, whatever is sometimes in act and sometimes in potentiality is measured by time. But the intellect of a separate substance is above time, as we have just shown.[1] Therefore, it is not sometimes in act of understanding and sometimes not.

[3] Moreover, there is always actually present in every living substance some vital operation with which it is endowed by its very nature, although other operations are sometimes present potentially. Thus, the process of nourishment is perpetual in animals, but not sensation. Now, as preceding considerations make clear,[2] separate substances are living substances, and the only vital operation which they have is understanding. It follows that they are by their very nature always actually understanding.

[4] Then, too, the philosophers teach that the separate substances move the heavenly bodies by their intellect. But the movement of the heavenly bodies is always continuous. Therefore, the act of understanding exercised by separate substances is continuous and perpetual.

[5] And the same conclusion follows even if that teaching is denied, because separate substances are higher than the heavenly bodies; so that, if the proper operation of a heavenly body, namely, its movement, is continuous, for all the more reason will the proper operation of separate substances, namely, understanding, be continuous.

[6] Furthermore, whatever sometimes operates and sometimes does not operate is moved either through itself or by accident. Changes occuring in the sensible part of our nature, then, are responsible for the fact that we are sometimes understanding and sometimes not understanding, as Aristotle observes in *Physics* VIII.[3] But separate substances are not moved through themselves, since they are not bodies, nor are they moved by accident, because they are not united to bodies; so that in them understanding, which is their proper operation, is not intermittent, but continuous.

1. See above, ch. 96.
2. See above, ch. 91.
3. Cf. Aristotle, *Physics*, VIII, 6.

CHAPTER 98.

HOW ONE SEPARATE SUBSTANCE
UNDERSTANDS ANOTHER

[1]   Now, if separate substances understand those things
which are intelligible through themselves, as was shown,[1] and
if separate substances are intelligible through themselves, since,
as we have also seen,[2] freedom from matter makes a thing intelligible through itself, then it follows that separate substances
have separate substances as the proper objects of their understanding. Each of them, therefore, knows both itself and
others.

[2]   Indeed, each separate substance knows itself otherwise
than the posible intellect knows itself. For the possible intellect exists as in potency in intelligible being, and becomes
in act through the intelligible species, just as prime matter is
actualized in sensible being by a natural form. Now, nothing
is known, so far as it is only in potentiality, but so far as it is
in act. That is why the form is the principle of the knowledge
of the thing which becomes in act through the form. And the
cognitive power likewise is rendered actually cognitive through
some species. Thus, our possible intellect knows itself, thanks
only to the intelligible species whereby it becomes in act in
intelligible being; and for this reason Aristotle says in De
anima III that the human intellect "is itself knowable in the
same way as other things are,"[3] namely, through species derived from phantasms, as through proper forms. But separate
substances by their very nature enjoy intelligible being actually;
so that each of them knows itself through its essence, and not
through the species of another thing.

[3]   Now, as the likeness of the thing known is in the
knower, so in every case is the knowledge. But, one separate

1. See above, ch. 96, ¶3.
2. See above, ch. 82, and SCG, I, ch. 44.
3. Aristotle, De anima, III, 4 (430a 3).

substance is like another as regards the nature of the genus that such substances have in common, while they differ from each other in species, as was made clear above.⁴ It would then seem to follow that the one separate substance knows the other, not according to the proper nature of the species, but only as regards the common nature of the genus.

[4] Some therefore say⁵ that one separate substance is the efficient cause of another. Now, in every efficient cause there must be the likeness of its effect, and, similarly, in every effect the likeness of its cause must be present; for every agent produces its like. Thus, in the higher separate substance there exists the likeness of the lower, as in the cause resides the likeness of the effect; and in the lower is the likeness of the higher, as in the effect dwells the likeness of its cause. Now, in non-univocal causes the likeness of the effect exists in the cause in a higher mode, while the likeness of the cause is in the effect in a lower mode. But the higher separate substances must be non-univocal causes of the lower ones, since the former, placed in diverse grades, are not of one species. Therefore, a lower separate substance knows a higher substance in a lower way, according to the mode of the substance knowing and not of the substance known; whereas the higher knows the lower in a higher way. This is expressed as follows in the work *On Causes*: "An intelligence knows what is below it and what is above it, according to the mode of its substance, because the one is the cause of the other."⁶

[5] But, since it was shown above⁷ that separate intellectual substances are not composed of matter and form, they cannot be caused except by way of creation. We have also proved⁸ that to create belongs to God alone. One separate substance, therefore, could not be the cause of another.

[6] It has been demonstrated, moreover, that all the principal parts of the universe are created immediately by God.⁹ Hence,

4. See above, ch. 93 and 95.
5. Cf. Avicenna, *Metaphysics*, IX, 4 (foll. 104va–105ra).
6. *Liber de causis*, VIII (p. 168).
7. See above, ch. 50 and 51.
8. See above, ch. 21. 9. See above, ch. 42, ¶5–9.

one of them is not caused by another. Now, each of the separate substances is a principal part of the universe, much more than the sun or the moon; since each of them has the nature of a species all its own, which is nobler than that of any corporeal things. Therefore, one separate substance is not caused by another, but all are immediately from God.

[7] So, according to what was said above, each of the separate substances knows God, by its natural knowledge, after the manner of its substance; and through this knowledge they are like God as their cause. But God knows them as their proper cause, possessing in Himself the likeness of them all. Not in this way, however, could one separate substance know another, since one is not the cause of another.

[8] We must, therefore, consider that, since none of these substances is by its essence a sufficient principle of the knowledge of all other things, there must accrue to each of them, over and above its own substance, certain intelligible likenesses, whereby each of them is enabled to know another in its proper nature.

[9] Now, this can be made clear as follows. The proper object of intellect is *intelligible being*, which includes all possible differences and species of being, since whatever can be, can be known. Now, since all knowledge is brought about by way of likeness, the intellect cannot know its object wholly unless it has in itself the likeness of all being and of all its differences. But such a likeness of all being, can be nothing other than an infinite nature: a nature not determined to some species or genus of being, but the universal principle of all being and the power productive of all being; and this, as was shown in Book I,[10] is the divine nature alone. Indeed, no other nature can be the universal likeness of all being, since every nature except God is limited to some genus and species of being. It therefore remains that God alone, by His essence, knows all things. Every separate substance, on the other hand, is by its nature possessed of a perfect knowledge only of its own species; while the possible intellect knows itself not at all in this way, but through the intelligible species, as we remarked already in this chapter.

10. *SCG*, I, ch. 25, 43, and 50.

[10] Now, from the very fact that a substance is intellectual, all being lies within the scope of its understanding. Since it is not endowed by its nature with actual understanding of all being, a separate substance, considered in itself, is in potentiality, as it were, to the intelligible likenesses whereby all being is known, and these likenesses will be its act, so far as it is intellectual. It is, however, impossible that these likenesses should not be several. For we have already shown that the perfect likeness of all being cannot but be infinite. And just as the nature of a separate substance is not infinite, but limited, so an intelligible likeness existing in it cannot be infinite, but is limited to some species or genus of being, so that a plurality of such likenesses is required for the comprehension of all being. Now, the higher the rank of a separate substance, the more is its nature like to the divine; and thus it is less limited, inasmuch as it approaches nearer to the perfection and goodness of the universal being, enjoying, therefore, a more universal participation in goodness and being. The intelligible likenesses existing in the higher substance are, consequently, less numerous and more universal. And this is what Dionysius says in *The Celestial Hierarchy*,[11] namely, that the higher angels have a more universal knowledge; while in the book *On Causes* we read: "The higher intelligences have more universal forms."[12] Now, the apogee of this universality is found in God, who, through one thing, namely, His essence, is cognizant of all things; whereas its lowest realization is in the human intellect, which for each intelligible object needs an intelligible species appropriate to that object and on a par with it.

[11] Consequently, in the higher substances, knowledge acquired through forms of greater universality is not more imperfect, as it is with us. For through the likeness of *animal*, whereby we know a thing only in its genus, we have a more imperfect knowledge than through the likeness of *man*, whereby we know the complete species; since to know a thing only in terms of its genus is to know it imperfectly and as though in potency, while to know a thing in its species is to know it

11. Pseudo-Dionysius, *De caelesti hierarchia*, XII (PG, 3, col. 291).
12. *Liber de causis*, X (p. 170).

perfectly and in act. Occupying the lowest place in the order of intellectual substances, our intellect requires likenesses particularized to such a degree that there must exist in it a proper likeness corresponding to each proper object of its knowledge. That is why, through the likeness of *animal* it does not know *rational*, and therefore neither does it know *man*, except in a relative manner. The intelligible likeness present in a separate substance is, however, more universal in its power, and suffices to represent more things. Hence, it makes for a more perfect, not a more imperfect, knowledge; because it is universal in power, after the fashion of the productive form in a universal cause which, the more universal it is, the greater its causal range and its efficacy. Therefore, by one likeness the separate substance knows both *animal* and its differences; or, again, it knows them in a more universal or more limited way according to the order of such substances.

[12]   We have examples of this, as we remarked, in the two extremes, the divine and human intellects. For through one thing, His essence, God knows all things; whereas man requires diverse likenesses in order to know diverse things. And the higher his intellect, the more things is he able to know through fewer; and so it is that particular examples must be presented to the slow-witted to enable them to acquire knowledge of things.

[13]   Now, although a separate substance, considered in its nature, is potential with respect to the likenesses whereby all being is known, we must not suppose that it is deprived of all such likenesses; for this is the condition of the possible intellect *before it understands*, as Aristotle points out in *De anima* III.[13] Nor must we even think that it is possessed of some of those likenesses actually, and of others only potentially; in the way in which prime matter in the lower bodies has one form actually and others potentially, and as our possible intellect, when we are presently knowing, is in act with respect to some intelligibles and in potentiality as regards others. For, since these separate substances are not

13. Aristotle, *De anima*, III, 4 (429a 23).

moved, either through themselves or by accident, as we have shown,[14] all that is in them in potency must be in act; otherwise, they would pass from potentiality to act, being moved, in that case, through themselves or by accident. Thus, they have in them potentiality and act as regards intelligible being, as do the heavenly bodies as regards natural being. For the matter of a heavenly body is perfected by its form to such an extent that it does not remain in potentiality to other forms; and the intellect of a separate substance is likewise wholly perfected by intelligible forms, so far as its natural knowledge is concerned. Our possible intellect, however, is proportionate to the corruptible bodies to which it is united as a form; for it is so constituted as to possess certain intelligible forms actually, while remaining in potentiality to others. And so it is said in the book *On Causes*[15] that *an intelligence is full of forms,* since the whole potentiality of its intellect is fulfilled through intelligible forms. Accordingly, one separate substance is able to know another through intelligible species of this sort.

[14] Because a separate substance is intelligible by essence, someone may see no necessity for holding that one such substance is understood by another through intelligible species, but may think that one understands another through the very essence of the substance understood. For, in the case of material substances, knowledge through an intelligible species seems to result accidentally from the fact that such substances are not by their essence intelligible in act; and that is why they must needs be understood through abstract intentions. This, moreover, seems to agree with the remark made by Aristotle in *Metaphysics* xi, that *intellect, act of understanding, and thing understood are not different in the case of substances separate from matter.*[16]

[15] The admission of this point, however, involves a number of difficulties. For, in the first place, *the intellect in act is the thing understood in act,* according to the teaching of

14. See above, ch. 97, ¶6.
15. *Liber de causis,* X (p. 170).
16. Aristotle, *Metaphysics,* XI, 9 (1075a 3).

Aristotle,[17] and it is difficult to see how one separate substance is identified with another when it understands it.

[16]   Then too, every agent or operator acts through its form, to which its operation corresponds, as the operation of heating to the form of heat; thus, what we see is the thing by whose species our sight is in-formed. But it does not seem possible for one separate substance to be the form of another, since each has existence separate from the other. It therefore seems impossible that the one should be seen by the other through its essence.

[17]   Moreover, the thing understood is the perfection of the one who understands. But a lower substance cannot be the perfection of a higher one. Hence it would follow that the higher would not understand the lower, if each were understood through its essence, and not through another species.

[18]   Also, the intelligible is within the intellect as to that which is understood. But no substance enters into the mind save God alone, who is in all things by His essence, presence, and power. It therefore seems impossible for a separate substance to be understood by another through its essence, and not through its likeness present in the latter.

[19]   And, indeed, this must be true for Aristotle, who asserts that understanding occurs as the result of the thing actually understood being one with the intellect actually understanding; so that a separate substance, though actually intelligible of itself, is nevertheless not understood in itself except by an intellect with which it is one. And it is in this way that a separate substance understands itself through its essence. Accordingly, the intellect, the thing understood, and the act of understanding are the same.

[20]   On the other hand, according to Plato's position, understanding is effected through the contact of the intellect with the intelligible thing. One separate substance can, therefore, understand another through its essence, when it is in contact with it spiritually; the higher substance understanding the

17. Aristotle, De anima, III, 4 (430a 3).

lower through enclosing and containing it, so to speak, by its power; the lower understanding the higher, as though grasping it as its own perfection. Wherefore Dionysius likewise says, in *The Divine Names*, that the higher substances are intelligible "as the food of the lower."[18]

Chapter 99.

THAT SEPARATE SUBSTANCES KNOW
MATERIAL THINGS

[1] Thus, through the intelligible forms in question a separate substance knows not only other separate substances, but also the species of corporeal things.

[2] For their intellect, being wholly in act, is perfect in point of natural perfection, and, therefore, it must comprehend its object—intelligible being—in a universal manner. Now, the species of corporeal things are also included within intelligible being, and the separate substance, therefore, knows them.

[3] Moreover, since the species of things are distinguished as the species of numbers are distinguished, as noted above,[1] the higher species must contain in some way that which is in the lower, just as the greater number contains the lesser. Since, then, separate substances are above corporeal substances, it follows that whatever things exist in corporeal substances in a material way are present in separate substances in an intelligible way, for that which is in something is in it according to the mode of that in which it is.

[4] Also, if the separate substances move the heavenly bodies, as the philosophers say, then whatever results from the movement of the heavenly bodies is attributed to those bodies as instruments, since they move in being moved, but is ascribed to the separate substances which move them, as

18. Dionysius, *De divinis nominibus*, IV (*PG*, 3, col. 695).
1. See above, ch. 95, ¶2.

principal agents. Now, separate substances act and move by their intellect. Hence, they are actually causing whatever is effected by the movement of the heavenly bodies, even as the craftsman works through his tools. Therefore, the forms of things generated and corrupted enjoy intelligible being in the separate substances. And that is why Boethius, in his book *On the Trinity*,[2] says that *from forms that are without matter came the forms that are in matter.* Separate substances, then, know not only separate substances, but also the species of material things. For, if they know the species of generable and corruptible bodies, as the species of their proper effects, much more do they know the species of the heavenly bodies, as being the species of their proper instruments.

[5]   Indeed, the intellect of a separate substance is in act, having all the likenesses to which it is in potentiality, as well as being endowed with the power to comprehend all the species and differences of being; so that of necessity every separate substance knows all natural things and the total order thereof.

[6]   But since *the intellect in perfect act is the thing understood in act,*[3] someone may think that a separate substance does not understand material things; for it would seem incongruous that a material thing should be the perfection of a separate substance.

[7]   Rightly considered, however, it is according to its likeness present in the intellect that the thing understood is the perfection of the one who understands it; for it is not the stone existing outside the soul that is a perfection of our possible intellect. Now, the likeness of the material thing is in the intellect of a separate substance immaterially, according to the latter's mode, not according to that of a material substance. Hence, there is no incongruity in saying that this likeness is a perfection of the separate substance's intellect, as its proper form.

2. Boethius, *De Trinitate*, II (PL, 64, col. 1250).
3. Aristotle, *De anima*, III, 4 (430a 3).

Chapter 100.

THAT SEPARATE SUBSTANCES KNOW
SINGULARS

[1] Now, the likenesses of things existing in the intellect of a separate substance are more universal than in our intellect, and more efficacious as means through which something is known. And that is why separate substances, through the likenesses of material things, know material things, not only in terms of the nature of the genus or the species, as our intellect does, but in their individual nature as well.

[2] For, since the species of things present in the intellect must be immaterial, they could not in our intellect be the principle of knowing singulars, which are individuated by matter; the species of our intellect are, in fact, of such limited power that one leads only to the knowledge of one. Hence, even as it is impossible for the likeness of the generic nature to lead to the knowledge of the genus and difference so that the species be known through that likeness, so the likeness of the specific nature cannot lead to the knowledge of the individuating principles, which are material principles, so that through that likeness the individual may be known in its singularity. But the likeness existing in the separate substance's intellect as a certain single and immaterial thing is of more universal power and, consequently, is able to lead to the knowledge of both the specific and the individuating principles, so that through this likeness, residing in its intellect, the separate substance can be cognizant, not only of the generic and specific natures, but of the individual nature as well. Nor does it follow that the form through which it knows is material; nor that those forms are infinite, according to the number of individuals.

[3] Moreover, whatever lies within the competence of a lower power a higher power can also do, but in a higher way. That is why the lower power operates through many instru-

ments; the higher, through one only. For the higher a power is, the greater its compactness and unity; whereas the lower power is, on the contrary, divided and multiplied. This accounts for our observation of the fact that the one power of the common sense apprehends the diverse genera of sensible objects which the five external senses perceive. Now, in the order of nature the human soul is lower than a separate substance. And the human soul is cognizant of singulars and of universals through two principles, sense and intellect. Therefore, the separate substance, which is higher, knows both universals and singulars in a higher way, through one principle; namely, the intellect.

[4] A further argument. The species of intelligible things come to our intellect in an order contrary to that in which they reach the intellect of a separate substance. For they reach our intellect by way of analysis,[1] through abstraction from material and individuating conditions; that is why we cannot know singulars through them. But it is as it were by way of synthesis[2] that intelligible species reach the intellect of a separate substance, for the latter has intelligible species by reason of its likeness to the first intelligible species—the divine intellect—which is not abstracted from things, but productive of them. And it is productive not only of the form, but also of the matter, which is the principle of individuation. Therefore, the species of the separate substance's intellect regard the total thing, not only the principles of the species, but even the individuating principles. The knowledge of singulars, therefore, must not be denied to separate substances, although our intellect cannot be cognizant of singulars.

[5] Moreover, if, as the philosophers say, the heavenly bodies are moved by the separate substances, then, since separate substances act and move by their intellect, they must know the movable thing which they move; and this is some particular entity, for universals are immovable. The new places, also, which result from movement are certain singular realities that cannot be unknown to the substance which exercises movement by its intellect. Therefore, it must be said

1. Literally, "resolution."
2. Literally, "composition."

that separate substances know singulars belonging to these material things.

Chapter 101.

WHETHER SEPARATE SUBSTANCES HAVE NATURAL KNOWLEDGE OF ALL THINGS AT THE SAME TIME

[1] Now, since "the intellect in act is the thing understood in act, just as the sense in act is the sensible in act,"[1] and since the same thing cannot at the same time be many things actually, it is seemingly impossible, as we observed above,[2] that the intellect of a separate substance should be possessed of diverse species of intelligibles.

[2] But it must be known that not everything is actually understood, the intelligible species of which is actually present in the intellect. For, since an intelligent substance is also endowed with will, being, thereby, master of its own acts, it is in its power after it possesses an intelligible species to use it for understanding actually, or, if it have several intelligible species, to use one of them. That is why we do not actually consider all the things of which we have scientific knowledge. Therefore, an intellectual substance, being cognizant of things through a plurality of species, uses the one that it chooses, and thereby actually knows at the same time through the one species all the things which it knows; for they are all as one intelligible thing so far as they are known through one, even as our intellect knows at the same time several things brought together or related to one another as one individual thing. On the other hand, the things that the intellect knows through diverse species, it does not know at the same time. And, consequently, just as there is one understanding, so is there one thing actually understood.

[3] Therefore, in the intellect of a separate substance there

1. Aristotle, *De anima*, III, 2 (425b 27); III, 5 (430a 20).
2. See above, ch. 98.

is a certain succession of understandings, but not movement properly so called, since act does not succeed potentiality; rather, act succeeds act.

[4] But the divine intellect knows all things at the same time, because it knows all things through one thing, its essence, and because its action is its essence.

[5] Wherefore, in God's understanding there is no succession, but His act of understanding, wholly and simultaneously perfect, endures through all the ages. Amen.

prime matter,
_____ God as its cause, 53
_____ is ungenerated and incorruptible, 264
_____ its eternity argued, 100
_____ its rank, 327

relations,
_____ as predicated of God, 42–46

sense,
_____ as defined by Plato, 270
_____ how it differs from intellect, 201–02
separate substances,
_____ are caused by divine creation only, 331–32
_____ are completely unmoved, 329, 335
_____ are intelligible by essence, 335
_____ are not the species of sensible things, 319
_____ are required for the perfection of the universe (see
            substance, the intellectual), 314
_____ are superior to the celestial movers, 318
_____ contain but one individual of the one species, 320–
            22
_____ differ in species from the soul, 322–23
_____ genus and species in, 323–25
_____ how they know the species of material things, 337–
            38
_____ how they know singulars, 339–41
_____ how they know themselves and other things, 330–37
_____ move the heavenly bodies, 329
_____ the existence of, 18–19
_____ the great number of, 316–20 (see also substance, the
            intellectual)
_____ their knowledge, not derived from sensibles, 325–28
_____ their motionless understanding, 328, 341–42
_____ their perpetual act of understanding, 328–29
_____ understanding, their only vital act, 329
soul, the,
_____ defined by Aristotle, 191, 300
_____ does not partake of God's nature, 287–90
_____ in brutes perishes with the body, 267–72
_____ incorruptibility of the rational soul, 254–58
_____ is not a body, 199–201
_____ is not a harmony, 198–99
_____ is not a temperament, 197–98

Moos, M. F., 22
Moses, 130, 135

Nemesius, 23, 197

Origen, 15, 23, 131–35, 274, 278–79, 284, 316, 325

Paul, St., 80, 130, 279
Pegis, A. C., 12, 22, 24–25
Penido, M. T.-L., 24
Plato, 22, 168–75, 204, 223, 228–30, 234, 240, 248, 257–58,
    269–72, 277, 280, 282, 284, 286, 336
Porphyry, 22, 260
Pythagoras, 124

Rickaby, J., S. J., 24
Riedl, J. O., 25
Ross, W. D., 20

Sertillanges, A. D., O. P., 24–25
Simon Magus, 128
Smith, G., S. J., 24
Solomon, 258
Steele, R., 20

Théry, G., 21

Wild, J., 25

Zeno, 258